ISSUES IN SOCIOLOGY
Edited by Robert G. Burgess

Families

Diana Leonard
*Senior Lecturer, University of London Institute of Education and
Convenor of its Centre for Research and Education on Gender (CREG)*

John Hood-Williams
Senior Lecturer, Thames Polytechnic

MACMILLAN
EDUCATION

First published 1988

Published by
MACMILLAN EDUCATION LTD
Houndmills, Basingstoke, Hampshire RG21 2XS
and London
Companies and representatives
throughout the world

Printed in Hong Kong

British Library Cataloguing in Publication Data
Leonard, Diana
Families. —— (Issues in sociology).
1. Family
I. Title   II. Hood-Williams, John
III. Series
306.8'5   HQ728
ISBN 0–333–37192–5

ISSUES IN SOCIOLOGY

Families

Contents

Series Editor's Preface

The aim of the *Issues in Sociology* series is to provide easy access to debates and controversies in different fields of study within sociology. In particular, the series is designed for students who are beginning sociology as part of sixth form study or in further education, or in adult and continuing education classes.

The books in the series are written by authors who have wide experience of research and teaching in a special field of study where they have been directly involved in key debates. In this way, they are able to communicate the richness of the subject to the student. At the beginning of each volume, an introductory essay presents an outline of the field where key issues, problems and debates are identified. In subsequent chapters, the student is provided with commentaries, sets of materials, questions for discussion, essays and guides to further reading. The result is a workbook that can be used by the individual student or by teachers working with small groups or a whole class.

Altogether the material in each volume seeks to convey the way in which sociological research involves a knowledge of theory and method as well as a detailed understanding of an area of study.

For some time sociologists have been concerned with studying families alongside researchers drawn from a range of disciplines. Diana Leonard and John Hood-Williams convey the different ways in which debates among researchers within and beyond sociology have influenced the shape of sociological investigations on families. They have provided an excellent guide to the study of families by highlighting key controversies and major debates. In addition, they have presented students with a series of stimulating questions about sociological inquiry that will generate much interest in this field of study.

Robert G. Burgess
University of Warwick

Authors' Preface

This book has been written within the clearly defined format of the *Issues in Sociology* series. We were attracted to the idea of producing a book that was organised in this way, even though conforming to formats is not easy. The idea of the series is to produce short, relatively cheap, introductory books on specific aspects of sociology, by presenting students with debates going on within the discipline. These debates are represented by extracts from the original writings of sociologists who have made important contributions to the fields.

We believe this is an excellent idea and one that can present sociology in a way that captures an important aspect of the discipline: namely that sociology is a debate – an informed scientific debate between authors who not only hold different competing sociological 'perspectives', but rather who disagree about substantive empirical and political issues. Many of the most interesting debates within sociology are between sociologists who are in broad theoretical agreement. Furthermore there is rather more shared interest between many major sociological thinkers than is, we believe, often acknowledged.

In selecting debates we have tried to strike a reasonable balance between our own interests as researchers within the sociology of the family and those of current A Level examiners. It has not been our task to 'cover the syllabus', although we think that readers familiar with the field will recognise a re-ordering of themes that in some cases have a long and honourable history. We hope that with this book we will be able to move examination boards on to asking new questions on the family and we are sure that the format of the series is well geared towards future changes in the A Level examination format, which are bound to require more active and critical engagement with the texts of sociology. A Level examiners themselves complain that they cannot ask new questions when there are no new texts to support them; and publishers, in their turn, demand that new books are written 'for' the syllabus! We hope we have achieved a selection that allows for some development.

We think that the (dare we say, 'new') sociology of the family is interesting, stimulating and of considerable relevance to the lives of students. We want you to enjoy studying it. We hope therefore that the study format, with its textual, essay and examination questions does not inhibit that enjoyment. The questions should stimulate enquiry and not be a dead hand on the text.

Acknowledgements

The authors would like to thank Yvonne Beecham, Bob Burgess, Molly Dawson and Kate East.

The authors and publishers wish to thank the following who have kindly given permission for the use of copyright material:

Academic Press Inc. (London) Ltd for extracts from 'Class struggle and the persistance of the working-class family' by J. Humphries, *Cambridge Journal of Economics*, 1977.
M. Anderson for an extract from *Approaches to the History of the Western Family, 1500–1914*, 1980, Macmillan Publishers Ltd.
Associated Book Publishers (UK) Ltd for extracts from *Politics and Power*, eds D. Adlam *et al.*, 1980, Routledge & Kegan Paul Plc; *Class, Codes and Control Vol 3* by B. Bernstein, 1976, Routledge & Kegan Paul Plc; *The Process of Schooling*, eds M. Hammersley and P. Woods, 1976, Routledge & Kegan Paul Plc; *Family Socialisation and Interaction Process* by T. Parsons, 1956, Routledge & Kegan Paul Plc; *The Symmetrical Family* by M. Young and P. Willmott, 1973, Routledge & Kegan Paul Plc; and *Women United, Women Divided*, eds P. Caplan and J. M. Bujra, 1978, Tavistock Publications.
The Associated Examining Board, University of Cambridge Local Examinations Syndicate, University of London Schools Examinations Board and University of Oxford Delegacy of Local Examinations for questions from past examination papers.
Basil Blackwell Ltd for extracts from *Dual Career Families Re-examined* by R. and R. N. Rapoport, 1976 and *The Changing Experience of Women*, eds E. Whitelegg *et al.*, 1982, Martin Robertson in association with Open University Press.
Blackwell Scientific Publications Ltd for extracts from *Child and Adolescent Psychiatry*, eds M. Rutter and L. Hersov, 1985.
Cambridge University Press for extracts from *Communes, Sociology and Society* by P. Abrams and A. McCulloch, 1975; *Household and Family in Past Time* by P. Laslett, 1972; *Families in Former Times* by J. L. Flandrin, 1979; and 'Who Cares for the Family?' by H. Land, *Journal of Social Policy*, Vol. 7, 3, 1978.

Jonathan Cape Ltd for extracts from *The Naked Ape* by D. Morris, 1968.

Century Hutchinson Publishing Group Ltd for extracts from *The Policing of Families* by J. Donzelot, 1980; *The Empire Strikes Back*, ed. C.C.C.S.; *Losing Out: Sexuality and Adolescent Girls* by S. Lees, 1986; and *Close to Home* by C. Delphy, translated by D. Leonard, 1984.

The Controller of Her Majesty's Stationery Office for an extract from the Report of the Committee on One-Parent Families, Cmnd 5629.

Croom Helm Ltd for extracts from *Power and the State*, ed. G. Littlejohn *et al*, 1978 and *Fit Work for Women*, ed. S. Burman, 1979.

Ronald Frankenberg for extracts from *Communities in Britain*, 1966, Penguin Books Ltd.

Gower Publishing Group for extracts from *Rethinking Social Inequality*, eds D. Robbins *et al.*, 1982.

Houghton Mifflin Company for extracts from *Comparative Family Systems*, ed. M. F. Nimkoff. Copyright © 1965 by Houghton Mifflin Company, Boston, adapted with permission.

International Creative Management, Inc. for an extract from *Women in the Kibbutz* by L. Tiger and J. Shepher. Copyright © by L. Tiger and J. Shepher.

New Socialist for 'Family Fables' by H. Land, *New Socialist*, May/June 1983.

The Open University for extracts from D207, *Introduction to Sociology*, Unit 20, 1980 and E353, *Society, Education and the State*, Unit 12, 1981. Copyright © 1980 and 1981, The Open University Press.

Penguin Books Ltd for extracts from *The Family and Marriage in Britain* by R. Fletcher. Copyright © Ronald Fletcher 1962, 1966 and 1973; and 'Homosexual Couples' by K. Plummer in *The Couple*, ed. M. Corbin. Copyright © Ken Plummer.

Prentice Hall Inc for extracts from *The Family* by W. J. Goode. Copyright © 1964 by Prentice Hall Inc, New Jersey.

Rights of Women for an extract from *Lesbian Mothers on Trial*, 1984.

Robson Books Ltd for extracts from *How to Survive as a Second Wife* by M. Drummond, 1981.

C. Smart for extracts from 'From disregard to disrepute' by J. Brophy and C. Smart, *Feminist Review*, No. 9, 1981.

South End Press for extracts from *Women and Revolution*, ed. L. Sargent, 1981.

Trouble and Strife magazine for extracts from an interview with Jean Breeze, 'A Family of Women', No. 7 Winter 1985.

Unwin Hyman Ltd for extracts from *Seven Years Old in the Home Environment* by J. and E. Newson, 1976, George Allen and Unwin.

Virago Press Ltd for extracts from *Independent Women* by M. Vicinus, 1985.

J. Woods for 'Groping towards sexism: boys' sex talk' in *Gender and Generation*, eds A. McRobbie and M. Nava, 1984, Macmillan Publishers Ltd.

Every effort has been made to trace all the copyright holders but if any have been inadvertently overlooked the publishers will be pleased to make the necessary arrangement at the first opportunity.

Introduction

The family is an institution much discussed; much worried over. The press writes articles and television mounts programmes enquiring as to its health and progress. The churches study and pronounce on ways to behave towards it and within it. The medical profession, at least until 1985, offered its annual guidelines on 'Getting Married'. None of the political parties has yet implemented a minister for the family but at each party conference they all stand as being the 'party of the family' and the leaders' husbands, or wives, rush on stage to make their annual hand-holding appearances. What this means is that although the family is often said to be a personal and private institution it is also, clearly, one with a high public profile and one in which everyone is presumed to participate. In the new jargon, our society is 'familialised'.

The family is also an institution about which there is a good deal of contradictory feeling. On the one hand there is massive public acclaim and support. Charles and Diana's wedding, perhaps *the* public spectacle of the decade, was not just a celebration of monarchy but of the family values in which almost everybody shared – if only momentarily. The lesser, but more recent, Andrew and Fergie event drew on those same wells of family feeling. There is a whole printing industry sustained by interest in, and support for, marriage and the family. The advertisers' images of happy families sell products and services from Bisto to package holidays and confirm the values of family life. But on the other hand, for centuries, radical groups have sought to 'smash the family' and we only have to watch the soap operas, all of which take family relationships for the stuff of their story-lines, to be reminded of the extent of in-fighting, rivalry, jealousy and hatred in families. And of course, when the wife's body is found, detectives interview the husband first.

The subject then is complicated, contradictory and (what is in some ways worse for a student) close to our everyday experiences. Oddly enough the sociological study of the family, which is of course a particular kind of study of the subject, did not reflect these difficulties at all until fairly recently. The subject used to be, in our view, rather dry, distant, moralistic and lacking in any immediate application to the debates that go on around us every day. However as we make clear below, that has changed. The sociology of the family can now help to make sense of the contradictions and explain some of the difficulties in what C. Wright Mills called the 'series of traps' in which we find ourselves. It does help us to understand day to day life. We think it is revealing, uncomfortable and also fun! We are going to introduce our book of social science debates on the family by charting this change, outlining the forces behind it and the legacy that has been left.

Considerable changes in the sociological study of the family have taken place over the last 20 years. In the immediate post-war period and up until the 1960s, various kinds of functionalism, which we discuss below, dominated the field. These retained a considerable influence on family studies long after criticisms by writers such as Alvin Gouldner (see also Further Reading to Chapter 1) had very much reduced their influence in other areas of sociological inquiry. The family was also a low status area of study and this was one of the reasons that it remained untouched by developments in other areas of sociology. The subject was treated rather uncritically as the study of a more or less inevitable institution that was very largely a social response to certain biological features of human life – such as humans' 'natural' desire for (hetero)sexuality and affection; their need to reproduce (in the wide sense of bringing up children as citizens); their need for security and shelter. On the other hand, although the study was uncritical it was also unrecognisable as an account of actual families. The stuff of much of the writing of the time was the creation of elaborate systems of interrelationships between role occupants, and between the family and other institutions in society. Abstract diagrams of boxes and two by two tables filled the texts. Much of this seemed to bear little relationship to the experiences of family life held by students or for that matter their teachers, nor to the growing sophistication of sociological theory and methodological debates.

□ The Sociology of the Family and the 1960s and 1970s

Changes in the study of the family had as their background a period of relative economic prosperity throughout most of the Western World as economies expanded in post-war recoveries. However, genuine improvements in post-war living standards masked the continuing relative differences that persisted in the prosperity of the different classes. Whilst England, and particularly London and the South East, was 'swinging', poverty was banished from the popular imagination and ideology (in the sense of political and class divisions) was declared to be at an end.

This period, the swinging 1960s and early 1970s, was marked by the imprint of cultural changes that we describe below. The most obvious surface features were changes in fashion and popular music – conjured up by reference to miniskirts and the Beatles. We were all said to be middle class or 'embourgeoised' then. The new difference between groups was thought only to be the worrying difference between youth and adults, or the pleasurable difference between male and female. However, when the fragile economic bubble burst in the mid 1970s it was revealed, as a few had stressed all along, that behind the gentrified squares stood the new tall slums; behind the façade of affluence waited the old spectre of poverty; underneath the fashionable regional accents the advantages of class bit hard; and the lives of women and the black population remained not only different to those of men and Whites, but also disadvantaged. White racism rapidly discovered a convenient cause for many of these ills – the presence of small but concentrated groups of black immigrants and their British-born children living, precisely, in those areas where the economic disadvantage hit hardest.

The boom years were marked by party political consensus and growing radical movements. The Conservative and Labour parties and governments broadly agreed to continue a wide range of policies, established immediately after the war, covering education, health, housing and social welfare arrangements generally. Macmillan, Wilson, Heath, and Callaghan were all, loosely speaking, social democrats and had rather more in common with each other than with anything that was to happen politically after Thatcher came to power.

Post-war class struggles went on outside the parliamentary and party political systems and produced some spectacular eruptions. In France in 1968 the President, De Gaulle, was so convinced that the revolution had come that he arranged his flight out of the country. In Britain in 1974 a miners' strike helped to topple a government, and in Portugal in the same year an 'old style' revolution occurred. The same decades witnessed the emergence of a politicised student movement whose sit-ins, demonstrations, campaigns and protests took place across much of the Western World. There were also successive waves of youth cultures moving from teds to mods and rockers, to punks, to skinheads, to rasta, to new romantics, to casuals. Civil rights movements in the USA gave birth to the more radical, separatist, black power groups; and Gay and Women's Liberation Movements often took their initial inspiration, strategies and tactics from these black groups and anarchist forms of organising. Anti–nuclear groups and Green movements grew. All these, either together or separately, found much to criticise in the world they lived in – the conditions of waged labour, authoritarian teaching and narrow curricula in the universities, the Vietnam war, the oppression (or lack of rights, depending on the analysis) of black peoples, women and homosexuals, establishment music, media, fashion and 'life styles' and even, as we've seen, the state itself. These critical attitudes to society found their way into the social sciences, many of whose members could trace their own involvement to these groups.

In the specific case of the sociology of the family, five critical influences have had important consequences for the direction of current thinking. The first were the radical psychologists and the most influential of these writers was R.D. Laing. His early interest was in constructing a more telling explanation of the behaviour of schizophrenics than was available in the conventional psychiatry of the time. He believed that it was far more possible to *understand* people diagnosed as mentally ill than was generally believed. Such an understanding came, essentially, from exploring the social context of their lives – principally their family life and especially the power relations within their families. He believed that the family backgrounds of his patients could help to explain the apparantly bizarre and meaningless behaviours they displayed. Along with David Cooper and his co–worker Esterson, Laing developed a powerful criticism of family life as a place where parents who were called 'normal' got their children to love them by terrorising them, and where the 'normal' behaviour could include sending loved sons out to die in Vietnam and building fall-out shelters against nuclear weapons.

The families described by Laing are fairly dislocated environments. They have no location in place or time. They have few relationships with the wider world and they seem only to consist of power relations between 'adults' and 'children' with little reference to husbands and wives or sons and daughters. Nevertheless, his work is a powerful evocation of the family as a place of suffocating, emotional intensity where beneath the surface calm, a nightmare of complicated webs ensnare the members in complex and painful patterns. His influence has been to direct us to view the darker side of family life even if it has offered few suggestions for change.

The second, and what has proved to be more sustained and practical influence in the sociology of the family has come from the Women's Liberation Movement. From its earliest writings in the late 1960s, the WLM took a keen interest in the family since it was clearly a social institution that had great influence on women's lives and their standing in the wider society. It is often said that 'a woman's place is in the home' and it is clear that the roles of wife and mother are crucial to the lives of all women – even those few who do not end up occupying them. Like the radical psychologists, much feminist writing on the family is critical, but it is more varied. It has looked at such things as the hours of unrecognised housework and caring done in families, at violence, and sexual double standards, at the influence of the industrial revolution on men, women, and children and at employment and family life. Also, unlike radical psychology, it has been concerned to propose practical ways in which change should occur.

A third major influence on the sociology of the family has been the development of work on the history of the family, women and sexuality. These developments are not entirely separable from the second influence, since many of the major historians – although certainly not all – were themselves feminists. The growth of family histories shaped recent sociological work partly because the historians were able to show that many of the claims about social change and the development of industrialisation and modernisation made by functionalist theorists did not stand up to historical analysis. For example, it used to be argued that the small 'nuclear' family had developed as a response to the enormous growth of production in factories using waged labour in England during the nineteenth century. Historians have demonstrated that small households were usual in pre–industrial, pre–capitalist England, and that North West Europe has had a characteristic family system since medieval times. Indeed this characteristic of Europe may help to explain why capitalism developed widely in Britain first. The whole argument concerning the relationships between family size and structure and family values and industrialisation and capitalism has been opened up for further questioning. We present some aspects of this new debate in Chapter 5.

The fourth major influence on family sociology has come from the growth of Marxist writing and of Marxist–feminist writing in particular. Although Marxism, as a developed study, has existed among economists, political scientists and sociologists in Europe throughout this century, it was only strongly represented in English academic study in history until the 1960s. By the late 1970s, however, there existed a developed canon of Marxist scholarship and a corresponding spread of its influence on social science curricula in the Anglo-Saxon world. Marxist study of the family took a number of forms. In its crudest variants it asked questions very much like those asked by functionalism but with a disapproving tone. For example it was interested in the relationship between the family and the wider society – like functionalism. Like functionalism it too suggested that the family–household system fitted the needs of (capitalist) society. Unlike functionalism it did not represent society as a smoothly running machine but as an organisation that had conflict and contradiction at its heart, and it regarded this 'fit', between family and society, as unwelcome: as one through which the unpaid, working class, family provided capitalist enterprises with new generations of (male) factory fodder, at little cost to the enterprises themselves, and a stabilising haven for the alienated worker who might otherwise have fermented revolution. Additionally the wives themselves comprised a reserve army of low-paid labourers holding down wage rates. The 'fit', according to such Marxists, is thus not a convenient, logical outcome of history but a deliberately procured arrangement that advantages one sector of the society – the bourgeoisie.

Since the late 1960s, Marxism has been much influenced by feminism, and a whole series of less crude formulations of the 'fit' between capitalism and the family have been proposed. These stress how the family and the wage labour system *also* oppress women. Some of them are represented in Chapters 5 and 6.

The final critical influence came from 'life style politics' in the New Left, hippies, the WLM and gays, in a specific concern to develop and live alternatives to the nuclear family. Academics sympathetic to such groups looked at the deliberate attempts of the past and present to establish new domestic and sexual lives and new parent-child relations. They created some alternative living arrangements for themselves and worked to counter the ideology that suggests that the 'normal' family – in the sense of both the most common and the proper domestic group – is the man, wife and 2.4 children. We consider some of the findings and debates generated by these groups in Chapter 7.

Since the 1960s, there has slowly come awareness of the diversity in family structure and culture represented by various ethnic groups. Some of these communities are of long–standing – single Irish people, for example, have been coming to England (particularly) to find work for centuries, establishing sub-cultural groups; and there have been periods of successive immigration by Jewish, Italian, Polish, Afro-Caribbean, Asian, Cypriot and other groups.

Such sociological attention as has been given to ethnic minorities and black British people has tended to be of a race-relations variety, stressing the problems and difficulties for the minority (and the majority) population of mass immigration, with little attention to racism. Some attention has been paid to the family (see Chapter 3) because it is seen to be the site of socialisation of the new generation. However, relatively little actual empirical research (demographic or ethnographic) has been done. This means that much of the plentiful assertion about the character of such families is based on stereotypes and informal experience rather than on systematic research.

At the same time as these major social movements were influencing writings on the family, demographic changes were occurring and being commented upon. These were also influential in shaping both popular and scientific thinking. Demographically, after an immediate post-war peak, there were steady levels of divorce until the mid 1960s. Then came a sudden jump, much commented upon at the time, up by 66 per cent between 1965 and 1970. Since then the divorce rate has continued to rise on a steep upward climb and in 1980 there were twice as many divorces as in 1971. The most recent figures show some stabilisation, since the 1984 figure was the same as that for 1980 (12 per 1000 of the married population). Nevertheless, despite the usual noise of crisis that surrounds these figures, the number of people who currently divorce each year, taken as a percentage of all married people, only amounts to about 1 per cent – a figure well below rates experienced in the United States for over ten years. On the other hand, the figures do mean that each year all married couples have, theoretically, a 1 per cent chance of divorcing. This small figure, dripping away year by year adds up to high absolute numbers of men, women and children who now experience divorce at some time in their lives.

The popularity of marriage increased fairly consistently from the 1950s through to the early 1970s. It began to look as if marriage was becoming pretty well a universal experience in England and Wales. Since then there has been a steady and progressive decline in the annual number of marriages. First marriage rates have fallen by over 40 per cent since their 1972 peak, and re-marriage rates have also been falling steadily – down by 18 percent in the same period. Thus the total number of people marrying has followed an overall downward trend since 1972. This has occurred at a time when overall population figures, which are clearly a major relevant variable, have been *rising* slowly. (Since 1951 the size of the overall population has increased by something over 10 percent.) However these figures do not necessarily indicate any profound change in attitudes towards marriage. In the first place, we are considering relatively short time periods. Secondly, in a period of economic recession we would expect couples to delay their first marriages and this has indeed been happening. By 1984 only one in six spinsters marrying was a teenager; in 1974 the figure was one in three. During the 1970s as a whole the number of teenage spinster marriages halved. Finally, co-habitation rates have been climbing alongside falling first marriage rates as couples decide to live together without marrying. However, since co-habitatees typically end up getting married the number of people who never marry is likely to remain small.

The first five years of the 1960s were also part of the second great 'baby boom' of this century. This had begun in 1956 and it tailed off after 1965. Average family size remained about the same, at about two children per family, but the longer term trend was towards smaller families. On the other hand, fewer couples were childless or had only one child and there was a growing uniformity in family size across the whole population.

The number of elderly people over 65 was climbing sharply throughout the period and increased by a million between 1960 and 1970 and, perhaps even more significantly, their numbers as a percentage of the population as a whole increased dramatically. Since 1971 and for the rest of this century the number of over-65-year-olds is and will be 16 percent of the population – over two and a half times the figure for the beginning of this century. Within this figure, the number of the very elderly (those over 85) will increase by 50 per cent.

In all these developments what excited the contemporary commentators most was indications of family instability and neglect of family responsibility. Evidence of stability and continuance do not make headlines! Most attention was given to the climbing divorce rates and the increased number of women in waged work, together with their 'latch key' children. The image of children carrying their own door keys and returning from school to empty homes haunted educators and other experts of the 1950s and 1960s.

At the beginning of the 1960s a further indication of change in family life was taken to accompany the newly available (contraceptive) pill for women. Initially its consumption was largely confined to middle class, married women. Despite much heralding at the time it was still, by 1976, less popular than the sheath. Nevertheless it does seem to have had the effect of making *all* contraception more easy to talk about and acceptable to use and, over the longer term, has made pre-marital heterosexuality a great deal more common and admissable.

A final significant development of the period that we want to draw attention to is what David Morgan has called the 'medicalisation' of the family. From the late 1960s there has been a sustained growth in both writing and in the practice of therapies that explicitly operate within a model that regards family and marriage 'problems' as if they were diseases. The Family Therapy movement, fed by the Family Welfare Association and the National Marriage Guidance Council, have spread a view of the family ordered around the notion of 'family pathologies' which may be 'treated', or 'cured' by a new army of human relations technicians. These experts operate in therapist–client relations that mirror those adopted by doctors or psychiatrists. A growing research literature is derived from policy-focused action research that uses accounts given in therapy as data for theories of how the 'healthy' family can be promoted.

This movement has had considerable influence on current writing and thinking on the family, particularly in official circles. The idea of 'the problem family' brings together a set of (largely) state agencies that were hitherto unrelated, or at least not closely related, creating new notions of what family life is or is supposed to be. As Morgan points out, however, it is not easy to know if, as the literature claims, marital disharmony is a 'family problem' leading to (or underlying) personal distress which in turn leads to (or underlies) economic problems. It might be that personal distress or economic problems lead to marital disharmony. Significantly little attention has been given to the effects of, for example, unemployment on family life.

These then are the major historical developments and influences behind what we could call the new sociology of the family. However it would be a partial presentation that did not also recognise the legacy left to the study of the family by the earlier forces of functionalism and community studies. In our book we have represented these older influences less widely and it is only right that we outline here their contribution to family sociology.

□ Founding Work in the Sociology of the Family

The earlier sociology of the family was shaped by two main theories: British social anthropology associated with such writers as Radcliffe-Brown and the American sociology of Talcott Parsons. The first was influential in the field of community studies within which much early sociology of the family in Britain was written, and the latter in developing a theory of social action and of social systems, which gave particular attention to the family as a key institution for socialising individuals into the values and roles which maintain the stability of societies.

From the 1920s through until the 1960s, British anthropology described distant cultures and made them intelligible to an audience of Western colonial and intellectual elites. Rather than dismiss the, to Western eyes, strange rituals and kinship systems of such societies as the products of primitive mentalities or survivals from preceeding social forms, Radcliffe-Brown insisted they be explained rationally in terms of the functions they performed for the societies as a whole both here and now.

Community studies likewise began by treating British society as a set of sub-cultures to be discovered. They did not assume that we already *knew* what life in Britain – particularly in working class, rural or Celtic Britain – was like. They created a body of writing describing a variety of community settings, including farming in Lowland Scotland and Devon, Irish and Welsh villages, coal mining communites, fishing ports, market towns, black immigrant ghettoes in West London and Italian immigrants in Battersea, indigenous, white working class settlements in Bethnal Green and housing estates in Oxford, Swansea and Guildford. Clearly, the family holds a central role in the heart of such communities and such studies focused upon it. Kin relations, patterns of childcare and personality development, the effects of housing renewal and rural–urban migration were all observed and reported upon. Even today much of our empirical knowledge on families still derives from such work.

The second, major, early post-war influence on the sociology of the family was Talcott Parsons. Parsons was first and foremost a great synthesiser who imaginatively combined the ideas of a number of important thinkers into grand theories. He used elements of the writings of Weber, Durkheim, Alfred Marshall, Pareto, and Freud in developing a theory that was intended to operate on a grand scale. At the heart of his theory was an attempt to explain human action – something he considered poorly accounted for in economic theory – and the stability of social systems. In his view, what held society together in an orderly way was not the free market economic system but a commitment to a moral order created out of a common core of institutionalised values and complex, integrated inter-relationships between, and within, the systems and sub-systems that make up the social whole.

In his work on social systems Parsons stressed the functional interdependent parts of the whole in maintaining the structure, and how institutions had become specialised for particular functions (see Weber's conception of rationalisation). For example, he saw the modern form of the family as operating in such a way as to facilitate, externally, certain workings of the economy such as the operation of the individualised, competitive, mobile (and male) labour market, and he saw the interrelating roles of husband and wife as facilitating, internally, the social and psychic stability of the family, which was specialised for the functions of socialisation and the maintenance of the emotional stability of adults.

The chapters of our book show the legacy of both structural functionalism and Parsonian systems theory functionalism, for the sociology of the family. However the major intention of the book is to show the extent to which the field has moved on. We have tried to do this within the format of the series, which means not covering the A Level syllabus as such, but rather showing something of the enterprise of sociology itself: the debates and arguments that make up the stuff of the discipline. The design of the book is intended to encourage a critical, enquiring attitude to sociological study by introducing you to the arguments that go on within the discipline. These arguments are common to the development of science in general rather than to sociology in particular. By presenting the discipline in a way that reflects its own characteristics we hope to give you a better sense of the sociological enterprise itself.

Nowadays the study of the family is less tidy than it used to be. It picks up influences from a wide range of writings. It is much less interested in grand theory and total systems, with the exception of the theories of the state and the economy and some family therapy theory which draws on cybernetics. Because it is critical and more directly concerned with the everyday experiences and politics of family life, it is on the one hand much more accessible and interesting and on the other a little more disturbing. We hope that you will enjoy both looking at the sociology of the family and re-looking at your own experiences of family life, and that both do indeed turn out to inform each other.

Further Reading

D.H.J. Morgan, *Social Theory and the Family*, contains an excellent critical discussion of the sociology of the family of the 1950s and 1960s and assesses the influence of Parsons, radical psychology, feminism and Marcuse.

D.H.J. Morgan, *The Family, Politics and Social Theory*, looks at developments since his earlier book and considers the influence of family therapy, family history, phenomenology and medicine.

HMSO *Social Trends*, is an annual publication from the Office of Population and Census Surveys. It contains a section on households and families, providing the latest government statistics on marriage, divorce, family size, etc.

Family Policy Study Centre, 231 Baker Street, London NW1 6XE. This Centre is concerned with linking together family trends and public policy. It produces a regular bulletin and occasional pamphlets, briefing papers and fact sheets on family trends, family policy, community care, social security. These give up-to-date figures and an informed commentary.

Three useful general reviews of recent work on the family have recently been published by sociologists:

Diana Gittins, *The Family in Question: changing households and familiar ideologies*, uses historical and contemporary findings to 'answer old questions in new ways' – e.g. why do people marry and have children? and how do we explain violence in families? It has an excellent bibliography.

Graham Allan, *Family Life* stresses how the division of tasks and responsibilities within the home today is both shaped by and in turn itself shapes divisions and inequalities occurring outside it.

We shall indicate which sections in these books are relevant further reading for each of our chapters.

In addition, Faith Robertson Elliot, *The Family: Change or Continuity*, reviews many of the debates considered in this collection in a concise, clear dispassionate fashion.

David Lee and Howard Newby, *The Problem of Sociology*. Chapter 16, 'Societies as systems: functionalist models of social order' and Chapter 17, 'Functionalists, family and gender' give a full account of the influence and problems of functionalist analysis. The authors distinguish 'soft' and 'hard' functionalism, which corresponds pretty well to our distinction between anthropological structural functionalism and Parsonian systems functionalism.

1 Is the family universal?

This chapter presents some of the arguments concerning the prevalence of the family. Does the family exist in all societies or only in some? It is also concerned with the further question of why social science should have been so preoccupied with this debate.

It rapidly becomes clear that any such discussions presuppose assumptions about the definition of the family. Writers must say *what* it is they are talking about before they can consider *whether* it is (or is not) universal.

Like many debates within sociology, this argument is interwoven with general theoretical concerns about the character of society and how it works. We will illustrate these concerns in a moment, but first it should be noted that to stress this interweaving in relation to the sociology *of the family* is unusual. As we said in the Introduction, this branch of sociology often appears as a rather discrete field of study, somehow separate from general sociological concerns and development, and untouched by them. The separation of the sociology of the family is frequently coupled with an assumption that the family itself is somewhat 'outside' of society – private and personal, more natural and less social than most institutions.

For some writers included in this chapter, the idea that the family *is* universal largely removes it from the concern of sociology, de-socialises it and puts it into the provenance of zoology or biology. Writers such as Desmond Morris, the zoologist author of Reading 2, and more recently the biologist E.O. Wilson, stress that the unit of a man and wife in a long term sexual relationship, with the female rearing children, is 'natural' because humans, as animals, exhibit certain biological characteristics that compel them to develop certain ways of living if they are to be successful as a species. Morris argues that during the evolution of the human species these biological characteristics have interacted with those ways of living, which we can call culture, in such a way as to develop a quite specific genetic 'human nature'. On the other hand anthropologists such as Roger Keesing stress that no one family arrangement is to be found throughout the world. There are rather a great variety of ways of living and this means that there are no fixed ways in which human biology has to be lived out. All humans have to eat, but the rotted meat that makes the mouths of a New Guinea tribe water would be rejected by a hungry Westerner. This leads to the opposing view that there is no fixed and specific 'human nature' at all.

It may be that this gives the clue to why so much time is spent arguing over the universality of the family. What is at stake is the idea that the family (especially the family as we in the West know it) is a *good* thing, the way that we '*ought*' to live. If the family is a universal, a natural thing, its worth and desirability is self-evident. Using 'nature' and 'natural' as synonyms for real, necessary and good is a key ideology in the West. (As one simple example of this think for a moment of how often and in what ways advertising uses these terms.) Those who seek to demonstrate that the family is natural and universal are almost invariably engaged in proving that it is 'good'. As such the relevance of these arguments extends beyond the social sciences and into wider political debates. For this reason, critics of western family life are more likely to line up against the universalists.

The second theoretical concern in the debates represented here is between those who pay particular attention to the meaning or sense-making activities of humans and those who stress the social facts of family life with less concern over what people think of them. The first group, often referred to as interactionists, stress that if people believe situations to be real (true) then they are real in terms of their consequences. The second group, sometimes referred to as positivists, stress the extent to which the social world of classes and groups exists independently of what people think about it – indeed may be aware of – and that it constrains them, notwithstanding their views (or lack of knowledge).

These two positions are implied in conflicts over the definition of the family. Although there is some agreement among our various readings as to what aspects of social life are relevant to a discussion of 'the family', there are disagreements as to how these elements are to be understood. Whilst some see enormous problems in establishing which relationships are recognised as 'kinship' and what form of mating is advocated in various cultures, and in knowing how people feel and why they behave as they do, other writers consider such criteria as co-residence, household structure and kinship to be empirically self evident. By co-residence social scientists usually mean people who habitually live in the same dwelling, by household structure they mean the pattern of the relationships between co-residing people, and by kinship they mean people who are related to each other by what their own culture recognises as some kind of descent relationship (for example, mother and child) and/or some kind of marital relationship.

A third theoretical concern connects to this second one and revolves around issues of functionalism. As we have said in the Introduction, post-war sociology of the family has been enormously influenced by both anthropological structural functionalism and Parsons' systems functionalism, both being broadly within a positivist tradition. Both analyse societies as a complex set of institutions, or systems and sub-systems, which interrelate with one another, each performing functions necessary for the continuance and well being of the social body. The family is defined by authors within this tradition in terms of the functions it performs for society; and roles within the family are defined in terms of their function for the maintenance of the family as a whole. (For critiques of functionalist writing see Further Reading.)

Whilst all the readings we include seem to agree that it is necessary to meet certain universal requirements for a society (in any recognisable sense of the word) to continue, they interpret this very differently. Human mortality and physical frailty require the bearing and rearing (in the fullest sense) of new members, and the provision of food, sleep and shelter for existing members. But to go on from this to say that whatever social arrangement performs these tasks or functions – no matter how differently from us it does them – is a family, seems to some writers unacceptably to widen the definition of 'family'. If this is how 'the family' is defined, then it is inevitable that it will be regarded as a universal institution because the argument is circular. Certain universal functions define the institution, the functions are universal, therefore the institution is universal. If too wide a definition is accepted, the whole debate is pointless. It would be rather like economists arguing over whether all societies (or only some) have economies, defining the economy as the production, distribution and consumption of products. But economists do not debate whether 'the economy' is universal; they debate what kind of economies societies have and what diverse social forms there are concerned with these activities. Perhaps sociologists of the family should do the same.

☐ The Unnatural Family

Anthropological research provides fascinating details of the variety of ways in which different cultures around the world organise their domestic lives and kin relationships. In every society children are born incapable of surviving on their own; people are subject to the processes of ageing and dying and the facts of human sexual reproduction pertain. But, social life and its interrelationships with these facts is enormously varied. That babies are born dependent does not tell us who shall have the responsibility for caring for them, nor how, or for how long, they remain dependent. Human reproduction does not tell us who shall mate with whom, or what sort of relationship they shall have before and after they have done so. *Social* rules determine these questions. Felicity Edholm here stresses that the full extent and significance of the variability in domestic relationships has not always been recognised even by anthropologists, because their own Western assumptions about 'normal family life' have prevented them exploring fully the very different understandings other cultures have of what *we* see as natural or biological relationships and sentiments.

Reading 1

Anthropologists, in their attempt to understand the ways in which societies other than their own function, have inevitably constructed unfamiliar social relations in terms of those with which they are familiar; they have developed conceptual tools which have been formulated from within the constraints of their own culture, which inevitably relate to their own world.

It was, and still is, widely argued that some form of the family, and, in some cases, of the nuclear family, was universal, and was found in all societies. Only recently has this accepted wisdom been challenged and it has still not been dislodged. One major reason for its resilience in anthropology, apart from the crucial political, economic and ideological significance of the family in the nineteenth and twentieth century western world, is that groups very similar to those which we identify as the family do exist in the majority of societies known to anthropologists. Furthermore, anthropologists have tended to assume that an adequate explanatory definition of any given social or cultural trait [in one culture, i.e. their own] can be extended to similar traits in other cultures. But as one anthropologist has commented:

> because the family seems to be the predominant unit we must not be bemused into thinking that it is the 'natural' or 'basic' one . . .

We have to look . . . at the crucial exceptions, to re-examine the seemingly familiar, family-like groups, to question the given assumptions about human relations and social forms that we almost inevitably have. . . .

When anthropologists talk about the family, it is primarily in terms of kinship. At its simplest, kinship refers to the ties which exist between individuals who are seen as related, through birth (descent) and through mating (marriage). It is thus primarily concerned with the ways in which mating is socially organized and regulated, the ways in which parentage is assigned, attributed and recognized, descent is traced, relatives are classified, rights are transferred across generations and groups are formed. Such relationships are seen as constructed within the basic constraints and imperatives on the organization of human life; production and reproduction, mating, dependence, the need for enculturation and the life cycle. Kinship is above all concerned with relationships which are socially constructed; relatives are not born but made.

When we look at the societies studied by anthropologists and at the variation in kinship systems, it is clear that the range of social options is enormous, that the constraints on human behaviour do not produce uniformity, and that those assumptions we make about what is 'natural' in respect of fundamental human kinship relations, are profoundly challenged by the evidence from widely different societies. If we take some of these assumptions, we can then look at some anthropological data on kinship and become aware of the extent to which we are profoundly ethnocentric in our outlook. . . . [For instance] The question of who our kin, our relations are is answered in numerous ways, even for the primary parent-child relation. Notions of blood ties, of biological connection, which to us seem relatively unequivocal, are highly variable. Some societies of which we have anthropological record recognize only the role of the father or of the mother in conception and procreation. The other sex is given some significance, but is not seen, for example, as providing blood . . . as having any biological connection. Only one parent is a 'relation', the other parent is not.

In the Trobriand Islands, for example, it is believed that intercourse is not the cause of conception, semen is not seen as essential for conception. Conception results from the entry of a spirit child into the womb; the male role is to 'open the passage' to the womb, through intercourse, and it is the repeated intercourse of the same partner which 'moulds' the child. A child's blood comes from its mother's side and from her siblings, her mother and mother's brother, not from the father. A child will not be related by blood to its father, but will look like its father since he has through intercourse created its form. Fathers continue after birth to have a very close and intimate relationship with their children and it is this contact which also is seen as creating the likeness, as moulding the child in his/her father's image. . . .

The Lakker of Burma on the other hand consider that the mother is only a container in which the child grows; she has no blood connection with her children, and children of the same mother and different fathers are not considered to be related to each other.

These cases are extreme but have important implications in that they indicate not only that relations which seem to us to be self-evidently biological, are not universally seen as such. 'Natural', 'biological' relations are not inevitably those which organize human relations at a very fundamental level, since what is understood as 'biological' is socially defined and therefore is expressed in different ways.

F. Edholm, 'The Unnatural Family', in E. Whitelegg *et al.* (eds), *The Changing Experience of Women*, pp. 166–9.

Questions

1. Why does Edholm call her article, 'The Unnatural Family'?
2. How does she define the family?

☐ The Naked Ape

The popularising zoologist Desmond Morris sweeps aside Edholm's type of argument, saying that her examples are exceptions, from backward and unsuccessful cultures. His book was published in 1968 but his kind of ideas have recently enjoyed a resurgence of popularity under the name 'sociobiology'. As the name implies, this argues that the laws of human biology *do* have considerable effect in determining the social organisation of societies. Morris does not claim that the nuclear family is universal but that the nature of human beings – as 'naked apes' – means that it is necessary to have a nuclear family form for a culture to be successful. In particular Morris is concerned with specific aspects of family relations – sex and parental roles, and the relationships between adult men. These must be of a particular kind for societal 'success'.

The obvious question to be asked of these accounts is, what is meant by a successful culture? Many cultures, though not industrialised or highly technical, have achieved remarkable stability and, for example, harmonious relationships with nature. On the other hand our own culture although spectacularly successful in some areas, still has apparently fundamental problems that it seems unable to resolve.

Reading 2

The earlier anthropologists rushed off to all kinds of unlikely corners of the world in order to unravel the basic truth about our nature, scattering to remote cultural backwaters so atypical and unsuccessful that they are nearly extinct. They then returned with startling facts about the bizarre mating customs, strange kinship systems, or weird ritual procedures of these tribes, and used this material as though it were of central importance to the behaviour of our species as a whole. The work done by these investigators was, of course, extremely interesting and most valuable in showing us what can happen when a group of naked apes becomes side-tracked into a cultural blind alley. It revealed just how far from the normal our behaviour patterns can stray without a complete social collapse. What it did not tell us was anything about the typical behaviour of typical naked apes. This can only be done by examining the common behaviour patterns that are shared by all the ordinary, successful members of the major cultures – the mainstream specimens who together represent the vast majority. Biologically, this is the only sound approach. . . .

Because of the extremely long period of dependency of the young and the heavy demands made by them, the females found themselves almost perpetually confined to the home base. In this respect the hunting ape's new way of life threw up a special problem, one that it did not share with the typical 'pure' carnivores: the role of the sexes had to become more distinct. The hunting parties, unlike those of the 'pure' carnivores, had to become all-male groups. If anything was going to go against the primate grain, it was this. For a virile primate male to go off on a feeding trip and leave his females unprotected from the advances of any other males that might happen to come by, was unheard of. No amount of cultural training could put this right. This was something that demanded a major shift in social behaviour.

The answer was the development of a pair-bond. Male and female hunting apes had to fall in love and remain faithful to one another. This is a common tendency in many other groups of animals, but is rare amongst primates. It solved three problems in one stroke. It meant that the females remained bonded to their individual males and faithful to them while they were away on the hunt. It meant that serious sexual rivalries between the males were reduced. This aided their developing co-operativeness. If they were to hunt together successfully, the weaker males as well as the stronger ones had to play their part. They had to play a central role and could not be thrust to the periphery of society, as happens in so many primate species. What is more, with his newly developed and deadly artificial weapons, the hunting ape male was under strong pressure to reduce any source of disharmony within the tribe. Thirdly, the development of a one–male–one–female breeding unit meant that the offspring also benefited. The heavy task of rearing and training the slowly developing young demanded a cohesive family unit. In other groups of animals, whether they are fishes, birds or mammals, when there is too big a burden for one parent to bear alone, we see the development of a powerful pair-bond, tying the male and female parents together throughout the breeding season. This, too, is what occurred in the case of the hunting ape.

In this way, the females were sure of their males' support and were able to devote themselves to their maternal duties. The males were sure of their females' loyalty, were prepared to leave them for hunting, and avoided fighting over them. And the offspring were provided with the maximum of care and attention. This certainly sounds like an ideal solution, but it involved a major change in primate socio-sexual behaviour and, as we shall see later, the process was never really perfected. It is clear from the behaviour of our species today that the trend was only partially completed and that our earlier primate urges keep on re-appearing in minor forms.

This is the manner, then, in which the hunting ape took on the role of a lethal carnivore and changed his primate ways accordingly. I have suggested that they were basic biological changes rather than mere cultural ones, and that the new species changed genetically in this way. You may consider this an unjustified assumption. You may feel – such is the power of cultural indoctrination – that the modifications could easily have been made by training and the development of new traditions. I doubt this. One only has to look at the behaviour of our species at the present day to see that this is not so. Cultural developments have given us more and more impressive technological advances, but wherever these clash with our basic biological properties they meet strong resistance. The fundamental patterns of behaviour laid down in our early days as hunting apes still shine through all our affairs, no matter how lofty they may be. If the organisation of our earthier activities – our feeding, our fear, our aggression, our sex, our parental care – had been developed solely by cultural means, there can be little doubt that we would have got it under better control by now, and twisted it this way and that to suit the increasingly extraordinary demands put upon it by our technological advances. But we have not done so. We have repeatedly bowed our heads before our animal nature and tacitly admitted the existence of the complex beast that stirs within us. If we are honest, we will confess that it will take millions of years, and the same genetic process of natural selection that put it there, to change it. In the meantime, our unbelievably complicated civilisations will be able to prosper only if we design them in such a way that they do not clash with or tend to suppress our basic animal demands.

D. Morris, *The Naked Ape*, pp. 9–10.

Questions

1. Morris points out that primates have a long period of infantile dependency.
   (a) What does he argue follows from this?
   (b) Why do these things follow from this?
   (c) What alternative social arrangements *could* follow at each stage?
2. Morris argues that 'pair bonding' developed to solve the problems.
   (a) What were the three problems?
   (b) For whom were they problems?
   (c) Upon what assumptions is the existence of these problems based?

□ Household and Family in Past Time

Peter Laslett, head of the Cambridge Group for the Study of Population and Social Structure, has played a leading role in countering some of the myths which existed about the history of the Western family. In particular, his historical demographic approach, building up accounts of particular villages and parishes from church records, censuses and diaries, has shown that households in North Western Europe in the past were not large and extended. Rather the average (small) size and kinship structure found today has been commonplace for three centuries at least. In this reading he defends his particular definition of the family as the basis for comparative research.

Reading 3

The particular subject of this book . . . [is] . . . the comparative history of the domestic group. A preliminary definition of the family in this sense in contrast to the other senses which are possible is to be found in everyday experience. The domestic group is the family which the suburban worker leaves when he catches his bus in the morning, and returns to in the evening: it was the family which the English husbandman or petty farmer of our pre-industrial past sat with at table and organised for work in the fields. It consists and consisted of those who share the same physical space for the purposes of eating, sleeping, taking rest and leisure, growing up, child-rearing and procreating (those of them belonging to the class of person whom society permits to procreate). In earlier times, and nowadays in undeveloped societies, this same space was also where the domestic group worked at those tasks which could not be done in the open air, and these were not a few, even in agriculture. In the households of craftsmen, the industrial producers and service workers of that era, and in those engaged in commerce, everything went forward within this living space; such households made up fully a third of all domestic groups in pre-industrial England. Since the insistence is on residence, the full term to be defined is the *coresident domestic group*, and our interest is in changes in the structure and size of that group over time.

Even when spelt out in this way, the definition of the domestic groups is by no means sharp and unambiguous in all societies, ... Apart from the problem of the actual boundaries of the household even in social situations which can now be observed, the great difficulty of the study of the domestic group in the past is that we ourselves cannot literally go back in time and examine any one such group or any number of them with the criterion of residence, or of shared activities, or of consumption, or of production, or of authority in mind.

All we have is some knowledge of the law and custom of our chosen areas and a few documents left behind by a handful of the myriads of communities which have consisted of such domestic groups. These documents consist of lists of inhabitants, and the task is to exploit them in such a way that the exactest possible comparison can be made. For this purpose it is essential to lay it down who is to be included in the coresident domestic group and who excluded from it.

I must insist that in doing this no theory of domestic group organisation is being advanced, simply the rules which have to be observed if surviving documentary evidence is to be made usable for comparative domestic group analysis. If faced with the challenge to answer the question what exactly is meant here by the terms family and household the only appropriate response would be an appeal to the past persons who created that evidence. The lists they left behind them consist of series of names of individuals in blocks, with clear indications of where one block ended and the next began; unless they made out exactly such lists their evidence has not been admitted. It requires no great perspicuity to see that these blocks of names must have been families, or households, and we know that the men of the past called them by these titles. Nevertheless we have to assume that in order to qualify for such descriptions the shape of these blocks was very far from being arbitrary, and in fact was determined by three main considerations. Persons would only appear together within those blocks if they had the three following characteristics in common; they slept habitually under the same roof (a locational criterion); they shared a number of activities (a functional criterion); they were related to each other by blood or by marriage (a kinship criterion). . . . In this volume the first two criteria are taken to be universal.

P. Laslett, *Household And Family in Past Time*, pp. 23–5.

Questions

1. Laslett restricts his definition of the family to the 'co-resident domestic group' of people, comparing those from different centuries and different continents. Bearing in mind the arguments of Reading 1 concerning what is usually included in the meaning of 'family', can you think of any problems with Laslett's approach?
2. Compare his definition of 'co-resident domestic groups' with the Census definitions of 'household' and 'family'.

☐ Families in Former Times

Flandrin, a French historian, disagrees with Laslett because he believes we should focus on meanings not lists in records. He argues that our contemporary concept of the family is new and like

Edholm he stresses that it is a social construction. In the pre-industrial period in Britain and France 'family' meant two things which were then regarded quite separately: co-residence and kinship. It is only in the last century that these two senses have been brought together. This means that contemporary usage is anachronistic when applied to households that existed in Europe in the past.

Reading 4

Nowadays the word 'family' refers to different things. In the widest sense of the word, it is 'the entirety of persons mutually connected by marriage or filiation', or 'the succession of individuals who descend from one another', that is to say, 'a line', 'a *race*', 'a dynasty'. There is also, however, a narrower sense, in much more common use, which the dictionaries usually put in first place and which is the only one, generally speaking, taken into account by the sociologists. In this sense, the word designates 'related persons living under the same roof', and 'more especially, the father, the mother and the children'. These two elements defining the family in the narrower sense can be reconciled in so far as, and only in so far as, it is rare, in our society, for persons other than the father, the mother and the children to live together in the same house.

This apparently was not the case from the sixteenth to the eighteenth centuries. If one consults the older English and French dictionaries, one finds that the concept of the family was divided between the notions of co-residence and kinship, which one finds amalgamated in the definition that has become most current today. In former times, the word 'family' more often referred to a set of kinsfolk who did not live together, while it also designated an assemblage of co-residents who were not necessarily linked by ties of blood or marriage. . . .

It was the *notion of co-residence* which was mentioned first in the older English dictionaries. That of Samuel Johnson (1755) gives, as the first sense of the word 'family', 'those who live in the same house' and, as a synonym, 'household'. Usage confirmed the fact that the servants and other domestics were part of the family. Thus, Samuel Pepys wrote in 1660, at the beginning of his famous *Diary*,

I lived in Axe Yard, having my wife, and servant Jane, and no more in family than us three.

. . . The concept of kinship, without any indication of co-residence, was, on the other hand, given a prominent place in all the French dictionaries and most of the English ones. . . . It [the word family] is used in this sense of 'those who are of the same blood in the male line', 'all those who descend from one and the same stock and who are, consequently, of the same blood', and of 'those descended or claiming descent from a common ancestor; a house, kindred, lineage'. The *Encyclopédie* adds a significant nuance of meaning when it asserts that the word 'famile' is usually understood to mean the entirety of several persons united by ties of blood or of affinity. . . .

. . . 'The word *family* is understood in an even narrower sense', according to the French dictionaries: 'that of the nearest kinsfolk.'. . . . This sense of the word approximates so much more closely to the sense in which the word is used today that it was given after that of 'household'. But who were these kinsfolk? What were the criteria and the limitations of their proximity? The few dictionaries that concern themselves with this question give different answers, of varying degrees of explicitness. 'In this sense, under the name of the *Royal Family*, one includes the children and grandchildren of Kings', according to Furetière and the *Dictionnaire de Trévoux*. . .

Is it possible to discern any progression in this third sense of the word, the tendency to separate from the rest of the extended family the father, the mother and the children? . . .

In England there was a. . . [historical] development: this sense of the word 'family' is still missing from Johnson's Dictionary (1755), but it is given by Murray, in the nineteenth century, with the first indisputable example dating from 1829. One has to wait until the nineteenth century for the concepts of co–residence and of close kinship to be united in concise formulas, in definitions whose very succinctness bears witness to the fact that they no longer constitute any problem. 'Persons of the same blood living under the same roof, and more especially the father, the mother and the children', in the words of Littré, writing in 1869. . . .

The concept of the family, therefore, as it is most commonly defined today, has only existed in our western culture since a comparatively recent date.

J.L. Flandrin, *Families In Former Times*, pp. 4–9.

Questions

1. What are the different things that the word family refers to today, according to Flandrin?
2. Give examples of contemporary households in which people who are not related by ties of blood or marriage co-reside and say whether (and why) these should or should not be considered to be 'families'.

□ The
Family
and Democracy

This reading is taken from one of the most important publications on the family of the 1960s, W.J. Goode's, *World Revolution and Family Patterns*. In this book he sought to describe and interpret the main changes in family patterns that have occurred over the past half century in Japan, China, India, the West, Sub-Sarahan Africa and the Arab countries and to relate them to various changes in other institutions in those societies. In this passage he is not concerned with what the family is, or was, but with American sociologists' use of the family as an ideal type and with 'the conjugal family' (which he defines as fewer kinship ties with distant relatives and a greater emphasis on the 'nuclear' family unit of couple and children) as an ideal, and as an ideology. Goode suggests that this idea of family life has had considerable force world-wide and he is particularly interested in its influence in non-Western countries. His very interesting notion is that in such countries the idea of the nuclear family has had the political effect of promoting the ideas of democracy and individualism in the societies at large.

Reading 5

As now used by family analysts, the term 'conjugal family' is techni-cally an *ideal type*; it also represents an ideal. The concept was not developed from a summary or from the empirical study of actual United States urban family behavior; it is a *theoretical* construction, derived from intuition and observation, in which several crucial variables have been combined to form a hypothetical structural harmony. Such a conceptual structure may be used as a measure and model in examining real time trends or contemporary patterns. In the ensuing discussion, we shall try to separate the fundamental from the more derivative variables in this construction.

As a concept, the conjugal family is also an *ideal* in that when analysts refer to its spread they mean that an increasing number of people view some of its characteristics as *proper* and legitimate, no matter how reality may run counter to the ideal. Thus, although parents in the United States agree that they *should* not play an important role in their children's choice of spouse, they actually do.

Relatives *should* not interfere in each other's family affairs, but in a large (if unknown) percentage of cases they do. Since, however, this ideal aspect of the conjugal family is also part of the total reality, significant for changes in family patterns, we shall comment on it as an ideology.

[In the process of industrialisation of contemporary third world societies] One important source of change is the *ideology* of 'economic progress' and technological development, as well as the ideology of the conjugal family, and spokesmen for both appear in non-Western countries before any great changes are observable either in industrial or family areas of life.

Elders may deplore both ideologies, but both appeal to the intellectuals, often trained in Western schools, and to the young, to women, and generally, to the disadvantaged. The ideology of the conjugal family is a radical one, destructive of the older traditions in almost every society. It grows from a set of more general radical principles which also arouse these groups *politically* in perhaps every underdeveloped country. Its appeal is almost as universal as that of 'redistribution of the land'. It asserts the equality of individuals, as against class, caste, or sex barriers.

The ideology of the conjugal family proclaims the right of the individual to choose his or her own spouse, place to live, and even which kin obligations to accept, as against the acceptance of others' decisions. It asserts the worth of the *individual* as against the inherited elements of wealth or ethnic group. The *individual* is to be evaluated, not his lineage. A strong theme of 'democracy' runs through this ideology. It encourages love, which in every major civilization has been given a prominent place in fantasy, poetry, art, and legend as a wonderful, perhaps even exalted, experience, even when its reality was guarded against. Finally, it asserts that if one's family life is unpleasant, one has the right to change it.

Obviously, no actual conjugal family system genuinely lives up to these principles, but they express family values which, at some levels of consciousness and in many strata, arouse people the world over, just as in their political form they exhibit great power to move men and women. This is not to say that the majority accepts the ideology in either its political or familial form, but rather that people everywhere have *some* resentments against and objections to their family or social system, for which this ideology presents a beguiling alternative. The philosophy of the conjugal family enters each society as a set of general value assertions rather than as a specifically 'Western' ideology, and though Christian missionaries have also preached most of these notions, the effect of the ideology is independent of its ultimate origins. Its principles are sometimes attacked *because* of these origins, but their acceptance stems rather from the opportunities they offer to men and women who feel their family ties bind them harshly.

W.J. Goode, *World Revolution and Family Patterns*, pp. 7, 19.

Questions

1. What does Goode mean by the family as
   (a) an ideal type?
   (b) an ideal?
   (c) an idelogy?
2. How does the family, according to Goode, stand for equality and individuality?

☐ The Ideology of the Family

Our final two readings introduce a debate over the universality of the family within Britain today. The authors of the first reading, Michèle Barrett and Mary McIntosh, like Goode, point to the importance of the *idea* of the nuclear family; although unlike Goode they are not pleased by the extent of this ideological influence because they do not follow his view that the family idea has promoted beneficial effects. They stress that although ideologically dominant, the nuclear family, in fact, is no longer centrally important to the way people actually organise their lives.

Reading 6

[More] importantly for an understanding of the contemporary family, this institution is the focal point of a set of ideologies that resonate throughout society. The imagery of idealized family life permeates the fabric of social existence and provides a highly significant, dominant and unifying, complex of social meaning. . . .

The structure and values of family life play a very important part in the organization and ethos of institutions [such as schools] rightly thought of as 'social' but wrongly contrasted with the family as an exclusively 'private' affair. No such opposition between family and society exists. Just as the family has been socially constructed, so society has been familialized. Indeed it can be argued that in contemporary capitalist society one dominant set of social meanings is precisely an ideology of familialism. The meaning of family life extends far beyond the walls of concrete households in which the proverbial 'co-residing close kin' go about their business of marrying and raising children.

It is hardly necessary to point to the saturation of the media, advertising and popular entertainment in familial ideology. . . . If there were a direct correspondence between the imagery of the family represented in the media and the actual composition of households, we would find the majority of the population living in nuclear residences of children and their parents. Yet, if the 1971 census is to be believed, fewer than a third of Britain's households were enmeshed in such an arrangement and only one in ten was organized in the normatively sanctioned pattern of paternal breadwinner and maternal full-time housewife.

We live in a society where the 'average family' is continually evoked. We are continually addressed as belonging to it . . . [and] . . . this hegemonic family form is a powerful ideological force that mirrors in an idealized way the characteristics attributed to contemporary family life. [However,] it has only a tenuous relation to co-residence and the organization of households as economic units. It dominates, rather than is dominated by, the social organization of kinship. The major significance of 'the family' in Britain today is ideological.

M. Barrett and M. McIntosh, *The Anti-social Family*, pp. 29–34.

Questions

1. What evidence do the authors give to support their view that the nuclear family is ideologically significant?
2. What similarities and what differences can you see between Goode's discussion of the ideology of the family and this reading and how would you account for them?

□ Some Facts of Family Life

This reading is a direct response to those who, like the authors of Reading 6, see the nuclear family as having ideological importance but as having only a tenuous relation to the way in which people actually organise their family and domestic lives nowadays. It argues that, currently, the vast majority of the population are living within households which are clearly structured around the development cycle of the nuclear family.

Reading 7

Most adults still marry and have children. Most children are reared by their natural parents. Most people live in a household headed by a married couple. Most marriages continue until parted by death. No great change seems currently in prospect.

As headlines, such facts are the demographic equivalents of small earthquakes in Chile with nobody killed. They seem a far cry from current preoccupations about the family. Attention has focused on the rise in divorce, cohabitation and one-parent families, and the fall in marriage and birth rates.

Social alarmists fear the death of the family. This same thing is welcomed by radical voices which assert the need for alternatives. The casual belief is fostered that only a diminishing minority now lives in the traditional 'nuclear' family of two parents with their children. The facts give no justification for these beliefs.

Of course, some changes have occurred in marriage and family patterns. Their importance cannot be ignored. But they must be seen in the context of major continuities in family life. Let us begin by looking at families and households. What is really going on here?

Much play is made of the supposed pluralism and diversity of contemporary family forms. The first column of the table [see overleaf] shows that only 40 per cent of households consist of married couples living with children. Figures like this lead to the claim that it is wrong to describe the typical family as a unit of parents plus children, and that this cannot be used as a basis for policy-making, either. It is further said that a stricter stereotype – breadwinning husband plus housewife – applies to only 15 per cent of households and, more restrictively still, that men with two dependent children and a non-employed wife constitute only 5 per cent of all workers. Statements of this kind have a formal truth. But they are severely misleading if they are looked at in isolation.

The second column of the table shows that you get a very different picture if you consider people, rather than the units they live in. In fact, six out of ten people (59 per cent) are currently in parents-plus-children households. A further 20 per cent of people are married couples who mostly have had, or will have, children. The 8 per cent living alone are mostly the elderly widowed, or else younger people who are likely to marry. At any one time, about 80 per cent of people live in households headed by a married couple. Threequarters of these families contain children, who represent 83 per cent of all children.

Households and people in households: 1981

Type of household	% of households	% of people
one person	22	8
married couple	26	20
married couple with dependent children	32	49
married couple with independent children	8	10
lone parent with dependent children	4	5
other	9	8

Source: modified from *Social Trends, 13*; figures for Great Britain

The point is that snapshots of *household types* are misleading about *families*, and they ignore the life cycle. Even with universal marriage and parenthood, and no divorce or early death, there would always be many non-nuclear-family households, because the parents-plus-children unit is a developmental phase. But it is one which is normal and is still experienced by the great majority.

Nor does the fact that only 15 per cent of households consist of breadwinner husband plus housewife, undercut the social import-ance of nuclear families. This means insisting that the definition must include a fully-dependent housewife, which makes it rather an Aunt Sally argument. One significant family change is the proportion of wives with jobs: up from 22 per cent in 1951, through 38 per cent in 1966, to 58 per cent now. Employed wives are thus now statistically normal in Britain. But employed married mothers are still (just) a minority at 49 per cent. Only 14 per cent of all married mothers have full-time jobs, and most of these have older children.

The pattern is of married women withdrawing from the labour force to become mothers, and some of them taking (mostly part-time) work as their children mature. This is important for family life, but it is scarcely a drastic re-ordering of the conventional model. The new pattern seems established and accommodating enough to be dubbed the 'neo-conventional family'. Certainly, it does not mean that the nuclear family has been abandoned as the normal experi-ence.

Robert Chester, 'The Rise of the Neo-Conventional Family', *New Society*, 9 May 1985, pp. 185–8.

Questions

1. Which two statistics does Chester call 'misleading' when quoted in isolation?
2. What evidence does Chester give to counter the 'social alarmists' and to show the continuities in family life?
3. What changes in family life does Chester say *have* taken place recently?

Essay Questions

1. 'The phrase "the typical British family" is stereotypical and is misleading.'
   (a) Why is this so?
   (b) What are the consequences of the use of this stereotype? (AEB 1984)
2. The modern nuclear family has been described as 'anti-social'. Can it be described as a beneficial social institution? (Cambridge 1985)
3. 'The family is unlike all other institutions because it is natural.' How might a sociologist respond to this remark?
4. 'Mothering is a cultural role not a biological instinct.' Discuss. (London 1983)
5. Although forms of marriage vary, all societies forbid or deny the possibility of marriage between specified individuals or social groups. How would you account for this? (London 1983)

Further Reading

Interesting critiques of sociobiology have been produced by American scholars, but they are not easy to get hold of. One accessible source is

Rayna R. Reiter (ed.), *Towards an Anthropology of Women*, articles by: Lila Leibowitz, 'Perspectives on the Evolution of Sex Differences', Sally Slocum, 'Woman the Gatherer: male bias in anthropology', and Kathleen Gough, 'The Origin of the Family'.

If possible refer to
Lila Leibowitz, *Females, Males, Families: a biosocial approach*. This book challenges the 'new' biological view of human sexual behaviour from an evolutionary perspective. It looks at animals, primates and humans, stressing the diversity of ways humans organise families, arguing that what is characteristic of us as a species is our flexibility, our 'expanded behavioural plasticity'.

Elaine Morgan, *The Descent of Woman*, gives a very different interpretation/invention of the evolution of the human species from that of Desmond Morris.

E.R. Leach, *Rethinking Anthropology*. Chapter 1 is a difficult but important argument for a structuralist anthropology of family and kinship. Leach argues against technical classificatory terms, which import English language patterns of thought and private psychological theories, and which are often developed to analyse particular societies. He tries instead to relook at ethnographies in terms of more general categories and 'the logic of possibilities'.

Jean La Fontaine, 'Anthropological perspectives on the family and social change', *Quarterly Journal of Social Affairs*, Vol. 1, No. 1 (1985).

M. Anderson, *Approaches to the History of the Western Family, 1500–1914*. A very good short summary of its subject. It contrasts further Laslett's demographic and Flandrin's sentiments approaches.

Raynor Rapp, 'Family and Class in Contemporary America' in B. Thorne and M. Yalom (eds), *Rethinking the Family*. Rapp argues for keeping 'family' and 'household' as distinct concepts. She explores how the two vary among differing class sectors in contemporary America.

Veronica Beechey and James Donald (eds), *Subjectivity and Social Relations* includes a section on 'Familial Ideology' with useful papers by:
V. Beechey, looking at different analyses of various familial ideologies in works influenced by marxist and Foucauldian frameworks and analyses based upon semiology and Lacanian psychoanalysis, and
R. Coward on media representations of the Royal Family (taken from her book *Female Sexual Desire*).

R.N. Rapoport, M.P. Fogarty and R. Rapoport (eds), *Families in Britain*, 26 articles covering the variety of forms and recent changes in families in Britain.

Diana Gittins, *The Family in Question*, Chapter 3, 'What is the family? Is it universal?'

Graham Allan, *Family Life*, Chapter 1, 'The family in society'.

2 | Is the family in crisis?

For the last 200 years at least there have been writings referring to a contemporary crisis in the family. Our own period is no exception. Like earlier writings, contemporary pundits' talk of crisis is accompanied by a nostalgic looking back to a golden age when the family was harmonious and stable, when parents were respected, and family members cared for one another. In different periods the focus of concern alters although many of the central worries seem perennial.

In the 1950s, according to Ronald Fletcher, the concerns were the rapid changes that were being brought about by industrialisation and urban change, and the growth of the welfare state. These were said to be disrupting the order of old communities, diminishing the importance of the family, increasing the instability of marriage, and promoting moral decay. Fletcher did not believe these concerns to be justified and wrote his book, *The Family and Marriage in Britain*, largely as an attempt to prove that the family had not declined in importance and was not less stable or less moral. Indeed his conclusions were that the family was increasing in importance. Unlike Talcott Parsons (who thought the family important but specialised in its functions), Fletcher thought the number of its functions was increasing and that they were being carried out more effectively than previously.

Nevertheless, while the sociology of the family of the 1950s, 1960s and 1970s in works by Young & Willmott, Fletcher, Rosser & Harris, John & Elizabeth Newson, Elizabeth Bott and Colin Bell, stressed the strength and stability of (particularly working class) family life, there were plenty of worried voices, including those of politicians, churchmen, journalists and headteachers. Concern was expressed over the growth in the numbers of 'working' mothers, whose absence from home (allegedly) led to maternal deprivation, 'latch key' children returning to empty homes, and therefore juvenile delinquency. Divorce rates climbed substantially as we have pointed out in our Introduction and the popular press worried over the future of marriage. The swinging 1960s supposedly led to greater promiscuity and marital faithlessness;

and successive waves of youth culture were thought to show children rebelling against their parents. Urban renewal was held to have led to isolation on estates and in tower blocks.

The current 'family in crisis' debate is basically about family (and community) *breakdown*. Concern is primarily expressed over the ending of marital relationships and the consequences of this breakdown for children and the public purse (in maintaining ex-wives). In addition there is a continuing worry over parental authority and the state of community relations, often expressed in the same breath as a lament about the 'inner city' and Black 'immigrants'; and a new concern about the care of the rapidly growing number of elderly people.

In stark and surprising contrast to all this there is a virtual silence on the effect of unemployment on the family. Unemployment is popularly presented as something that happens to individuals, not to people as members of a class or a family – except when it is a question of 'massaging' the statistics. Then only the 'real' unemployed (men with dependents) apparently need to be considered. There is some consideration in sociology of the effects of the present economic situation on young people's transition from school to work/non-work, but almost nothing on how it affects their transition from minors (family dependents) to adults (householders).

Concern over breakdown takes several forms. Firstly, there is now some recognition of the need to know what exactly is meant by 'breakdown' before rushing to conclusions as to its consequences for various parties. We need to evaluate the quality of relationships, which are not easily identified by the term 'breakdown'. It may be that continuous relationships where there is no thought or possibility of separation or divorce are damaging to those involved; whereas divorced or separated parties may be leading lives with supportive relationships.

Secondly, the separation of marital (or non-marital) partners may very well have specific consequences for children, but just what *are* they? Is there evidence of psychological damage to children when their parents separate or they lose one of them? What happens if they only ever had one? Since divorce almost invariably means a lowering of the standard of living for the children and usually for the wife, how important are economic consequences? What factors are important in reducing the effects of disharmony or deprivation? Is the presence of strong sibling support, or secure income, crucial? Does the obligation to maintain drive a wedge between parent (father) and child? What effect does re-marriage and step-parenting have on children, and adults?

In the 1970s the main debate over divorce statistics was between those who believed that they signalled the end of marriage and those who believed they marked an increasing demand for a higher standard of marital relationship, because they showed people's refusal to tolerate bad marriages. This debate is now largely over. It is now commonly recognised that marriage as such is not about to end, since divorce rates, though still high, are matched by high re-marriage rates. However a series of complex issues on divorce remain unsolved, and debate around these intensified in the early 1980s. Perhaps the most bitter exchanges have been over the question of financial settlements and child custody. The view promoted by such groups as Families Need Fathers and The Campaign for Justice in Divorce is that the legal changes of the 1970s unfairly advantaged first wives and disadvantaged husbands and second wives, while Rights of Women argue that it is unfair to take away such protection as marriage offers women until their overall situation in society is improved. We represent these views in Readings 3 and 4.

The broad strategy of the final years of the last Labour government and of the three Conservative governments under Margaret Thatcher has been to restrict state expenditure. The effect of this is to be seen in state policies which relate to our family crisis debate. There have been a series of moves to reduce benefits, to promote community (read family) care, and to force people to 'stand on their own feet' – or at least only to depend on kin.

This can be seen with respect to divorce. Recent legal changes first (1974) promoted the mutual dependence of ex-spouses and then (1984) promoted a 'clean break' with each to stand on their own feet. Either of these two strategies ensures that the cost of divorce does not fall on the state.

This same strategy can be seen with respect to a quite different family problem – that of the elderly. We referred in our Introduction to the dramatic increase in the absolute numbers, and the proportion of elderly people in the population. This will continue until at least the end of the century. The issue is presented as being who is going to look after this group since they are depicted as, unambiguously, a drain on the nation's resources, with nothing to contribute to everyday life. The interest of the government has been to try to ensure that the potentially enormous cost does not fall on the state. One way in which this has been done, according to Reading 5, has been by promoting the idea of 'Victorian family values'. This implies women should go 'back into the home' and care for the elderly, thus neatly reducing the twin pressure for jobs and for hospital beds. Another side to this tidy solution is discussed in the reading.

Finally the worry over the condition of the community continues unabated. The 'Law and Order' issues that were a prominent feature of the 1979 general election campaign have surfaced intermittantly throughout the 1980s. There is a strong racist and classist element in this debate (see Lawrence, Reading 7 in Chapter 4), a concern with criminal, riotious, Black (male) and rough, working class youth. This has been coupled to a concern over the decline of 'community' – itself often linked to black immigration and settlement in inner city areas.

The idea of stable, supportive, close knit, working class communities, often revolving around central mother figures, has often been stressed in sociology, with the privatised, home-centred life of the suburbs and embourgeoised new working class, who lack supportive kinship networks, as the other side of the coin. But before we can be confident there is any substance to the reported widespread 'loss of community' we need to be clearer about what exactly is meant by the term. Various uses of the word have been run together in a confusing way, making it difficult to be sure what, if anything, is different today from yesterday, and also how these relate to concerns about the family. Such empirical studies as exist, point in different directions.

□ Marriage Breakdown

A continuing note in the noise of crisis surrounding the family is the theme that broken homes breed juvenile delinquency: that single parenting is inadequate and produces problems for society. Reading 1 is an extract from a report that argues that no easy causal relationship exists between such families and delinquency, and that the rhetoric of 'family breakdown' disguises enormous difficulties in actually defining what is meant by this term. The report is a prestigious two volume publication by the 1974 Parliamentary Committee on One-Parent Families chaired by Sir Morris Finer. It argues at length that the real problems for one-parent families, especially fatherless families, are lack of adequate income and lack of public support services. It suggested a series of measures to improve this situation, but these have not been implemented.

Reading 1

For the last quarter of a century, such terms as 'marriage break-down', 'parental deprivation' and 'broken home' have been used in the study of situations where children lack the continuous support of two parents. Although many of these investigations have seemed to demonstrate a causal connection between broken homes and disturbed or delinquent behaviour in chidren, such critics as Lady Wootton have observed that:

> attempts fairly to assess the significance of their findings are . . . thwarted, first, by the absence of precise definition of what constitutes the 'breaking' of a home, and, second, by lack of any information as to the frequency of the 'broken home' amongst the population in general.

The first difficulty arises from the multiplicity of causes of breakdown. Marriages may collapse as a result of death or of *de facto* or *de jure* separation or of the prolonged absence of a partner for voluntary or involuntary reasons. On the other hand, some relationships may be consummated and result in the birth of children but never be celebrated as marriages. This wide range of possibilities was reflected in the Committee's own suggested framework for written evidence which explained that:

> a one-parent family, for working purposes, shall simply be defined as a family in which there is an adult and dependent child or children, one parent or partner is absent (for whatever reason), there is no reasonable prospect of his or her return within a fairly short period and there is no effective parent substitute.

Other difficulties result from the need when estimating the consequences of parental deprivation upon children to allow both for their ages at the time of breakdown as well as for the great diversity of upbringings which may follow. It is vital to relate children's ages at the time of breakdown to their subsequent behaviour, and it clearly makes a great difference whether the child is a baby or an adolescent when his parents part; or whether he is subsequently brought up by his mother alone, or by his mother and her next partner, or in an institution. The children of broken homes may experience two or more families and occupy a different ordinal position in each.

Few studies have faced up satisfactorily to the difficulties here noted. But sometimes the concept of breakdown has been extended to include a discordant but continuing relationship between parents. If the findings of Illsley and Thompson that 'it is not broken homes, but unstable parental and family relationships which produce traumatic effects' upon children is true generally, then the hope of measuring the significance of broken homes becomes indeed a chimera. These considerations reinforce the conclusion of Illsley and Thompson that the general concept of the broken home, however phrased, must be treated with extreme caution:

> Broken homes do not possess a monopoly of marital disharmony and childhood unhappiness – many children from intact homes suffer from family insecurity and emotional deprivation. Conversely many children from broken homes lead a happy normal life. This is particularly true in post-war Britain where social services and concern for child welfare have softened many of the harsher consequences of parental loss. Whatever its past usefulness this highly generalised concept should be abandoned in favour of a more intensive study of defined categories of family and childhood experience in both broken and intact homes. Such studies would help to determine what kinds of experience produce lasting deleterious effects and concentrate attention and therapy where it is most needed.

M. Finer and O. R. McGregor, *Report of the Committee on One-Parent Families*, pp. 38–40.

Questions

1. Give two examples, from the reading, of the 'difficulties' in defining the 'broken home'.
2. If we are to abandon the concept of broken home, as suggested, what new concepts should we develop in its place?

☐ Separation, Loss and Family Relationships

With divorce increasingly seen as the main indicator of marital breakdown, concern has shifted to its specific effects on children's psycho-social well-being. What are the (harmful?) effects of loss of a parent, and what are the (beneficial?) effects of parental remarriage?

In a recent collection of articles for child psychologists and psychiatrists, Michael Rutter and Stephen Wolkind outline current knowledge of the long term effects of such family stresses. They reassert the importance of parental co-operation and harmony before and after divorce and the significance of socio-economic factors.

Reading 2

It would be quite misleading to see divorce as basically the loss for the child of one parent, usually the father . . . To begin with, the life event tends to have a long history; often divorce follows years of marital strife. But, also, divorce has lasting consequences. In many cases there is a drastic reduction in the standard of living; frequently the parents go through a prolonged period of emotional disturbance; sometimes discord continues or even escalates after the marital separation; patterns of child care alter; and in many cases there is the further 'event' of parental remarriage with all its further consequences . . . These multiple influences need to be taken into account in dealing clinically with children's problems following divorce . . . Family discord before and after divorce constitutes one of the most important risk factors. Of course, this is also the case in families that remain intact . . . The implication is that, if parents cannot live amicably together, the maintenance of a tension-ridden discordant marriage 'for the sake of the children' is not a good solution. Equally, however, it is clear that: divorce does not necessarily bring an end to the marital conflict; divorce frequently makes things worse for parents and children before it makes them better; and it is crucial for the children that the parents strive to establish harmony and cooperation over the divorce arrangements and, most especially, to support each other's relationships with the children. [Among] older children . . . the sibship emerges as a powerful supportive network, not only to buffer the family ordeal, but also to provide the basis for well-functioning affectionate relationships. In [various] studies, it was important for the parents to have the support of good relationships outside the marriage; the re-establishment of a new intimate relationship was particularly important. However, for parents and children other sources of self-esteem and accomplishment (as at school and at work) aided successful adaptation. . . .

It is not the separation as such that causes persistent psychiatric disturbance. Rather, the poor outcomes arise because the separation leads to poorer quality child care . . ., because it sets in motion a train of other adverse experiences . . ., or because the separation itself stems from a pattern of chronic psychosocial adversity. . . .

The proportion of children in the United States who will spend at least part of their lives being brought up by a single parent now approaches 50% . . . accordingly the pattern can scarcely be regarded as highly atypical, although it may well be disadvantageous for optimal psychological development. Obviously, one-parent families do not constitute a homogeneous group. Many arise as a result of parental death or divorce – with results as already discussed. In both instances, it is difficult to differentiate the effects of rearing by one parent from the many other adverse family features with which it is associated. Moreover, frequently the one-parent family situation is temporary, as parents remarry. In other cases, the one-parent status is a consequence of an illegitimate birth. However, here too the one-parent situation is usually temporary. Of the illegitimate children in the British National Child Development study who were not adopted as infants, two-thirds were living in two-parent families at the age of 11 years . . . However, the illegitimate children did not differ from others solely in terms of having a period of being reared by a mother on her own; their socioeconomic circumstances tended to be well below average and they were more likely to have had an admission to foster care or a children's home . . .

Numerous studies have shown that, as a group, children in one-parent families have a somewhat raised rate of both educational difficulties and emotional/behavioural disturbance. . . . To an important extent the increased level of psychosocial difficulties seems to be a function of poor material circumstances, but, even when these have been taken into account, illegitimate children show more social maladjustment than legitimate children. . . . [It has been] found that this was particularly the case when they were living with a step-parent – a finding that suggests that it is family difficulties rather than the absence of a father *per se* that causes the damage.

Nevertheless, it is likely that parenting may be a more difficult task when undertaken without the support of a marriage partner. . . . [One study suggested that single] parents tended to be more socially isolated than married couples and to experience more stressful life events. They found that, within a single parent group, mother–child interaction was better when there were fewer stressors and more parenting support.

S. Wolkind and M. Rutter, 'Separation, Loss and Family Relationships', in M. Rutter and L. Herson (eds), *Child and Adolescent Psychiatry: Modern Approaches*, pp. 43–8.

Questions

1. If the authors do not think separation or divorce *itself* causes problems, what do they think causes difficulties?
2. To what extent does this reading answer the concerns of the paragraph by Illsley and Thompson in Reading 1?

☐ The Case of the Ex-Husband and the Second Wife

The next three readings show that a good deal of heat has been generated by disagreements over the financial and child custody arrangements that should follow divorce. This first reading, written on behalf of ex-husbands and second wives, argues that the divorce reforms of 1974 unjustly advantaged women, firstly as ex-first wives and secondly as mothers. It recommends three principles: firstly that divorce should be a 'clean break' in which the parties should separate as absolutely as possible, as quickly as possible; secondly that only 'rehabilitative' maintenance should be paid (i.e. maintenance should only be paid for a short while to enable the wife/mother to get back on her feet); finally the question of conduct – and especially of who is the guilty partner – should be re-introduced and taken into account in these matters. All these principles are in fact now enshrined in the Matrimonial & Family Proceedings Act 1984.

Reading 3

The financial aftermath of divorce makes a mockery of the concept of the 'clean break' – it is more like a very messy divide across which both sides continue to hurl abuse long after the marriage is legally dead and buried. While no one disputes the obligation of a father to provide for his children, there is growing doubt about the justice of letting an ex-wife live off her husband for the rest of her life. Despite legally enforced equality of opportunity, and that a third of the country's workforce are women, half of them married, Britain clings to archaic family laws. . . .

The overriding principle, laid down in the Matrimonial Causes Act 1973, says that post-divorce financial settlements should place the parties, so far as is practicable, and, having regard to their conduct, just to do so, in the financial position in which they would have been if the marriage had not broken down'. This is clearly pie in the sky for all except the very rich. For ordinary mortals it is clearly impossible to keep two people separately for the price of one. It leaves those at the middle and lower levels of the income scale with the right to remarry but without the means.

Among the lawyers and theoreticians there are two schools of thought. One view is that all maintenance for ex-wives (though not for children) should be abolished. Maintenance should be paid only when there are very young children involved or for a limited period when an ex-wife is looking or training for a job. The opposing view is that it is all very well to talk about the equality of women and claim that they can work for a living – but the fact of the matter is that time at home rearing children means lost career opportunities and, therefore, less pay. So, the ex-wife should be compensated.

However, many divorced women break up their homes against the wishes of their husbands. And there is many a bewildered and financially battered husband left wondering how and why he has lost his children, his wife, his home and a large portion of his income forever through no particular fault of his own. In the old days things were a little different. If a woman ran off with the milkman and was divorced for adultery, she would not expect maintenance. If, on the other hand, her husband eloped with his secretary and his wife divorced him, she would, as the innocent party, receive maintenance. The 1969 Act abolished the idea of a 'guilty' party. When it comes to fixing the financial provisions, conduct is usually ignored. . . . That is what most people find hardest to understand – why on earth should a man be forced to pay for the pleasure of being deserted? The answer is that we have more or less done away with the idea of the matrimonial offence. It appears only as evidence of the breakdown of a marriage, not as the grounds for ending it. So a wandering wife who brings the dissolution of her marriage on herself will find her claim to a share of her husband's income intact . . .

The present laws were supposed to do away with those long juicy divorce cases that provided the Sunday newspapers with so many stories and the private detective with so much employment. 'Guilt' was supposed to be a thing of the past. The trouble is that, when one party is paying money and the other receiving it, it feels to the husband that he is being punished. And not only the husband. A second wife will find that an ex-wife who has not conveniently died or remarried will take priority over her when it comes to sharing out the income. One woman's maintenance is often another woman's pay packet.

M. Drummond, *How to Survive as a Second Wife*, pp. 85–7.

Questions

1. What are the two schools of thought on maintenance payments referred to here? Can you think of other viewpoints on this issue?
2. What do you think the consequences of these views will be for
   (a) divorced women with young children, and
   (b) housewives who are divorced in middle age?

□ The View from Divorced Wives and Mothers

A counter argument to the view that the family law favoured women (before the 1984 changes) is provided here by Julia Brophy and Carol Smart. They suggest that it was the state's concern to avoid picking up the bills for welfare and child care – either in the form of Supplementary Benefit payments or in state nurseries – that produced laws that attempt to force ex-partners (in practice, men) to support each other (their wives) and their children. The authors argue that the anomalies through which divorced wives and mothers appear to benefit, come from the fact that the family is a sex-role segregated institution within a sex-segregated society which gives males the advantage. Women are encouraged into economic dependence on men in the family, not least by a waged labour market that offers the best pay and conditions to male workers, and women are given responsibility for housework and child care. On divorce the dubious privilege of this position becomes the source of an attack, in which women are presented as idle, as living off husbands – the famous 'alimony drones'.

Reading 4

There is, it would seem, a popular belief that twentieth century women have now achieved equality with men. In fact this century has been described as the 'woman's epoch' because of the volume of legal reforms which have apparently ameliorated the position of women in the family and in economic and political spheres. In addition, women are perceived as not only achieving equal rights with men but, in some instances, as receiving special treatment from the law. This is particularly the case in the area of family law where women usually receive the custody of children and are usually entitled to maintenance from their husbands. . . .

The view that the 'pendulum' has swung back too far and, in mitigating the effects of nineteenth century legislation, has come to favour women unfairly, is now common currency. For example, there is now a growing emphasis on fathers' rights to custody, and pressure groups such as Families Need Fathers (FNF) argue that men are unfairly denied rights over their children. There is also a growing belief, fostered in particular by the Campaign for Justice on Divorce (CJD), that wives, even common-law wives, can financially exploit men and remain a drain on their economic resources for life. . . .

The introduction of reforms to family law in the early 1970s . . . to a large extent removed the contentious issue of a wife's behaviour and its effects upon her claim to maintenance or her right to accommodation. In addition it formally recognized the value of domestic labour as an indirect contribution to the acquisition of assets. A wife's adultery (in theory) could no longer wipe out a consideration of the economic value of her unwaged labour to her husband. In reality, however, . . . the courts take other factors into account and the most important is not a wife's indirect economic contribution but her status as a mother. The benefits wives now appear to enjoy on divorce (the custody of children, the occupation of the matrimonial home and the receipt of maintenance) are not benefits or rights that simply accrue to women-as-wives. They flow from juridical concern over the welfare of children. It is because women tend to have the custody of children, that they also tend to be awarded the matrimonial home or to have the tenancies of rented accommodation transferred to them. . . . the law is not so much operating to improve the rights of wives against those of husbands, but is acting to protect children and provide them with an 'appropriate' caretaker. . . .

The (partial) removal of the concept of matrimonial offence has had very important implications for the position of the husband in family law. Essentially it means that he can no longer evade the duty to maintain his wife regardless of her adultery or desertion, and consequently he, and not his wife, has been constituted as the central figure. It is his willingness or ability to maintain his dependants that occupies the law, not the quality or degree of his wife's misbehaviour. Family law no longer argues, as it once did, that it is against 'public policy' to award maintenance to a guilty wife. On the contrary it now argues that it is in the interests of preserving 'public funds' that all husbands should support their dependents. The aspects of family law which used to punish the wife in order to discourage other wives from disobedience is less evident now. Instead it is the husband who is scrutinized. . . .

This gradual shift from a focus on wives to husbands has obscured the law's relation to women. Because family courts now
concentrate on, and have gained greater powers to enforce obligations on husbands, wives *appear* to occupy a privileged position.
But a wife's economic position is not necessarily improved by this
strategy because the policy of the courts is not to benefit wives but to
protect the 'public purse' and to deflect the economic costs of the
disintegration of the family away from the welfare state and onto
individuals. Although this policy is not new it has never been an
unconditional policy within family law as it has been in welfare law.
Family legislation is now moving closer to welfare legislation and is
also adopting interventionist strategies that have been more common to the latter. For example the courts have increasing powers to
investigate incomes, to deduct monies at source, to vary property
ownership and to investigate the family through the agency of
welfare officers. Intervention into and surveillance over the family is
becoming more extensive and the prevailing strategy of family law is
not to construct a semi-autonomous institution within which one
patriarch has absolute power, but to regulate family members (positively and negatively) and to contain economic dependency within
the family unit.

. . . Legal discourse celebrates the individual relation between a
mother and her child and consistently reinforces ideologies of motherhood in which the biological bond between mother and child is given
primacy. However legislation has failed to contribute in a material
sense to the economic viability of the mother/child unit outside of a
family structure; whilst celebrating motherhood the law has retained
the economic dependency of the mother on either a 'wage-earner' or
the state. In effect mothers are prevailed upon to provide vital duties
with regard to children but the only really viable means for them to do
so is within the confines of the heterosexual family unit (whether or
not that unit is legitimated by marriage). So it is not motherhood in
isolation that is revered by the courts but motherhood within a familial
structure.

. . . the contemporary debate about the disproportionate advantages accorded to women in marriage, which has recently been
fuelled by groups such as CJD and FNF, argues that the burden that
is placed on husbands to maintain their wives is now an anachron-
ism because the legal status of wives has improved so much. . . .
This ignores the fact that the duty to maintain is not simply contingent
upon a husband's counter-balancing rights [notably his former right
to *own* his wife] but upon the fact that the division of labour between

husbands and wives places women in a position of dependency upon their husbands. The duty to maintain stems from an economic reality and not an eighteenth century legal right, so the loss of those legal rights should not automatically lead to a reduction in a husband's obligations.

The problem with these arguments . . . is that they conflate law and legislation with the reality of inequality within the family and within wider society. They ignore that women are still in a subordinate position, both in the domestic and waged economy in spite of legislation on equal pay, sex discrimination, domestic violence and matrimonial property rights. They also fail to recognize that law, as well as other social institutions, operates to constitute women as dependents within the family. This level of analysis locates the problem of dependency at the level of individual members of the family.

J. Brophy and C. Smart, 'From disregard to disrepute: the position of women in Family Law', in *Feminist Review*, No 9, 1981, pp. 3–16.

Questions

1. Why were wives, according to the authors, given benefits in law in the 1970s?
2. Readings 3 and 4 are in clear disagreement. Outline what you see as the strengths and weaknesses of both arguments and say which one you agree with more.

□ Who Cares for the Elderly?

A quite different but rapidly escalating 'crisis' around the family is the pressing question of who is going to be responsible for caring for the growing numbers of elderly people in Britain. As with the problems of divorce, government reactions seem primarily motivated by a desire to reduce public expenditure – or at least to prevent it increasing. This aim is certainly one strong element within the calls for a return to 'Victorian Values'.

This reading is from an article by Hilary Land in which she was responding to proposals that were 'leaked' in 1983 from the Conservative Government's Family Policy Group.

Reading 5

Some Ministers have expressed the view that families should be encouraged 'to reassume responsibilities taken on by the state, for example, responsibility for the disabled, elderly,. . . '.

Apparently they are unaware that in 1980 only 5% of the elderly lived in institutions, just over half in long-stay hospitals and that the single, widowed and childless were over-represented among them. At the turn of the century only one person in every 20 was aged 65 years or over and only one in every 82 was aged 75 years or more. Since then the elderly population has increased nearly fourfold so that in 1980 the figures had increased to one in 7 and one in 18 respectively.

Nevertheless, at the end of Victoria's reign, so admired by Mrs Thatcher, those who survived to old age were more likely to end their days in an institution (usually the workhouse) then they would be now. Today a third of the elderly have had, or have no surviving children, but of those who do, one in five live with one of them. Among the infirm the proportion is even higher: half of the bedfast elderly live with one of their children.

Study after study has shown that relatives not the state or voluntary services, provide the bulk of support to the elderly even if they do not all live under the same roof. A national study carried out in 1976 found that two out of every three elderly parents aged between 65 and 74 years, saw their children at least once a week. Among those aged 75 or older the proportion was three out of four.

The major reason given for infrequent contact was distance: half of the over-75s who were not visited said their offspring lived too far away (one sixth were living abroad). Has Mr Tebbit thought that if more of the unemployed heeded his exhortations to get on their bicycles, then more of the elderly might be isolated?

The Costs of Loving Care

Caring for a disabled or infirm person, even in the context of a loving relationship, is costly in terms of time, opportunity and resources. It is not an experience confined to a tiny minority of families. On the basis of a national study carried out in the 70s it was estimated that 'one half of the housewives between 35 and 64 can expect at some time or another to give some help to elderly or infirm persons.'

A more recent study in the North East found that at a given time there were more people involved in caring for handicapped or elderly dependants than there were mothers with children under 16 years. The period involved may be considerable: another study in 1978 found that a quarter of the carers had already been looking after a disabled relative for ten years or more.

Apart from their own ill-health, the most common reason for early retirement among women is the need to care for a sick relative and estimates of their weekly earnings forgone range from £80 to £120 (1980 prices). (It would be interesting to know how the Chancellor of the Exchequer proposes to encourage them to make better provision for their own pensions.) . . .

Apart from financial hardship, all the evidence we have suggests that what these families need is some relief from the daily and often nightly strains of caring. A small study conducted in 1980 looked at the amount of time spent caring for an elderly relative. The majority were spending between four and six hours daily. On average women were spending over three hours a day in caring activities, helped by their husbands for an average of 13 minutes.

Cuts in domicilary services, like home helps, day centres, or holiday relief schemes, which sadly the previous Labour Government set in train in 1976, and to which this Government has given a vicious momentum, makes the work of caring within the family even harder. It is quite clear that it is too little, not too much state provision which undermines a family's capacity to care.

To assert that families, meaning of course mainly women, could and should do more in the context of major cutbacks on community welfare services is an insult to those hundreds of thousands of women who do care and do so often at great cost to themselves and other members of their families. As for those who have no immediate family (and again they are mainly women – only a third of the over 75's and a quarter of the over 85's are men) what of their needs?

Spending Cuts the Aim

Of course, one of the FPG's major objectives is to cut public spending on welfare. That this should be presented as 'family policy' and as a means of strengthening 'the family' is significant but not new. The myth that families no longer care for the sick or the old as much as they did in the past, has a long history. The Poor Law Commissioners of 1834 appealed to it as they argued for a harsher, more deterrent and therefore cheaper (they hoped) system of poor relief. It was repeated 70 years later by those Edwardian politicians who opposed the Liberal welfare reforms such as state provision of old age pensions and school meals. . . .

Ideology and rhetoric cannot change demographic trends, however vehemently expressed.

H. Land, 'Family Fables', in *New Socialist*, May/June 1983, pp. 20–31.

Questions

1. According to this reading, what would be the real effects on the elderly of a return to Victorian values?
2. The elderly are frequently regarded as merely the recipients of care. What contributions, to their families and to society, are made by elderly people that you know?

□ What is a Community?

Our final readings refer to yet another type of crisis that involves the family. This is the widely expressed view that modern society has suffered from a loss of community. The terms family and community are often used almost as one joint term, but the exact relationship between them is by no means clear. Both terms are slippery, elusive, political concepts – a point made clear with respect to the family in Chapter 1. This reading helps to clarify the different meanings involved in commons usages of the term community and in so doing begins to challenge the common sense assumption that old rural communities were harmonious and stable – the ideal setting for family life, while new urban or suburban ones are fragmented and isolating.

Reading 6

It is a common observation that modern British society is characterized by a 'loss of community'. The phrase is often used in an oblique but poignant way to express the dissatisfaction which many people experience about the quality of life in the contemporary world. There is an implied antithesis between the past, when, so it is believed, the individual was integrated into a stable and harmonious community of kin, friends and neighbours, and the less palatable present . . .

The withering away of a spirit of community as an apparently endemic feature of our social condition is therefore offered as the diagnosis of a wide variety of contemporary social problems, ranging from the incidence of juvenile crime to the loneliness of the elderly. More generally this sense of loss raises doubts about the validity of 'progress' and our fears concerning the direction in which modern society appears to be moving. . . .

Unfortunately, however, it is not always clear precisely what is meant by community and whether, in what ways and how it has been lost. There is, for example, a constant danger of nostalgia in contrasting the past with the present, a tendency to take a highly selective and somewhat rose-tinted view of the 'good old days', which can convey a misleading account of the actual changes that have occurred. . . .

[One] sense in which a loss of community is said to afflict society concerns the decline of locality as a basis of modern social organization. In many pre-industrial societies. . . . local areas. . . . retained a fair amount of autonomy and there was a greater diversity of local traditions and customs. . . .

The growth of urban industrialism has, however . . . meant that most localities have become more dependent upon extra local sources of decision-making, thanks to increasingly nationalized and centralized forms of political and economic control. . . .

[Another] sense of loss of community . . . refers to the effects of rapid social and economic change. As slum clearance such changes are often welcomed, but as the tearing down of inner-city communities they are criticized. Not surprisingly, therefore, an often fierce public debate has been fought over the desirability of these changes, in which the notion of community has been central. . . .

A sense of loss of community has not, however, been limited to such urban areas, although it has been more visible there because of the actual demolition of Victorian neighbourhoods and their replacement by new housing estates. A similar sense of loss has afflicted the older inhabitants of many rural villages because of the recent transformation in the social composition of the countryside. Rural villages have lost many of their former agricultural inhabitants and received in their place an influx of ex-urban commuters, retired people and second-home owners. . . . A feeling that community has declined is not limited therefore to those areas that have undergone physical redevelopment. Rapid social change may also bring about a sense of dislocation. The former population may feel estranged and taken over by such changes. In urban areas, for example, such feelings are aroused by the 'gentrification' of former working-class neighbours (i.e. their colonization by professional and managerial newcomers) or by a rapid influx of overseas immigrants. Nevertheless it is worth pointing out that the newcomers themselves believe that they are creating community, albeit among themselves in many cases, rather than attempting to destroy it. . . .

In its most abstract sense the perception of a loss of community in modern society refers to changes in both the structure and content of personal relationships. Here community is used to denote a sense of common identity between individuals, and enduring ties of affection and harmony based upon personal knowledge and face-to-face contact. It is often contrasted with the impersonal and dehumanizing aspects of modern life, with the rise of a selfish individualism, a calculative approach to human relationships and the sense of social dislocation present under conditions of rapid social and economic change. . . .

Essentially the many and varied definitions of community are reducible to three.

1. Community as a fixed and bounded *locality* – that is, as a geographical expression, denoting a human settlement located within a particular local territory. . . .

2. Community as a *local social system* – that is, as a set of social relationships which take place wholly, or mostly, within a locality. . . .

3. Community as a *type of relationship*. More particularly, community is defined as a sense of identity between individuals (even though, in some cases, their mutual identification may never have resulted from any personal contact). . . .

Unfortunately sociologists in the past have tended to run all three of these definitions together. There has been a largely unexamined assumption that life in particular localities promotes a certain structure of relationships which results in the presence or absence of communion. However, the three definitions of community need to be considered separately and the relationships, if any, between them carefully examined. Prevailing cultural assumptions about rural and urban life often assume a unity between locality, local social system and communion which acts like a pair of blinkers on our perceptions. Rural villages are often assumed to consist of closely-knit inhabitants living in happy communion, while in cities there are only isolated, lonely individuals lacking any sense of mutual identity.

[We should also note that]. . . . one source of communion is the 'mutuality of the oppressed' – the almost unavoidable communality enforced by a shared existence on the edge of poverty. . . . the lifting of the constraints deriving from poverty will [probably] provoke the decline of communion – a point which is echoed in the 'myth of suburbia' and in much of the writing on working-class privatization. . . . It is equally plausible, however, to argue that communion can only be created voluntarily upon the basis of choice of life-style or interests. Freed from social and economic constraints, like-minded individuals may come together to share their experiences and develop a meaningful sense of communal identity. It is possible, for example, to regard the commune movement in this light. . . . or the many attempts to create communion on the basis of voluntary associations or social movements. Unlike the 'mutuality of the oppressed', however, these are usually quite conscious attempts to recapture a sense of belonging and frequently they have resulted from a deep disenchantment with certain aspects of modern society.

H. Newby, Community, Study Section 20 of *Social Sciences: a Second Level Course*, pp. 5, 6, 8, 11, 13, 35.

Questions

1. Why does Newby think it important to carefully distinguish between the three senses of community?
2. Why might poor people leave their communities if given the opportunity?

□ Housing Estates and the Loss of Community

Community studies of the changes in post-war housing have drawn attention to the differences between life in the close knit, urban, working class settlements of places such as the East End of London and the new out–of–town housing estates. The general argument put forward has been that the new estates are characterised by much more emphasis on a home–centred life. This is built around internal, nuclear family relationships (and especially perhaps around children), carried out behind closed doors, rather than by relationships with neighbours, between generations, or wider kin. It is claimed the old friendliness has gone and been replaced by hostility, family–(self–?) centredness, loneliness and vandalism.

One of the problems with this view of 'loss' is that it has been promoted by an earlier sociology which pictured 'traditional' working class life in a romantic light. No mention was made in the early studies of gossiping neighbours, wife battering, child abuse, the burdens of mothering larger numbers of children *and* elderly relatives, the sexual miseries reported in the problem pages of the women's magazines, or petty crime.

The next reading, by Ronald Frankenberg, is from a book in which he reviews a large number of community studies. It draws particularly on the contrasts between life in 'Greenleigh', a large London County Council housing estate in outer London, and Bethnal Green, an inner London working class area studied by Michael Young and Peter Willmott in 1953–55. Frankenberg takes a properly critical view of the material he discusses and he is well aware of the dangers of myth making, but he nevertheless stresses *changes* which took place with the move to the new estates.

Reading 7

. . . everyday life,. . . accentuates the dependence of husband and wife and immediate family upon each other and their isolation in the home. There is very often in housing estates (as in Greenleigh, Dagenham, Barton, and Coventry) nowhere else to go. In Bethnal Green there is one pub for every four hundred people and a shop for every fourteen households. In Greenleigh there is a pub for every five thousand and a shop for every three hundred people. It is no wonder that the number of television sets per hundred households increased much more rapidly in Greenleigh than in Bethnal Green.

All this has a profound effect on the relationships of men and women. In Bethnal Green there was a community of women which was almost self-sufficient. Men, except the retired, were cut off from it by their daily exile at work. When they came home the women included them in the community by passing on gossip. In Greenleigh it is the women's work of raising children and keeping house which cuts them off. This activity which was a 'factory industry' in Bethnal Green has become a cottage industry in Greenleigh. Like all cottage industries child rearing and home building tend to encompass all the family. The man is drawn in as well. Here is the mechanism of changing networks, changing roles in action. Men spend more time doing jobs in the house and garden and watching telly than they do in the pub and at the football ground. [As Young and Willmott say,]

The 'home' and the family of marriage becomes the focus of a man's life, as of his wife's, far more completely than in the East End. 'You lose contact with parents and relations once you move out here,' said Mr Curtis. 'You seem to centre yourself more on the home. Everybody lives in a little world of their own'.

... the key to the understanding of social relationships on housing estates. . . . lies in uncertainty. The Irish countrymen know what to expect as the response of others to their particular behaviour. The estate housewife does not. She knows how the hire-purchase companies behave, she knows what to expect of her family, but her neighbours are a mystery. Hence she seeks privacy – she does not want others to know her relationships with the commercial outside world – and she wants her relationships within the family to be played out according to its internal expectation uncomplicated by the discordant expectations of the outside world. The problem is, she does not and cannot know whether the outside expectations are discordant or not. She cannot choose between discordance and conformity because there is no reference group to help her. Hence the appeal to the mass media and the status race. . . .

Although active interaction with neighbours is at a minimum, their presence is felt. They are perceived as watchful eyes looking for faults in the housewife's craftsmanship as wife, housekeeper, and mother. The husband's job, often far removed from the estate, is no longer the main criterion of status. A family is judged (or thought to be judged) by its mother and its mother is judged by the appearance and affluence of her home and her children's appearance. The standards to which the neighbours are thought to impel one are paradoxically not local but national – the standards of the women's magazines, newspapers, and television commercials.

Consumer goods are acquired because they are useful and because others have them. Some, like cars and telephones, are a means of retaining contact with the old way of life in the context of the new. Visiting sisters on other housing estates may only be possible by car. Urban public transport tends to go from periphery to centre rather than linking places on the periphery.

I have suggested in earlier chapters that conflict within consensus is an essential part of community. In Bethnal Green I described the friendly rivalry between streets and sub-districts. In Greenleigh the only possible basis for such unity creating conflict are the nuclear families in their 'little boxes'. As Young and Willmott suggest, relationships are often window-to-window rather than face-to-face . . . The neighbours are ubiquitous but anonymous.

R. Frankenberg, *Communities in Britain*, pp. 229–32.

Questions

1. What does Frankenberg mean when he says housework and child rearing have returned to being 'cottage industry' as opposed to 'factory industry'? Do you think the metaphor is appropriate?

2. Give examples of things that encourage people on estates to live in little worlds of their own. Refer to examples given in the reading and also to other features that you can think of.

□ Women's Solidarity

A very different picture of community and women's interactions on a housing estate, this time Span housing in South East London in the early 1970s, is provided by an ethnographic study by Gaynor Cohen. Most of the men on the estate were in their 30s and either in professional posts or executives or managers. Cohen argues that the tasks assigned to women, far from isolating them, in fact prompt them to develop patterns of co-operation.

Reading 8

Most women with young children on this housing estate (that is the majority of families) subordinated their own interests to those of their husbands and children. The demands of husbands' careers were accepted as a necessary evil and women turned to neighbours, who were in a similar situation, for help with domestic duties, which (given different circumstances) they might have expected their husbands to provide.

The first contacts between wives were on the practical basis of exchanging equipment and services. They helped each other with the initial 'settling in' problems and borrowed kitchen, gardening, and home decorating equipment. They exchanged expertise – from advice on sewing children's clothes, to first aid assistance from mothers previously employed as professional nurses. Most important of all, as families with young children, they exchanged services: mothers took turns in entertaining a group of children for a morning or afternoon, or in ferrying children to and from school. They installed baby-sitting alarms along a row of houses and alternated the evening's guard on neighbours' sleeping children. This degree of co-operation has previously only been noted in working-class districts among female kin . . .

The distinctive feature of these co-operating activities was that they generated support among the women. Through this solidarity a distinct culture developed which provided a resource for women lacking support from husbands. This did not usurp the husband's role within the family, or force wives to consider their own status separately from that of their husbands. In short, solidarity was seen as substituting for the husband's involvement with wife and children, given the fact that his career demands made it impossible – at least temporarily – for him to share such tasks.

Solidarity between women went beyond offering each other support with practical tasks, and led to the development of a specific 'estate style'. Not only did it give the estate a separate identity from the area surrounding it, but it also distinguished it from other middle-class communities. . . .

Most women who participated in the estate culture had few contacts outside the estate. Many claimed that their network of contacts had narrowed since moving there, they had increasingly less time available for maintaining ties with friends or relatives from elsewhere. Daily routine involving shopping on the estate, collecting children from school, or attending the clinic meant that most wives were constantly meeting neighbours. Casual contacts were strengthened by the informal gatherings organized between the women themselves, such as coffee mornings, tea sessions, or sales parties of clothes, wigs, 'Tupperware', or make-up.

Dinner parties when husbands were home, lent further support to communication. At any such social gathering attended by both husband and wife, it was evident that husbands did not share or even fit into the estate culture. Communication between men was often spasmodic and superficial. Their attitudes were not based on shared experiences or interests, for men identified with the world of work – with their profession or their company. Their job consumed most of their time, and the estate culture was mediated to them by their wives.

Solidarity did not develop among all estate women, only among the majority who shared the common problem of raising children without support from husbands. Yet even among this group, there were differences – primarily of status, educational background, and attitudes – which had to be overcome. Despite the fact that the price range of the houses meant that the majority of house holders were likely to be middle class, the men's jobs varied considerably. Such differences were often accompanied by specific and conflicting family life-styles which, to some extent, were played down through an under-emphasis of the husband's actual job. One taxi-driver's wife reported that her husband had been convinced that when their professional neighbours discovered the nature of his work, they would be isolated. In fact it had been weeks before anyone had asked about her husband's job.

G. Cohen, 'Women's solidarity and the preservation of privilege', in P. Caplan and J.M. Bujra (eds), *Women United, Women Divided*. pp. 135–8.

Questions

1. How does the participation of husbands on this estate vary from that described for Greenleigh?
2. Which women do you suppose did not participate in the estate culture and why?
3. How would you explain the disparity between the last two readings?

Essay Questions

1. Do changing divorce rates indicate changing conceptions of marriage? (Oxford 1987)
2. What have been the major social consequences of the increase in the divorce rate? (Oxford 1985)
3. 'A sense of community has been lost in modern societies'. Discuss the evidence for and against this statement. (Cambridge 1986)
4. 'The growth of the welfare state has undermined family responsibility for the care of the sick and the elderly.' Is there any sociological evidence to support this view? (Oxford 1985)

Further Reading

Michael Anderson, 'How Has the Family Changed?', *New Society*, 27 October 1983, looks at today's families in the light of what Victorian family life was really like, and argues that few today would want to change places.

Anna Davin, 'Imperialism and motherhood', *History Workshop*, No. 5, spring 1978, looks at what was seen as the crisis around the family in 1900 – a concern about poor mothering and the 'unfit' breeding, and to improve infant life and child health, because a numerous, robust population was needed as a national resource.

Paul Willis, 'Youth Unemployment: thinking the unthinkable', *Youth and Policy*, Vol. 2, No. 4, 1984, and B. Roberts, R. Finnegan and D. Gallie (eds), *New Approaches to Economic Life*, papers by:
G.M. Breakwell, 'Young People in and out of work',
C.C. Harris *et al.*, 'Redundancy in steel: labour market behaviour, local social networks and domestic organisation',
L. McKee and C. Bell 'Marital and family relationships in times of male unemployment',
R. Turner *et al.*, 'The work ethic in a Scottish town with declining employment'.
These give some initial research findings on the effect of unemployment on family life, including the state of suspended animation that wageless young people are in, and their 'broken transitions into the possibility of adult roles'.

E. Ferri, *Growing up in a One-parent Family*, and Mavis Maclean and John Eekelaar, *Children and Divorce: economic factors*, together summarise past research on the social, psychological and educational effects of single parenthood and divorce on children, and present findings, based on a random sample, of the financial consequences of divorce.

Nicky Hart, *When Marriage Ends. A study in status passage*, and Catherine

Itzin, *Splitting Up. Single-parent liberation*. These two books present interestingly contrasted views on the experience and effects of divorce. Hart's is based on a study in a club for the divorced and separated in a Midlands city, and shows a slow and painful process of adjustment between two statuses. Itzin's case histories/stories describe the traumas but also the sense of freedom often involved, and has comments from her interviewees a few years on about the new lives they have built.

Equal Opportunities Commission, *The experience of Caring for Elderly and Handicapped Dependants: a survey report*, and Muriel Nissel and Lucy Bonnerjea, *Family Care of the Handicapped Elderly: who pays?* There is now an increasing literature on the extent of care provided within families for the elderly, handicapped and chronically sick. These two short pamphlets provide striking case histories and time-budgets to stress the labour of love and the lack of outside support.

R. Frankenberg, *Communities in Britain*. This is an interesting re-analysis of British community studies along a rural-urban continuum, stressing changes in family patterns. Ten years later, Frankenberg reflected on his earlier work in:
R. Frankenberg, '"In the production of their lives, men (?). . " Sex and gender in British Community Studies', in D.L. Barker and S. Allen (eds), *Sexual Divisions and Society: process and change*.

Leonore Davidoff, Jean L'Esperance and Howard Newby 'Landscape with Figures: home and community in English society', in J. Mitchell and A. Oakley, *The Rights and Wrongs of Women*. This draws fascinating comparisons between the ideal setting for women's lives being the home and the ideal setting for wider social relations being the village community. It looks too at the power relations (and form of legitimate authority) contained within each.

Errol Lawrence 'Just plain common sense: the "roots" of racism', and 'In the abundance of water the fool is thirsty: sociology and black pathology' in Centre for Contemporary Cultural Studies, *The Empire Strikes Back: race and racism in 70s Britain* on the pathologising of Black families.

Diana Gittins, *The Family in Question*, Chapter 8 'Is the family in a state of crisis?'

Graham Allan, *Family Life*, three chapters look at the effects, particularly on women, of recent changes in family patterns: Chapter 6 Divorce and single-parent families, Chapter 7 The elderly, the family and community care, Chapter 8 Unemployment and family life. Also Chapter 4 Home and leisure, considers the growth of home-centredness and its impact on leisure patterns and sociable activity.

3 | Is the family symmetrical or patriarchal?

Equality and power are some of the most discussed concepts in philosophy and sociology and both have a variety of different definitions and interpretations. Issues of equality and inequality concern the distribution of work and rewards, and the justice of this distribution. Debates around power involve who has control over whom: can A make B do what A wants; and what advantages accrue to A from this.

The sorts of problems which come up when people discuss equality include the following. Can we compare people if they do different work and receive different rewards? That is, can those who are fundamentally different be considered either equal *or* unequal? Is there consensus as to what are 'rewards' (what is socially desirable)? In so far as there are dominant values in society, are they ones we wish to support? May some people not be correct to prefer interesting or socially useful jobs to high salaries? Or again, should the education system be set up as a race where all have an equal opportunity to succeed, although most will not; or should positive action be taken to help those who come from disadvantaged backgrounds or have lower abilities, so that we achieve something near equality of outcome? Or is the latter the way to hold back the able and individual, a disasterous route to dull, stultifying uniformity?

The sorts of debates around power (see S. Lukes, *Power*) include: does the ability to win disputes relate only to occasions of perceived conflict, or should it include situations where one side has the power to fix the agenda, so that some things which might be contested are never even discussed? And does even the latter go far enough? Do we not need to include recognition of the extent to which the 'needs' people feel they have are socially constructed; and the extent to which certain categories and classes of actor have power because of their social structural position, rather than because they have resources to win in particular interpersonal interactions? Or should we rethink more radically (see Foucault, *The History of Sexuality*) and regard power not so much as a capacity to determine events that is centred on particular classes or practices, such as the law, but rather as a feature built into relationships (knowledge, technology and so forth) and widely diffused throughout society? (See the introduction to Chapter 6.)

Though these debates have not, until recently, been applied to the family, they are obviously relevant. Currently they are being increasingly developed thanks to the 'politicisation of the personal' by feminism.

It is, for example, relatively easy to show there are profound differences in the everyday lives of family members: men, women and children. But are these differences inequalities? Are they bad? Should they be changed – or does the status quo not have something to be said for it? Who, if anyone, benefits from the differences between the lives of men and women? If 'the system' or some group is thought to benefit, how do they, and how is the system maintained so that they continue to benefit?

It is relatively easy to construct an argument that women are disadvantaged in the labour market; that their situation *vis-a-vis* men is unequal and that this is unfair. The waged work women do compares unfavourably with the work men do. There are men's jobs and women's jobs in both the middle and the working class, and women's jobs are much more restricted (two-thirds of all women work in just 3 of the census's 27 occupational groupings), and they are less well paid. It is more difficult to explain how and why this came about, though there are various suggestions, some of which are included in the readings in Chapters 5 and 6.

But the argument that women are disadvantaged within the family is more contentious.

1. TV comedians suggest women rule the roost and it is quite commonly suggested that women are the ones who are advantaged by marriage because they do not have to earn their own living and yet they secure most of the children's affection.

2. It is more commonly argued that families are reasonably egalitarian: that husbands and wives roles are different but equal, and that this form of division of labour has much to be said for it.

3. Others insist women are oppressed within the family and that this is the root of their oppression outside, so the family must change if women are to be liberated.

The debate in sociology is currently between these latter two positions, which we are here calling the 'symmetrical' and the 'patriarchal' view. Symmetry is defined in Reading 1 and patriarchy in a quotation from Michèle Barrett in Reading 6.

In the symmetrical view, which is not far removed from Talcott

Parsons's analysis of marital roles, it is recognised that the sexual division of labour may produce certain strains on partners (e.g. the stress of bread-winning responsibilities on husbands, and women's confinement to the home), but overall the exchange between the two is seen as fair. Each values and respects the other. In so far as there have been inequalities in the past, e.g. the husband/father being authoritarian, this has changed and will continue to change, and each partner now shares some of the responsibility, some of the strains, of his/her spouse.

The patriarchal view stresses the continuing rule of the husband/father; men's occupancy of a position within the kinship system through which they have power and authority over wives and children. In the nineteenth century the word patriarchy was almost always used as a term of approval. Writers talked of patriarchal virtues, and they interpreted the near absolute legal powers of husband/fathers over their dependents in terms of the responsibilities men had towards 'the weaker sex' and innocent children. Nowadays the term is used much more antagonistically, to stress the advantages and profit men derive from the subordination and work of women.

In this chapter we shall look at relations between husbands and wives, and in the next at generational relations. These are both aspects of patriarchy, though the term has become largely used by feminists in relation to gender relations. However, children too have their subordinate status determined by their position in the family: their work, rewards, rights and responsibilities. Children are family dependents whose exclusions from the labour market and legal status has many parallels with those of wives (see Chapters 5 and 6). Mothers, it is argued, face their children partly as delegates of their joint patriarch, with powers and controls largely derived from the patriarchal system.

We have had to be highly selective in our choice of extracts for this chapter. There has been a lot of recent work on marital decision-making and the division of household tasks and time budgets. We refer you to this in the Further Reading. It shows, not surprisingly perhaps, that women still usually do the bulk of domestic work – cooking, cleaning and the physical care of children, the sick and the elderly – usually in their capacity as wives, but sometimes as daughters and daughters-in-law. Husbands do household repairs, gardening, and help with the washing up and some childcare, but the time they spend is a small fraction (about one seventh) of the time spent on regular housework by women. Men have the major responsibility of earning income, but women's earnings are also important and most wives are now in part-time employment (see R. Chester, 'The Rise of the Neo-Conventional Family', Reading 7, Chapter 1). Women's paid work, however, is normally done *in addition* to housework. Even when men are unemployed, they do little housework.

We have chosen to include readings on men and women's relative share in the pleasures of childcare, in the distribution of food, in talk about sexuality, and the giving and experiencing of violence. We have also included a discussion of whether the term patriarchy can be equally applied to the experience of Afro–Caribbean women. These obviously do not exhaust all the areas where one might want to consider the justice of the distribution of work and rewards in the family, or the relative power of family members. We hope you will think of, and discuss, others.

☐ The Symmetrical Family

In 1970, twenty years after their famous researches into the family in Bethnal Green, Michael Young and Peter Willmott undertook a major historical and contemporary survey of the Greater London area. As a result of their work they clearly believed that a new form of post-industrial family had emerged, especially among the middle class and it was filtering down from them to the working class. This type of family is characterised by its home-centred emphasis on immediate family rather than on wider links with kin, by its economic importance as a major unit of consumption, and by having less segregated sex roles. Young and Willmott were not the first to comment on this (supposed) change. Various writers had noted it and named it and in this reading the authors explain why they have adopted and modified for their own use a term first used by Gorer.

You may like to compare this view of the family with Chester's 'neo-conventional family' discussed in Chapter 1 and, when you come to Chapter 7, with the idea of the 'dual career family' discussed by the Rapoports.

Reading 1

Inside the family of marriage the roles of the sexes have become less segregated. The difference between two contemporary families of the 1950s, with and without segregated roles, has been well described by Bott [in *Family and Social Network*].

> There was considerable variation in the way husbands and wives performed their conjugal roles. At one extreme was a family in which the husband and wife carried out as many tasks as possible separately and independently of each other. There was a strict division of labour in the household, in which she had her tasks and he had his. He gave her a set amount of housekeeping money, and she had little idea of how much he earned or how he spent the money he kept for himself. In their leisure time, he went to cricket matches with his friends, whereas she visited her relatives or went to a cinema with a neighbour. With the exception of festivities with relatives, this husband and wife spent very little of their leisure time together. They did not consider that they were unusual in this respect. On the contrary, they felt their behaviour was typical of their social circle. At the other extreme was a family in which husband and wife shared as many activities and spent as much time together as possible. They stressed that husband and wife should be equals: all major decisions should be made together, and even in minor household matters they should help one another as much as possible. This norm was carried out in practice. In their division of labour, many tasks were shared or interchangeable. The husband often did the cooking and sometimes the washing and ironing. The wife did the gardening and often the household repairs as well. Much of their leisure time was spent together, and they shared similar interests in politics, music, literature, and in entertainment. Like the first couple, this husband and wife felt their behaviour was typical of their social circle, except that they carried the inter-changeability of tasks a little further than most people.

Bott was writing fifteen years ago, and not many families have yet got as far as the second couple. Power has not been distributed equally in more than a few families. Division of labour is still the rule, with the husband doing the 'man's' work and the wife taking prime responsibility for the housekeeping and the children. . . . But the direction of change has, we believe, been from Bott's first to her second type.

Many different terms have been used for the new kind of family that is emerging. Since it has so many facets to it, a single apt word is not easy to find. Burgess and Locke said, a quarter of a century ago, that the family had moved from 'institution to companionship' and their words 'companionship family' have sometimes found favour, although not with us. The members of a family are more (or less) than companions. For the same reason we do not like 'companionate', as employed by Goldthorpe and his colleagues. We have ourselves talked about 'partnership' and the 'home-centred' family, but these words too are open to objection, the former because it is so general as to be applicable to all forms of marriage, and the latter because, although it stresses one of the distinguishing characteristics we have just mentioned, it does not now seem to us to stress the most important of them, the desegregation of roles. The new family could be labelled simply egalitarian. But that would not square with the marked differences that still remain in the human rights, in the work opportunities and generally in the way of life of the two sexes. The term which is best, in our view, is the one used by Gorer, the 'symmetrical family', although the emphasis we want to give is not the same as his. He said that, 'In a symmetrical relationship A responds to B as B responds to A; the differences of temperament, of function, of skills are all minimised.' We think it is closer to the facts of the situation as it is now to preserve the notion of difference but ally it to a measure of egalitarianism. In this context the essence of a symmetrical relationship is that it is opposite but similar. (Amongst those given in the Oxford English Dictionary, the definition of 'symmetry' which is the nearest, though not identical, to what we have in mind is 'Exact correspondence in size and position of opposite parts about a dividing line or centre. As an attribute either of the whole or of the parts composing it.') If all segregation of roles ever disappeared (apart from that minimum prescribed by the dictatorship of a biology from which there is for most people no escape) then one might properly talk about egalitarian marriage. But to be fair to what has happened in this century a term is needed which can describe the majority of families in which there is some role-segregation along with a greater degree of equality.

M. Young and P. Willmott, *The Symmetrical Family*, pp. 30–1.

Questions

1. In your own words say
   (a) what Gorer means by a symmetrical relationship and
   (b) what Young and Willmott mean by a symmetrical relationship.
2. In what ways are husbands and wives more, and in what ways less, than 'companions'?

□ Are Husbands Good Housewives?

At about the same time as Young and Willmott were publishing Reading 1, Ann Oakley was completing the research reported here (see also Further Readings). After interviewing a random sample of 20 20–30-year-old mothers of young children in West London about their attitudes to housework, she concluded that not only was there a continuing, marked division of labour, but also that the changes that *were* taking place did not lead to greater equality. The wives she talked to generally strongly agreed that there were, and should be, differences in the work done by men and women, although the women wanted their husbands to be interested in their families. What Oakley points out is that pleasure and status are attached to doing certain tasks rather than others, and that these were generally the tasks being taken over by husbands. She also observed that the women were not happy with their situation, though they saw no alternatives.

Reading 2

One of the first facts that emerged is that husbands (and wives) commonly make a distinction between housework and childcare: the degree of sharing in one area may be quite different from the degree of sharing in the other. Traditionally, research has assumed a convergence between the two, but this seems to be untrue of marriages in this sample. . . .

The most usual pattern was for husbands to share more in childcare than housework. . . .

Overall, class differences appeared rather more in the area of help with housework than with childcare, as the table below shows.

Husband's help with housework and childcare, by social class

	No. of respondents	Housework			Childcare		
		high	medium	low	high	medium	low
working class	20	2	1	17	2	8	10
middle class	20	4	9	7	8	4	8

Four questions proved invaluable as a means of finding out beliefs held about roles in marriage. The first of these, perhaps somewhat surprisingly, is: 'Does your husband ever change a dirty nappy?' (or where there were no children still in nappies, '*Did* your husband . . .'). This question was deliberately aimed at the boundaries defining the father's role in childcare, and the responses it received suggest that it does indeed do just this.

Here are some of the replies:

'You're joking! He says, "I'm not doing that – it's a woman's job".' (Working class: two children aged two and three.)

'He's changed a nappy once or twice but he does not make a very good job of it. He wouldn't change a dirty nappy – I wouldn't expect him to.' (Working class: three children aged four, two and a half and eight months.)

'No! He absolutely refuses. He says, "No thank you, goodbye, I'm going out." If I'm changing a nappy, he runs out of the room. It makes him sick. He thinks that it's my duty.' (Middle class: one child aged four months.)

'He might do it under protest. But I think he tends to think that's not what he *should* do.' (Middle class: one child aged four months.)

Clearly, the duties of even the most participant father rarely extend as far as this task. To the working class man, changing nappies which are dirty rather than merely wet is simply 'a woman's job.' Although the middle class father might not make exactly the same claim, he also appears to feel that this particular task cannot rightfully be expected of him.

These and other comments show just how much agreement exists in these marriages about what the husband/father's role should be. While a few of the women remarked that they would like their husbands to be prepared to change the occasional dirty nappy, even these women accepted, like the rest, that the physical side of childcare is basically the mother's responsibility. 'He's a very good father – he plays with the children' was a comment often voiced by both working class and middle class housewives. To play with the children in the evenings and at weekends; to take them off the mother's hands on a Sunday morning; to be interested in their welfare; and to act as mother substitute in times of illness or childbirth – this defines the father's role for these husbands and wives. . . .

One working class wife makes the distinction between help with the housework and help with the children quite clear: 'I agree with them looking after children and bringing them up with the wife, but I don't really agree with them doing housework. I don't think it's their job. I don't think it's their job to come home and do their wives' work in the evening.' . . .

While it appears true from this sample that men think of themselves as, in a sense, 'active' fathers, it seems that they limit their activities mainly to playing with or supervising children. Based on what the father does during his restricted hours at home, these assessments of fathers' participation could not be expected to show an absolutely equal division of labour between the sexes; but what they show is a lot less than this. To put it simply, these men seem to avoid all but the sheerly pleasurable aspects of childcare. The physical side, like the bulk of the housework, is in most cases avoided.

From a male-oriented standpoint, it is easy to see how playing with the children has been brought into the concept of the paternal role. It is a pleasant activity: changing dirty nappies is not. In fact, one could say that this enlargement of the father's role is an unfortunate development for women, who stand to gain nothing from it but temporary peace to do the household chores ('he plays with them in the evening while I'm washing up'), while they themselves stand to lose some of the very rewards childrearing has to offer.

The housework equivalent of 'playing with the children' is 'washing up.' Washing all the family clothes, cleaning the floors, making the beds, cooking the meals, remain feminine activities. It is perhaps less easy to see how washing up has come to be sanctioned as a male activity. Maybe it is because this task calls for limited time and energy and has to be done during the time husbands are at home. At any rate, the presence of British husbands at the kitchen sink does not appear to mean that they are fast becoming 'househusbands' in the sense in which women are 'housewives.' However great the dual-role problems of modern woman, modern man does not seem willing to solve them by creating the same dilemma for himself.

A. Oakley, 'Are Husbands Good Housewives?' in *New Society*, 17 Feb. 1972, pp. 337–40.

Questions

1. Many of the wives described their husbands as 'good fathers'. What did fathers have to do to earn this praise?
2. What is the evidence from Oakley's account that makes Young and Willmott's 'new' family seem unlikely to emerge?

☐ Consumption
   and the
   Family

Young and Willmott, and almost all other writers on the family who stress that a modern, changed family has developed, emphasise that the family continues to be important as a 'unit of consumption'. The family may have become less important as a unit of production – as a place where productive work is done, (see Chapter 5 – but it continues to be of major economic importance as a purchaser and consumer of goods and services that are now produced elsewhere. However the idea of the family as a 'unit' of consumption hides the question of whether or not the goods and services brought into the home are divided equally and equitably amongst all family members.

This reading uses historical material to suggest that inequalities *within* the family are of long-standing, even in families at a low standard of living where an absolutely equal distribution of, say food, would have meant a poor diet for everybody. The author, an American historian, suggests that unequal distribution – with men taking the lion's share of the little there was – was necessary to keep them, as the breadwinners, in good health and well-disposed towards their dependents.

Reading 3

In the late 1880s, social investigators and statisticians in England unwittingly developed a new tool for analyzing the welfare of women in laboring families. In their effort to answer questions about 'the condition of the people,' they moved beyond a general study of prices and money wages to collect intensive data on the budgets of individual working-class families. Historians have generally followed the pattern established by these poverty surveys and have discussed the standard of living of the English working class in terms of household units.

But some of these budgets could also be used to refine our concept of welfare still further. Several of the budgets suggest, in fact, that the members of a single family did not necessarily share a single standard of living. Working-class women, at least those married to low-paid unskilled laborers, apparently claimed a disproportionately small share of the household's food, medical care, and leisure time. Money-handling customs in poor families sometimes may also have added to the privileged position of husbands and the sacrifice of wives. . . .

The patterns revealed by the poverty surveys of the late 1880s [and onwards] may have originated before the industrial revolution. Evidence from other countries shows that cultural assumptions, rather than differences in physical size or type of work performed, often determined the allocation of food between men and women. Professor Natalie Davis, for instance, found that the tradition of giving males more food was a very old one in England. It applied where both were working on the same site or field and did not seem 'reasonably correlated' with energy needs or productivity. . . .

In rural Berkshire investigators were told [1913] that the women and children 'eat the potatoes and look at the meat.' Besides meat, including bacon, husbands sometimes ate extra vegetables, cheese, or eggs. In the country an added tradition meant that the husband ate better than the wife: some laborers still got meals with their wages, or rations of beer or cider. . . .

Money-handling arrangements that kept a part of the breadwinner's earnings out of his wife's hands often widened the standard-of-living gap even further. In almost all poor families and perhaps in the working class in general, money seems to have been divided into a portion for 'housekeeping' and a portion for the breadwinner's 'pocket money.' There were two major ways of dividing income into these portions. In some cases the wife was in control: her husband handed all his earnings to her and received back a fixed sum for his pocket money. In mining villages this custom was called the 'tip-up' and was sometimes performed before the front door so that the neighbors could witness and guarantee fair play. More commonly, the husband controlled the division of income. He would usually hand his wife a fixed sum out of his earnings each week. Most Victorian laborers earned irregularly to some extent. Some men fixed the housekeeping allowance around their average minimum earnings and reserved anything additional for their own pocket money. Tips, bonuses, or overtime as well usually went into pocket money. Often a woman did not even know what her husband had actually earned that week and reported the housekeeping allowance alone to investigators of family income. . . .

Pocket money . . . was . . . a device for diverting part of the family income to use for the wage-earner's pleasures, chiefly smoking and drinking. Some observers charged that up to a half of the intemperate man's wages went for beer, spirits, and tobacco, or a quarter in the case of a laborer who was never drunk. They repeated heart-rending stories of men who wasted their families' sustenance on gambling and drinking. . . .

In addition to claiming the lion's share of the meat and drink, husbands in many cases also got most of the health care that was available. . . . Although the working-class family scrimped to insure even the smallest child for funeral benefits, men often monopolized sickness insurance. In one prosperous, unusually well-insured Somerset village in 1909, for instance, nearly every working-class householder and most of the young men were in a benefit society for medical care and sick pay. But their families were not nearly so well covered. For the poorer families, sickness insurance was probably out of the question altogether, and one wonders whether a doctor's fee for anyone but the breadwinner could be spared out of such slender weekly budgets. The *Daily Herald*'s observation about Britain before the coming of the National Health Service was probably as true of the nineteenth century as of the twentieth. They asked their readers 'how many working mothers put up with a pain or a 'lump' for years for fear of costing her husband too dear – and died because urgent aid came too late?'. . .

What explains the strength of these arrangements in the family's economy? Helen Bosanquet once called the Victorian family a kind of 'mutual benefit society with extended benefits'. Since most of the extended benefits appear to have accrued to husbands, it seems strange that wives cooperated in the enterprise. We must remember, however, that by the mid-nineteenth century women were peculiarly dependent on their husbands. Bereft of the bye–employments of pre-industrial England, married women had to rely chiefly on the earnings of their husbands. Women who worked often earned barely enough to keep themselves, let alone to support their children. Home work, favored by married women, was the lowest-paid and most sweated labor of nineteenth–century England. A husband's sickness meant work and income lost; his death brought even greater calamity. The only alternative to poorly paid women's work was the Poor Law. The wife deferred to the breadwinner because without him her own situation would have been even worse. . . .

In 1914 Reeves defended married men against those who accused them of wasting their families' sustenance on their own pleasure. She argued that in laboring families the amount of self sacrifice required of a man, 'if he be at all tender-hearted towards his family, is outrageous. ' But the poorly paid man should not be expected to be superior to the middle-class man in the matter of self-denial and self-control. She found it understandable that a 'hard-working, steady, sober man' might spend 2d. a day on beer, 1d. on tobacco, and 2d. on tram fares 'without being a monster of selfishness, or wishing to deprive his children of their food.' That was obviously true. Nonetheless, it was the structure of the family's economy that allowed husbands to indulge themselves, however modestly, while wives could not.

Laura Oren, 'The welfare of women in laboring families: England, 1860–1950' in M. Hartmann and L. W. Banner (eds), *Clio's Consciousness Raised: New Perspectives on the History of Woman*, pp. 226–40.

Questions

1. What reasons are given in the reading to explain the husband's larger share of what were regarded as the good things of life?
2. In what way did men manage to get more individual spending money for themselves?
3. To what extent has the welfare state evened out inequalities between family members?

□ Status within the Family

This second extract dealing with consumption within the family agrees that differences exist in family members' access to the good things of life, but suggests that this is not due to constraint imposed from outside. It is not that, in a waged-based society, the wage earner must be kept well and happy or the whole family suffers. Nor is it a question of poor families living close to subsistence. Christine Delphy argues that differential consumption actually increases (not decreases) as the standard of living rises (for example within the middle classes) and that it involves goods which cannot be seen as simply necessary to maintain the husband's well being. Rather, she says, differential consumption is used to *mark out* differential status – to maintain and demonstrate adult men's superior position in the family.

How differential consumption is actually maintained varies. In our culture it is often left up to women themselves, as wives, mothers or daughters, to decide exactly how to show deference through self-sacrifice.

Reading 4

In Tunisia differential consumption is effected in a radically different way. Men have two or three meals a day while women have only one or two, and these meals never coincide. The women eat foodstuffs prepared once a year and obtained from second quality produce. The meals they make for men on the other hand use fresh and best quality ingredients. The rigorous separation of time, place and the basic substance of the meals makes any competition for the food between men and women impossible . . .

In France today men and women eat 'from the same table' (*au même pain et pot*). Differential consumption derives essentially not from prohibition on this or that food, but from attributing women the smallest and most mediocre share of each food. [There is a general principle that the household manager] . . . the wife and mother should always preserve the privileges of the husband and father, and 'sacrifice' herself. . . . only such a principle could give an account of the variability of content of differential consumption.

For instance, a young peasant farmer invited two city women to share his tea and opened a tin of paté. His aunt, an old woman who kept house for him because his mother was ill, was there. On her bread she put only the fat from around the paté, which had been scorned by the three other diners. The system not only requires women to restrain themselves, but also allows them a certain latitude by making them responsible for taking the decision as to the form of their restriction. Thus the meat of the paté had doubtless never been expressly forbidden to this old woman; but the obligation to leave the best part to others had been internalized as a moral imperative. She could have complied with it in a different way; she acted on her own initiative in giving herself the worst part; and above all the precise way of doing it was up to her. This attribution is experienced as a free choice and is often explained by the 'ordinary' motivation for choice: personal preference. When asked, the old woman replied that she liked fat. . . .

When one moves from the country to the town, and from low income sectors to higher sectors, consumption of food increases and differential consumption becomes less marked in this area. Since the level of food consumption is higher, it might be expected that basic needs are better covered and the differences of consumption would more and more concern less visible qualities and modalities. Indeed, food being sufficiently abundant, it might be expected that differences in food consumption would tend to disappear completely and be replaced by, or only exist in, other areas.

However, the flexible character of differential consumption, the fact. . . that it is not the specific content but the principles of attribution which are defined, allows other expressions of subordination when for one reason or another the household's scale of relative values is modified. One example can illustrate this move back to using food to express status differences, and this also illustrates the flexibility of the system.

In the last ten years France, and Paris in particular, experienced a shortage of potatoes which lasted for a fortnight. Since the demand for this basic commodity is relatively inelastic, prices rose and queues formed in front of the greengrocers. When questioned in one of these queues by a radio interviewer, a women replied: 'I'll keep the potatoes for my husband. The children and I will eat pasta or rice.' In spite of the relative expense of potatoes it would not have been beyond the budget of the family to get enough for everyone, given the subjective importance they attach to them. On the other hand, if the value of the gratification did not compensate for the budgetary sacrifice, as the renunciation by the wife and children suggests, the husband should also logically have eaten pasta and rice. The solution adopted seems to be explained neither by the physiological impossibility for the husband to absorb products (replacements in this particular situation) which were in any case consumed in almost as regular a way as pototoes, nor by the economic situation of the family, but rather by the symbolic necessity of marking privileged and statutory access to goods which are rare (or become rare) – this access being both the sign and at the same time the reason for the hierarchy of consumption.

. . . with growth in the part of the budget which is available for spending on things other than food, forms of consumption develop which were previously of little importance or non-existent. The raising of the general standard of living may thus allow the development of differentiation in certain existing areas. In addition, it allows the emergence of new areas of consumption which are fresh fields for the exercise of differentiation. For example, the acquisition of a car by a household in which previously everybody travelled by public transport, not only considerably increases the global difference in consumption – variance in the standard of living – between the user of the car and other family members, but above all it introduces differentiation into an area – transport – which up till then was undifferentiated. . . .

The study of differential consumption cannot [however] be reduced to the study of quantitative differences in access to particular goods,. . . it is also qualitative. Does a child being taken for a Sunday outing consume the family car in the same way as the father who drives it? Above all, does it consume the same outing? The problems which are currently being put forcefully in rural areas when two generations live together, reveal – if one listens to those concerned –

that the conflicts experienced divide not 'the generations', but rather concern the 'freely chosen' consumption which the 'invited' children want, and the 'compelled' consumption which is 'given' them (imposed) by their parent-hosts.

These examples seem to indicate that ways of consuming are perhaps more important than quantities consumed. But up to now the study of consumption has always been preoccupied with – has always meant exclusively – volumes, and the very existence of modes of consumption has not even been hinted at.

Christine Delphy, 'Sharing the same table: Consumption and the family', in *Close to Home*, pp. 52–4.

Questions

1. Explain in your own words the distinction Delphy makes between
   (a) *what* is consumed,
   (b) the principle of differential consumption, and
   (c) modes of consumption.
2. In your view is Delphy justified in dismissing the fact that the women she quotes say they 'chose' or preferred their different (low status) food?

□ Domestic
Violence

A major change in studies of the family over the last 15 years has been the re-recognition of the existence of the systematic use of physical force within the family: the recognition that babies, children, wives and the elderly are regularly 'battered', and that children, especially girls, may be sexually abused.

We say 're-recognition' because there have been times in the past when family violence was a cause of great public concern, for example, in 1878 with the publication of a pamphlet on *Wife Torture in England* by Francis Power Cobbe. However, getting the violence of husbands towards wives recognised in recent times has not been easy. Forcing it on to the formal political agenda – in the shape of the Parliamentary Select Committee on Violence in Marriage in 1974 – has been a major achievement of the Women's Liberation Movement. However, the first object of most feminist action in this area has been to give direct, practical aid to women (see Pizzey, *Scream Quietly or the Neighbors will Hear You* in Further Reading) and there has been as yet little research into the causes, consequences and extent of family violence.

A notable exception to this last generalisation has been the excellent research carried out in Scotland by Rebecca and Russell Dobash in 1975–6. They analysed police and court records in Edinburgh and in one large police district in Glasgow for all arrest reports, to see how many cases involved violence and how many of these involved particular forms of domestic violence. They also conducted in depth structured interviews with 137 women who were, or had been in refuges for battered women.

This reading from their book summarises some general positions that they arrived at. Their main argument, perhaps surprisingly, is that it is the marriage relationship *itself* that positively nurtures the seeds of violence. In other words the authority and power conferred on men by the role of husband (and the dependence conferred on women by the role of wife) actually promotes the likelihood of violence.

Reading 5

It is still true that for a woman to be brutally or systematically assaulted she must usually enter our most sacred institution, the family. It is within marriage that a woman is most likely to be slapped and shoved about, severely assaulted, killed or raped. Thus, it is impossible to understand violence against women without also understanding the nature of the marital relationship in which it occurs and to which it is inextricably related. . . .

Although it is not generally thought to be proper or masculine for a man to hit a woman, this constraint does not strictly apply to the treatment of one's wife. It is commonly believed that there are times when every woman needs to be taken in hand. Usually these are occasions when a woman challenges a man's authority, fails to fulfill his expectations of service, or neglects to stay in 'her place.' On such occasions men will treat women with disdain and use either subtle or obvious means to degrade, isolate, or ignore them. It is almost inconceivable that he would punch her in the jaw, unless, of course, she happened to be his wife.

It cannot be stressed too much that it is marriage and the taking on of the status of wife that make a woman the 'appropriate victim' of violence aimed at 'putting her in her place' and that differential marital responsibility and authority give the husband both the perceived right and the obligation to control his wife's behavior and thus the means to justify beating her. A social worker told us about a male client who in recounting a heated argument he had had with a woman commented, 'I would have hit her, but she wasn't my wife.'

Countless jokes are told about giving one's wife 'the old one-two,'. . . Punch has been beating the pulp out of Judy in front of audiences of delighted and impressionable children for centuries. But it is not humorous to read a newspaper account of an incident in which a man seen by policeman beating his wife in the street and told to stop replied, 'I can do what I like, she's my wife.' That it is the wife who is the victim of marital violence cannot be denied. See Tables 4 and 5.

Of the women interviewed, 77% did not experience violence until after marriage, but most of them had not been married very long when the first incident occurred. One woman we interviewed told us that she was first beaten on her honeymoon and when she cried and protested, her husband replied, 'I married you so I own you.' Forty-one percent of the women experienced their first violent attack within six months after the wedding, and another 18% within the first year. Another 25% were hit within the next two years, making a total of 84% within the first three years of marriage. Only 8% of the women did not experience their first attack until after five years of marriage. The husband's sense of ownership and control is immediate. It comes with the marriage contract, and all the social meanings and obligations associated with the words 'love, honor, and obey'.

Although both partners feel that marriage allows them to make some demands upon the other, there is a considerable difference in their abilities to achieve their own ends when there is disagreement. A wife's pleas, arguments, or demands that her husband meet his marital obligations as she perceives them may be met with compliance, excuses, indifference, or blows. A man should not be questioned by his wife (or at least not excessively) no matter what the reason. He is to be accorded the respect due his superior position and authority. So even if his wife has quite a legitimate demand, request, or complaint, she cannot go on too much about it because this is an affront to his authority. She must plead, cajole, and beguile and hope that he will be convinced. She is almost never in a position to coerce him by physical means and has neither learned the techniques of violence nor been taught to think in terms of physical control. The husband, on the other hand, feels he has a right to control his wife's behavior and authority over most, if not all, areas of her life; it is these beliefs, coupled with his desire to maintain authority, that lead to his first assault. The more general taboo that it is not correct for a man to hit a woman is qualified – 'unless she is your wife' – as immediate demands for control supersede demands for propriety. . . .

Arguments preceding the first attack are primarily associated with the husband's possessiveness and his ideas about his wife's re-

TABLE 4. Types of assault occurring between family members

	No.	%
Wife assault	791	75.8
Husband assault	12	1.1
Child assault	112	10.7
Parent assault	73	7.0
Sibling assault	50	4.8
Mutual assault	6	0.6
Total	1044	100.0

TABLE 5. Percentage of all offenses involving violence dealt with by selected police departments in Edinburgh and Glasgow in 1974*

	No.	%	Total
Wife Assault	759	(25.1)	Family
Alleged Wife Assault†	32	(1.1)	violence
Husband Assault	12	(0.4)	34.5%
Child Assault	112	(3.7)	No. = 1,044
Parent Assault	73	(2.4)	
Sibling Assault	50	(1.6)	
Mutual Assault	6	(0.2)	
Male-Male	1,169	(38.7)	
Male-Female	295	(9.8)	Nonfamily
Male-Police	288	(9.5)	violence
Female-Female	142	(4.7)	65.5%
Female-Male	53	(1.8)	No. = 1,976
Female-Police	29	(1.0)	

% 0 5 10 15 20 25 30 35 40

Total Number = 3,020

* This includes the reports for all of Edinburgh and one district of Glasgow that were subsequently prepared for and/or dealt with by the courts.
† The term alleged is used by police and courts, but from our reading of the cases there appears to be no significant differences between alleged wife assaults and wife assaults.

sponsibilities to him. These arguments center around sexual jealousy and domestic work but are often set off by what is thought to be
a violation of the husband's authority. In our interviews, expectations
concerning the preparation and serving of food commonly began
the first incident.

R.E. and R. Dobash, *Violence Against Wives*, pp. 75, 93–5, 246–7.

Questions

1. What arguments and incidents most commonly lead to domestic violence?
2. What evidence is there here to contradict the view that women marry
   violent men because they *like* violence?

☐ What the Experts Believe

We hoped that our next reading would be an extract from Erin
Pizzey's *Scream Quietly or the Neighbours will Hear You* in which
she argues that there are women who *seek* violent relationships. In
her later work she suggests this is because 'violence prone' women
become addicted to the hormone released by the threat of attack.
They therefore deliberately provoke attacks upon themselves in
order to get a 'fix'. Unfortunately we were refused permission to
use her work.

Instead we have selected an extract from a study of how profes-
sionals (doctors, social workers and solicitors – referred to in the
reading as 'practitioners') involved with marital violence view it
and what they believe to be its causes. The authors present these
views not as the explanation for domestic violence – they believe
that there is insufficient evidence to be sure about *any* causal
explanation, but as the 'intervening and distorting lens' through
which the phenomenon is commonly viewed.

Reading 6

We studied practitioners' explanations in two ways. First they were
invited to generalize by being asked:

> 'Do you have any views about factors which may precipitate
> marital violence? By precipitate we do not necessarily mean
> cause.'

Second, they were invited to particularize by being asked what factors they thought might have precipitated the violence in the latest case with which they had dealt . . .

In general, the evidence suggests that social structural explanations predominate in the interview samples, whereas individual personality explanations predominate in the case studies. In our view this distinction hinges on the question of where moral responsibility for behaviour lies, i.e. with elements in society, or with the individual? . . . people who do not themselves experience marital violence favour explanations that set them apart from those that do . . .

Another remarkable finding is that in the interview sample the personality of the woman consistently rates above the personality of the man as an explanation for the violence. . . . In spite of the fact that women are nearly always the victims of marital violence, it is they who are described as responsible for it, rather than the man who is the perpetrator. . . .

With regard to practitioners' use of explanations, certain propositions emerge from our evidence. First, it is not easy to identify the real causes of violence in marriage; second, busy practitioners tend to over-simplify; and third, there is a wide range of theory in use, often strangely blended with cultural stereotypes and morality.

May has studied the way previous generations viewed and explained family and marital violence and has shown the stereotyped images of domestic violence used by reformers and social workers of the Victorian and Edwardian eras. Our work indicates that many of these stereotypes are prevalent in the thinking of practitioners and academics today. Then, as now, the most common explanation was heavy drinking. Then, as now, poor housing and the emotionally impoverished cultural life of the poor, with its general roughness and violence, were considered important precipitating factors. Then, as now, social investigators were reporting the phenomenon of wives who take violence as a matter of course. Then, as now, references were being made to 'loud-mouthed viragos lacking domestic skills who often provoked their husbands' drunken assaults with their nagging tongues'. There is nothing new in seeing domestic violence in interactionist terms. Furthermore, not only is recent concern about marital violence a 'rediscovery' of a problem that was a public anxiety a century ago, but, as our research shows, the old explanations for it circulate once again.

M. Borkwoski, M. Merch. and V. Walker, *Marital Violence. The Community Response*, pp. 54, 60, 75–6.

Questions

1. List the factors used by the practitioners to explain marital violence and say whether they are compatible with the explanation offered in reading 5.
2. For what reasons might sociologists treat the explanations of practitioners as an 'intervening and distorting lens' (a phrase used by the authors of the extract) through which to view the phenomenon of domestic violence?

☐ Patriarchy and the Families of Black People

Use of the term 'patriarchy' by feminists, to refer to the dominance of old over young and male over female, especially rooted in the family, has been the subject of various critiques. Here Hazel Carby argues that this political usage shows the way feminism is blinkered by its origins among white middle class women.

She claims that relations between black men and women are different from those between white men and women, and structured by racism inseparably from sexism. The concepts used by white feminists to analyse the situation of white women cannot therefore necessarily be applied to the position of black women, who experience a different form of oppression from white men and black men, and from white women. She suggests that black families have been a source of resistance to racism. This is not unlike the argument of Jane Humphries (Chapter 5, Reading 9), who argues that the (white) working class family has been a source of resistance to class oppression.

Reading 6

In a recent comprehensive survey of contemporary feminist theory, *Women's Oppression Today*, Michèle Barrett sees the contemporary family (effectively the family under capitalism) as the source of oppression of women:

> It is difficult to argue that the present structure of the family-household is anything other than oppressive for women. Feminists have consistently, and rightly, seen the family as a central site of women's oppression in contemporary society. The reasons for this lie both in the material structure of the household, by which women

are by and large financially dependent on men, and in the ideology of the family, through which women are confined to a primary concern with domesticity and motherhood. This situation underwrites the disadvantages women experience at work, and lies at the root of the exploitation of female sexuality endemic in our society. The concept of 'dependence' is perhaps, the link between the material organisation of the household, and the ideology of femininity; an assumption of women's dependence on men structures both of these areas.

The immediate problem for black feminists is whether this framework can be applied at all to analyse our herstory of oppression and struggle. We would not wish to deny that the family can be a source of oppression for us but we also wish to examine how the black family has functioned as a prime source of resistance to oppression. We need to recognize that during slavery, periods of colonialism and under the present authoritarian state, the black family has been a site of political and cultural resistance to racism. Furthermore, we cannot easily separate the two forms of oppression because racist theory and practice is frequently gender–specific. Ideologies of black female sexuality do not stem primarily from the black family. The way the gender of black women is constructed differs from constructions of white femininity because it is also subject to racism. . . .

The use of the concept of 'dependency' is also a problem for black feminists. It has been argued that this concept provides the link between the 'material organisation of the household, and the ideology of femininity'. How then can we account for situations in which black women may be heads of households, or where, because of an economic system which structures high black male unemployment, they are not financially dependent upon a black man? This condition exists in both colonial and metropolitan situations. Ideologies of black female domesticity and motherhood have been constructed, through their employment (or chattel position) as domestics and surrogate mothers to white families rather than in relation to their own families. West Indian women still migrate to the United States and Canada as domestics and in Britain are seen to be suitable as office cleaners, National Health Service domestics, etc. In colonial situations Asian women have frequently been forced into prostitution to sexually service the white male invaders, whether in the form of armies of occupation or employees and guests of multinational corporations. How then, in view of all this, can it be argued that black male dominance exists in the same forms as white male dominance? Systems of slavery, colonialism, imperialism, have systematically denied positions in the white male hierarchy to black men and have used specific forms of terror to oppress them. . . . black men have not held the same patriarchal positions of power that the white males have established. Michèle Barrett argues that the term patriarchy has lost all analytic or explanatory power and has been reduced to a synonym for male dominance. She tries therefore to limit its use to a specific type of male dominance that could be located historically.

> I would not . . . want to argue that the concept of patriarchy should be jettisoned. I would favour retaining it for use in contexts where male domination is expressed through the power of the father over women and over younger men. . . . Hence I would argue for a more precise and specific use of the concept of patriarchy, rather than one which expands it to cover all expressions of male domination and thereby attempts to construe a descriptive term as a systematic explanatory theory.

. . . if we try to apply this more 'classic' and limited definition of patriarchy to the slave systems of the Americas and the Caribbean, we find that even this refined use of the concept cannot adequately account for the fact that both slaves and manumitted males did not have this type of patriarchal power. Alternatively, if we take patriarchy and apply it to various colonial situations it is equally unsatisfactory because it is unable to explain why black males have not enjoyed the benefits of white patriarchy. There are very obvious power structures in both colonial and slave social formations and they are predominantly patriarchal. However, the historically specific forms of racism force us to modify or alter the application of the term 'patriarchy' to black men. Black women have been dominated 'patriarchally' in different ways by men of different 'colours'.

H. Carby, 'White women listen: black feminism and the boundaries of sisterhood', in Centre for Contemporary Cultural Studies, *The Empire Strikes Back*, pp. 214, 215, 217–18.

Questions

1. How does Carby support her argument that
   (a) racism is gender specific and
   (b) sexism is race specific?
2. How might those who think the family *is* patriarchal explain the situation in which high male unemployment (black or white), or high rates of single parenthood or divorce, mean that women are not financially dependent upon their husbands?

□ Girls, Sex and Marriage

We have included the last two readings for three reasons. Firstly, because sexuality is an important element of the relations between men and women in the family. There is, however, in fact very little study of day to day marital sexuality on which we can draw. Sociologists have concentrated on the 'deviant' forms, such as 'pre-marital', 'extra-marital' or 'homosexuality'. Our readings feature adolescents' *talk* about heterosexuality and their attitudes show something of how they see the relationship between sexuality and marriage. The second reason for including these readings is that we cannot understand the character of relationships (including sexual relationships) within the family without considering the wider setting in which they are located and from which they, in part, derive. Both these studies were conducted with people who were still in the school system and who were developing attitudes to heterosexuality that they would take into courtship and marriage. Finally, these readings are more representative of interactionist sociology than any others in the chapter and as such bring us closer to people's experiences of issues central to family life.

The first reading analyses aspects of a predominately male vocabulary which purports to categorise and describe girls' sexuality. Sue Lees argues that use of this vocabulary serves to characterise girls' sexuality in a particular way, to attempt to control it and to try to constrain its expression. She believes that all of these things are of major importance in pressing girls to marry – despite their negative views of the marriages that they see around them.

Reading 7

Research on adolescents is almost exclusively about boys – or youth as they are commonly described. When girls do make an appearance in studies of youth culture they are usually seen in ways that are marginal, or which uncritically reinforce a stereotyped image of women. Discussions about them are often in the context of sex with such comments as 'obviously the boys are interested in girls – they clearly talk about girls and sex a good deal of the time they are together'. . . . This equating of girls with sex is a reflection of the way that women and girls are commonly represented in terms of their sexuality rather than as human beings. . . .

[In this study] the terms on which girls participated in any kind of social life were quite different from the terms on which boys did so. Sexual reputation constantly emerges both as a cause of concern for girls and a target of potential abuse from boys and other girls. The emphasis on the importance of a girl's reputation is shown up in a whole battery of insults which are in use by both girls and boys in their day-to-day life. The vocabulary of abuse raises many questions about the construction of sexuality, the place of marriage in the girls' lives and the social organization of gender relations. . . .

The most common form of sexual abuse, 'slag', which is commonly understood to mean a girl who sleeps around promiscuously, . . . often bears no relation to a girl's actual sexual behaviour. It can just as easily be applied to a girl who dresses, talks or behaves in a certain way. The only constraint on the use of 'slag' is its application to a girl who has no steady boyfriend . . . This leads to and reproduces a girl's subordination. . . .

There was a contradiction between the unromantic and stark picture of marriage that emerged from the girl's descriptions [of the marriages they saw around them] and their commitment – if somewhat resigned – to the idea of marriage. Most girls saw marriage as inevitable even if it involved financial dependency, domestic drudgery, isolation at home with young children and, at the extreme, even cruelty. This is less surprising when looked at in the context of the way female sexuality is socially constructed round the difference between slags and drags (one-man, marriageable 'nice girls'). The adolescent girl may sleep with her boyfriend but this does not mean that she is sexually free. A woman's femininity and active sexuality is rendered safe only when confined to the bonds of marriage and wrapped in the aura of 'love'. The very unfair way that sexual relations are structured and taken for granted throws some light on why male – female relations have changed so little.

The strategy that most girls adopt is to postpone this predicament for as long as possible or for at least ten years. As one girl said, 'marriage is something you end up with after you have lived'.

S. Lees, *Losing Out: Sexuality and Adolescent Girls*, pp. 14, 25, 27–8.

Questions

1. According to the reading, to whom is the term 'slag' applied?
2. Is Lees correct in writing as if the idea of slags/drags were of central importance to adolescents' ideas of female heterosexuality or are there other equally important influences?

☐ Boys'
Sex Talk

This reading is from a study of working class boys in a small mixed-sex centre for school 'disruptives', which the popular press called a 'sin bin'. The author recognises that boys sex talk does objectify women's and girls bodies, as sexual objects, and that such talk is a not unsuccessful attempt to have power over and to control girls' sexuality – and indeed their whole beings. However, without excusing such sexism, the author tries to explain why boys cannot easily break away from it.

Reading 8

One of the specific features of men's sexism is the dissecting approach that is taken to women's objectified bodies. This came out in the centre boys in numerous ways . . . and was a crucial element in their assessments of girls. It was externalised most frequently in sexist slang; the part of the language capable of holding the most sexist male meanings. This use of slang is common to the broader class culture to which the boys belonged . . . Perhaps part of its appeal was that it seemed to impart to the user a tenuous sense of control. . . .

The use of slang words for the bodies of *both* genders *by* both genders is a very old business (as even a cursory reading of Chaucer will show). It is doubtful whether the existence of such terms *per se* can be too simply linked to a patriarchial system, however old that system may be. Rather it is the tone, context, and use to which they are attemptedly put, that makes sexual slang part of sexist talk. In terms of the developing sexism of the centre boys it is the use of terms for parts of the body *combined with* the intent to assess the girls in crude and superficial ways that constitutes the element of attempted domination . . . any conversations between boys about women's bodies are premised on the idea that one can reasonably assess a person solely in terms of the male opinion (for it is men who presume to set the standards) of parts of their bodies. Further, these parts – 'arse', 'legs', 'tits', 'boat' (i.e. 'boatrace' = face) – seem to be almost interchangeable as 'good points' or at least one can be offset against another. Overhearing such an assessment discussion one might have got the impression that what was being discussed was some kind of grotesque snap-together doll. . . .

Early in a conversation the boys referred to Lorraine as 'a dog'.

This judgemental term (specifically on a girl's *looks*) is a very common term within the sexist mode. Sometimes it seems that all women who are not dogs ('dog rough' in the full phrase) are automatically 'tasty' or fanciable. Of course it is absurd even by sexist standards that 'dog' and 'tasty' should be a sort of binary opposition. However, in that absurdity may lie the secret of the power of the category. It relies for its power on the simplicity with which it attempts to sort out the whole female gender and, perhaps, *the emotions of the speaker.* How characteristic that is in fact of so much of the lack of subtlety of male sexism. If vacillation is imputed to women, then unwavering over-sureness may perhaps be, by negative implication, very male. Besides which, the *pose* of sureness is doubly 'functional' in that it obviates the need to find out if one really does know one's own mind.

One could ask why males feel the need of this false security? I follow Tolson's . . . main drift that masculinity has at its heart not unproblematic strength but often weakness, self-doubt and confusion. In the light of this anti-'commonsense' view of masculinity it is perhaps easier to understand why the boys make these superficial, dismissive judgements. Partly they are saying, 'we are the gender superior enough to judge women.' Looking down on the girls in the centre gave them an illusion of confidence. To put it another way, while the outward face of the sexist mode was characterised by confidence, brashness, fluency and 'presence' (the promise of power as Tolson puts it) the inward face was often the complete reverse. I think also the boys felt, obscurely, the need to by-pass the competitive relations between the sexes that their own behaviour perpetuated, but they were largely unable to do this. . . .

Throughout I have put a question mark beside the idea of a sexist mode being 'functional' for the boys, and yet I have half-retained the notion. There is always a danger of fixing an imbalance and of defeating opposition, or desire for change, by making structures seem *too* 'functional' and therefore impossible to alter. I do not want this analysis to be functional*ist* in that sense, but I do think it is vital not to flip over into complete voluntarism; we must look for structural (social and psychological) features of historically realised masculinity that are *not of individual men's choosing*, if we are to address the persistence of sexism and therefore stand a real chance of eradicating it.

J. Woods, 'Groping towards sexism: boys' sex talk', in A. McRobbie and M. Nava, *Gender and Generation*, pp. 58–61.

Questions

1. What two elements of talk did the boys combine in an attempt to dominate the girls at the centre?
2. What are the functions of sexist talk for the boys?

Essay Questions

1. Is it accurate to describe 'the modern family' as 'symmetrical'? (Cambridge 1986)
2. Show how feminist theory perspectives have helped to develop our understanding of one area of social life. (AEB 1984)
3. In what ways have feminist writers challenged earlier sociological accounts of the family? (AEB 1985)
4. To what extent can marriage in contemporary Britain be described as a partnership of equals? (AEB 1986)
5. How can violence in the family be explained sociologically? (Cambridge 1984)

Further Reading

D.M. Leonard 'Women in the Family' in V. Beechey and E. Whitelegg (eds), *Women in Britain Today*, contrasts the optimistic, evolutionary 'symmetrical' analysis of the family with those aspects stressed by recent feminist researchers.

A. Oakley, *Housewife*, and *Sociology of Housework*. A fuller report on work in Reading 2. Oakley studied housework in the manner of industrial sociology and hence stressed the idea of housework as work. She includes a history of housework, information on the division of household tasks, and time budgets.

Stephen Edgell, *Middle-class Couples: a study of segregation, domination and inequality in marriage*, is rather difficult reading, but contains some very interesting research findings on professional men's families and a general critique of studies of 'decision-making' and authority within the family.

Lorna McKee and Margaret O'Brien (eds), *The Father Figure*. A dozen essays look at what is happening to fatherhood, including men's experience of pregnancy and childbirth and being a lone parent, their participation in childcare, their legal status, and step-fatherhood. Especially recommended is Trevor Lummis on 'The historical dimension of fatherhood: a case study 1890–1914', based on oral history work with East Anglian fishermen and their families.

Janet Finch, *Married to the Job. Wives incorporation in men's work*, re-analyses existing studies of occupational communities to show how employers benefit from their male employees' wives' work, and how husbands' jobs affect women's lives.

Eva Gamarnikow *et al.* (eds), *The Public and the Private*, contains articles by:
L. Imray and A. Middleton, 'Public and private: marking the boundaries'
J. Hanmer and S. Saunders, 'Blowing the cover of the protective male: a community study of violence to women'
A. Murcott, '"Its a pleasure to cook for him": food, mealtimes and gender in some South Wales households'
C. Ungerson, 'Women and caring: skills, tasks and taboos'.

Julia Brennan and Gail Wilson (eds), *Give and Take in Families*. Different chapters look at the distribution of money, time, food, childcare, health and the impact of unemployment between family members.

Ann Whitehead, 'Sex Antagonism in Herefordshire', in D.L. Barker and S. Allen (eds), *Dependence and Exploitation in Work and Marriage*. Not a fetching title, but a fascinating 'ethnographic romp', showing the importance of men's control of the wives in their social standing in the local community, sex antagonisms expressed in joking, and the sexual harrassment of women who venture into male domains (like the pub).

Erin Pizzey, *Scream Quietly or the Neighours will Hear You*, provides a psychological approach to violence in marital relationships, in contrast to the sociological approach of Reading 5 of this chapter. Pizzey sees violence as resulting from particular personalities and from personal interactions and aims to help both the victims and those who use violence by working with both parties together.

Christine Delphy, *Close to Home*, is a collection by a major French theorist of the family, using a model of the family as a hierarchical set of labour relations. It looks at, amongst other things, the class position of women, divorce, and naturalising ideologies of the family.

Ray Pahl, *Divisions of Labour*. An interesting attempt to reconceptualise the nature of work, as opposed to employment – drawing together the study of production, reproduction and consumption; focusing on the household rather than the individual. It sees households as harmonious decision–making units.

Diana Gittins, *The Family in Question*, Chapter 2 Is patriarchy relevant in understanding families? Chapter 4 Why do people marry? Chapter 5 Why is women's work never done?

Graham Allan, *Family Life*, Chapter 3 Women, marriage and housework. How routine demands of domesticity shape the experience of women as wives and mothers and limit the opportunities open to them. Chapter 5 Marriage: an unequal relationship. The nature of contemporary marriage and the degree to which the tie continues to be one of inequality. Discusses different ways of measuring marital equality and links the structure of marriage to factors outside the domestic sphere.

4 | How do families socialise children?

The first reading in this chapter is by Talcott Parsons, who outlines his influential theory of the role of the family in the process of socialisation. The next few are by writers who, for various reasons, beg to disagree with him.

Parsons, like many sociologists, is interested in the 'problem of order' – the problem of knowing how societies hold together. He believes the answer lies, not in, for example, the unifying functions of the state (see Chapter 6) but in the existence of universally agreed norms and values. Because of this, socialisation is a key social process for him. He believes the teaching of these central values to each new generation is achieved, primarily, in the family and for this reason he sees the family as an extremely important institution.

The conventional wisdom underlying Parsons' theory is the view that a child is born into society without being a person. She has to learn the language, rules, patterns of behaviour, and systems of belief which make involvement in social life possible. Children are not born knowing these matters and the process of becoming social is carried out, primarily, in the family. The family and socialisation process thus stands between the growing child and the society that pre-exists it.

This view sees the child as a *tabula rasa* on which society is imprinted. Other common views see children as having an essential nature. One deriving from Christianity, sees children as inheriting the original sin of the human race following Adam's disobedience in eating the apple. Children are bad, flawed, imps of Satan who require control and discipline to make them human. Alternatively there is another long tradition, from the Romantic writing of philosophers such as Rousseau, and poets including Wordsworth and Blake which argues that children are essentially good, free spirits who become corrupted by the chains of society. The former is represented here in a reading from R.O. Blood; the latter can be found in the contemporary writing of John Holt or the educational theorist A.S. Neill, the founder of Summerhill school. As sociologists, we should treat ideas of essential nature very warily because sociological (as well as anthropological and historical) research demonstrates the enormous variety of ways in which human natures act (see Edholm, Reading 1 in Chapter 1).

One type of opposition to Parsons' view is based upon objections to assumptions he makes about the relationship between adults and children in his theory of socialisation. Writers in the Parsonian tradition see the continuance of the central values of society over time as pretty much the same thing as the relationship between parents and children. They take on the role of the parents and write about the mundane problem of *controlling* children as if it (the parents' problem) were a problem for sociological theory. Speier argues that young children are not blank surfaces waiting to have the culture of the society written upon them by their parents. Infact they have a culture of their own from an early age and influence their parents as their parents influence them. Additionally, although sociologists since Cooley have distinguished between primary and secondary socialisation, the overwhelming impression from authors like Blood is that socialisation is a business between parents and children alone. However since a minority of nuclear families in the West consist of parents who have one child, this means overlooking completely the influence of siblings upon siblings and also the influence of peer groups.

Speier is interested in children's rights and notices the imbalance of power between parents and children. He resents sociology parading one of its theories as a front for the continuance of a particular kind of historically specific relationship between parents and children. He believes the theory is wrong and the relationship is changeable.

Another objection has been made on the grounds that the concept of socialisation has operated as an 'umbrella' term. It covers an area of concern but it does nothing to explain it. To change the metaphor, the concept might therefore be likened to a black box, in which things are fed in and something comes out, but which sheds no light on the process. Among those that have made this objection is the author of Reading 6, Basil Bernstein, who once described the concept as having been trivialised because it had left unexamined the whole question of the structure, and changes in the structure, of culture and the ways in which culture is transmitted to new generations (and other groups).

Another objection is based on the argument that we should not think of society on the one hand and the individual on the other. Marx commented on theories that acted as if societies were made up of lots of Robinson Crusoes to remind us that the notion of the individual as separate from society, is itself a notion that belongs to class societies that stress the lone, competitive, individual struggling in the economic market. This particular critique is not easy to understand, since our sense of ourselves as *individuals* with society *out there* is entrenched in our thinking. Nevertheless this idea of ourselves as unified, separated individuals *is* a construction and if you think for a moment of the very different selves you present to your parents, your friends and your lovers you may get a sense of the effort involved in continuing to think of your 'self' as a unified centre of thought and action set apart from the social relations in which it was caught from the moment of conception.

The later readings in the chapter are not so much a complaint against the Parsonian tradition as an effort to explain more precisely the effects of socialisation within the families of different classes in terms of the cultures they transmit.

One prominent 'explanation' for the failure of working class pupils in the school system since the 1950s has invoked notions of poorly socialised children from deficient cultural backgrounds and pathological families. Educational programmes to overcome the disadvantages of a deficient culture have been common in both America and Britain. The reading by the Newsons is a good example of social scientific thinking on the child rearing of working class parents. (As we have already pointed out, child rearing practices can usually be interchangeably taken for socialisation in the tradition of writings that we are considering.)

Basil Bernstein has produced more sophisticated accounts of class *differences* (*not deficits*). He argues that these different class cultures involve different codes and that the characteristics of the middle classes advantage them in the education system. He is also interested in the relations between class cultures, changing family and school relationships and the production of different kinds of personality.

Bernstein's writing is often placed in a tradition noted for its interest in 'cultural reproduction'. The term socialisation deals with some similar concerns to the term 'reproduction', which is perhaps more often encountered in contemporary writings. In principle the term 'reproduction' invokes the whole question of how societies continue over time. As we have already pointed out this is certainly the meaning of socialisation in Parsonian theory. More particularly however reproduction is commonly used by Marxists of various kinds interested specifically in the reproduction of the class relations on a day to day basis, over time and also, biologically. It therefore signals an interest in a rather different model of society than that implied by socialisation and an interest in interruptions to this process (since these represent resistance in class societies) – something that Blood (Reading 2) unproblematically regards as 'criminal' or 'wild'.

Errol Lawrence, in the eighth reading takes up the related theme of 'popular' characterisations of black (as opposed to working class) families and black youth living in Britain. He argues that black families are different – but being different does not imply (as for example accounts in the popular press suggest) that these families are 'deficient'. For Lawrence there is no 'central value system' for youth to be socialised into either in contemporary Britain or indeed the America in which Parsons was writing. Accounts of black families assume that there is a unified white culture, that it is superior and that black families represent the continuation of an 'alien' culture 'over here'. This is patently racist.

If Bernstein is interested in cultural reproduction, the final reading is interested in economic reproduction. Fitz and Hood-Williams in their historical study of inheritance concentrate on the importance of economic features of the reproduction of societies and particularly on the transmission of property. They point out that capitalism itself has no formal mechanisms for passing capital through the generations to new individuals, and that this is done through families. The rules that govern this passage – rules of inheritance – are therefore of crucial importance to socialisation and the status of children. By determining who gets what, such rules reveal something of the norms of power, advantage and privilege underlying socialisation in Britain.

☐ Socialisation as a Key Function of the Family

In the introductory chapter to the collection of articles he wrote with Robert Bales and others, Talcott Parsons set out his thesis that the American nuclear family has become structurally differentiated from other institutions in society as it has become more specialised in function (here he draws on Weber's notion of rationalisation). The family now meets 'certain essential *psychological* conditions of continuity and conformity of society'.

Parsons starts from the observation that personalities are made not born: 'a *human* person exists only in so far as he has taken "society" into himself'. The family is the factory in this human manufacturing process. For children to be initiated into the central values of the society it is necessary for the adults around them to be themselves fully integrated into those values and the child's personality develops as it encounters successively more complex 'social object *systems*' through them. These are internalised and reinforced by the erotic attachment children have to their parents (here he draws on the work of Freud).

Reading 1

If, as some psychologists seem to assume, the essentials of human personality were determined biologically, independently of involvement in social systems, there would be no need for families, since reproduction as such does not require family organization. It is because the *human* personality is not 'born' but must be 'made' through the socialization process that in the first instance families are necessary. They are 'factories' which produce human personalities. But at the same time even once produced, it cannot be assumed that the human personality would remain stable in the respects which are vital to social functioning, if there were not mechanisms of stabilization which were organically integrated with the socialization process. We therefore suggest that the basic and irreducible functions of the family are two: first, the primary socialization of children so that they can truly become members of the society into which they have been born; second, the stabilization of the adult personalities of the population of the society. It is the combination of these two functional imperatives which explains why, in the 'normal' case it is both true that *every adult* is a member of a nuclear family and that every child must begin his process of socialization in a nuclear family. It will be one of the most important theses of our subsequent analysis that these two circumstances are most intimately interconnected. . . .

The central focus of the process of socialization lies in the internalization of the culture of the society into which the child is born. The most important part of this culture from this focal point consists in the patterns of value which in another aspect constitute the institutionalized patterns of the society. The conditions under which effective socialization can take place then will include being placed in a social situation where the more powerful and responsible persons are themselves integrated in the cultural value system in question, both in that they constitute with the children an *institutionalized* social system, and that the patterns have previously been internalized in the relevant ways in their own personalities . . .

But it is not enough to place the child in any institutionalized system of social relationships. He must be placed in one of a special type which fulfills the necessary psychological conditions of successful completion of the process we call socialization, over a succession of stages starting with earliest infancy . . . A few of them may . . . be noted here . . . In the first place, we feel that for the earlier stages of socialization, at least, the socialization system must be a *small* group. Furthermore, it must be differentiated into subsystems so the child need not have an equal level of participation with all members at the same time in the earlier stages of the process. We will show that it is particularly important that in the earliest stage he tends to have a special relation to one other member of the family, his mother.

We should like to suggest . . . that what we have called the 'isolation of the nuclear family' for the contemporary American scene, may, along with reduction in the average size of family, have considerable significance for the character of the contemporary socialization process. This significance would, we think, have something to do with the greater sharpness of the *difference* in status, from the point of view of the child, between members of the family and nonmembers. It will be our general thesis that in certain respects the modern child has 'farther to go' in his socialization than his predecessors. There seem to be certain reasons why the number of fundamental steps of a certain type is restricted. If this is true, each step has to be 'longer' and it is important that the 'landmarks' along the way, the 'cues' presented to the child, should involve extremely clear discriminations.

T. Parsons and R.F. Bales, *Family, Socialisation and Interaction Process*, pp. 16–19.

Questions

1. What, according to Parsons, is 'the central focus of socialisation'?
2. What does he see as the two basic functions of the family?
3. Why does Parsons think these two functions are 'intimately interconnected'?

☐ Parental Roles in Socialising Children

This reading is taken from a best-selling American textbook for college students on the 'Marriage and Family Living' courses common in junior colleges (somewhat like our Learning for Living in secondary school or YTS). The author identifies socialisation with the duties of parents to impose control and to restrain the young, wild individuals of each generation. Children are presented as not fully human creatures and socialisation is the process of turning unruly nature into conforming, responsible humanity. Not only should parents work on nature to produce law-abiding citizens but they should also work to curb extremes of sex stereotyping.

Reading 2

This chapter focuses on socialization, the next on education. The distinction is arbitrary, for the terms are often used interchangeably. But there is a difference between teaching self-control and teaching anything else. Self-control has a negative emphasis – keeping oneself from antisocial behavior. The remaining goals of child-rearing are positive – skills and knowledge that enrich the life of the individual and society. Many basic principles of learning and teaching underlie both socialization and education. Nevertheless, the practical implications are sufficiently different to justify separate treatment. . . .

Children are born with abundant potentialities but begin their lives undeveloped. The newborn child previously knew no distinction between himself and his warm, nourishing environment. Despite the birth trauma, he still considers himself the center of the universe. He is not aware that other people exist separately. Only gradually and painfully does the 'Copernican revolution' dawn. First he discovers that his mother is not part of himself, then that his father is distinguishable from his mother. Later he discovers they have needs of their own and other roles besides mothering and fathering him. Finally, he learns that his role is not simply to receive but to give, and that he must temper his impulses to meet the needs of others. Only then is he fully human.

This humanization is socially significant because the child graduates from the family into the outside world. If he has been properly humanized, society will not have to defend itself from his aggressive impulses and can depend on him to conform to social norms. The fabric of society would soon crumble were more than a few of its new recruits unsocialized. The machinery of justice can cope with a few criminals, but society relies on the inner controls of the vast majority.

To the family the stress of coping with an unsocialized creature comes early. Long before society encounters what the family produces, parents must live with what nature brings. No matter how great their generosity, their tolerance, or even their masochistic urge to be martyrs, parents must curb their 'little monster' if he is not to destroy their domestic tranquility. Every child is a potential 'Dennis-the-menace'. Although socialization sometimes occurs so swiftly that the threat is never apparent, its success is just as crucial to the family as to society.

To a child, being allowed to run wild seems delightful at first. But wild men end up in cages – either prisons or mental hospitals. The fact that society cannot tolerate unsocialized adults means that children who fail to learn conformity face a tragic future. For the child perhaps most pointedly, socialization is indispensable. . . .

So far I have ignored the fact that children come in two sexes . . . Research [has] suggested that boys and girls need to be treated differently for best results. The chief danger for boys is that they will be undersocialized, but many middle-class families oversocialize their daughters. To avoid these dangers, parents need to give their sons more affection and discipline than their daughters. They need to limit the extent to which they reject their daughters when they misbehave (since girls are so sensitive that 'a little rejection goes a long way – and very soon too far').

These prescriptions run counter to the usual tendencies. Most parents are free and cool with their sons, but strict and warm with their daughters. Yet the aggressiveness and independence of boys requires more vigorous discipline and warmer affection if they are to be socialized adequately.

R.O. Blood Jnr, *Marriage*, pp. 446, 457.

Questions

1. What is socialisation basically concerned with according to Blood?
2. What does he mean when he talks of middle class girls as 'over-socialised', boys as 'under-socialised' and criminals as 'unsocialised'?

□ Children as Actors: A Different View of Childhood Socialisation

The anthropologist, Matthew Speier, is critical of what he calls the classical formulation of the problem of socialisation. He regards this as simply a reflection of the general views that adults have about children. These views derive from adults' problem of managing children. Speier certainly implies that children are not wild, 'asocial beings' needing to be institutionalised into the central value systems of society – as the first two readings variously put it. He reminds us that children have their own culture, with its own rules and competencies which they acquire independently of adults. Speier also wishes to point out that when children and adults interact the adults have power over the children and can, to a considerable extent, determine the interactional rights that the children are to be accorded. For example adults often claim the right to determine when and if a child shall speak – although this and other claims do not go uncontested!

Reading 3

In sociology and anthropology alike, studies of children have come under the heading of socialization. . . .

A review of the literature in the field of socialization, particularly its standard references, will amply document that a set of working suppositions is deeply engrained in the choice of research problems and findings that result . . .

What this position amounts to very simply is that a child is treated as a special kind of social actor who is continually in need of learning how to participate in society . . . children are continually learning how to shape and fit their behaviour to an adult normative order which calls upon them to orient and conform to it. The over-riding interest the position therefore promotes is how well (or poorly) children go about working out that problem.

What the sociologist has overlooked, however, is that his attribution of this problem to the child is part and parcel of his own adult ideology as to what is socially important about children's behaviour. In actuality the child's problem is an adult's problem to the extent that an adult is committed to recognizing and obligated to helping the child work through that problem . . . The sociologist, then, has tended to adopt the position of an adult in his society when he has formulated research questions about child development and child rearing . . . To use a very crude metaphor,. . . sociologists have been going about their study of children mainly like colonial administrators who might be expected to write scientifically objective reports of the local populace in order to increase their understanding of native culture, and who do so by ideologically formulating only those research problems that pertain to native behaviours coming under the regulation of colonial authority. Such a 'science' would be designed to serve the successful management of the native culture; it would be a practical 'science' of human management. Commitment to such a practical 'science' would originate out of an ideological interest in controlling the native culture and not out of a 'passionate disinterest' in the culture for its own sake.

The metaphor of colonial administration, though not intended to be taken as more than a metaphor, is useful in two ways. It refers to a social situation in which two cultures are put into routine contact. It also refers to a situation in which one culture is in a position to manage the affairs of the other culture. . . . I want to propose that these two points be taken seriously. . . . A modification of outlook in our research should point innovatively to the recognizable existence of *children's culture* (or cultures). It is a culture which is separate from, but intimately related to its counterpart, adult culture. The *two cultures* are in routine contact with each other . . .

If there is any scepticism about the existence of children's culture, it is a reflection of our own adult ideological commitment which has all but obscured the fact of its existence. The work of parenthood consists mainly of the practical 'science' of child management in the family household. Likewise the work of a teacher is devoted largely to the practical 'science' of child management in the classroom and around the school establishment. Yet the Opies, for example, have documented the existence of children's culture among schoolchildren in Great Britain by accumulating a vast amount of data on children's traditional lore and games which do not originate out of the practical activity of child management. Likewise my own research on children's play activity at home, and my filming of children's interactions associated with school activity outside the classroom, indicates the existence of children's culture. It would appear to essentially be neither a miniaturized nor a half–baked adult culture, nor an imitated version of it – but a culture in its own right.

. . . some of the more significant general findings I have made pertaining to culture contact [concern] . . . adult-child conversational interactions . . . a child has a very special status as a conversationalist. This status is accorded him when adult members of his culture decide to speak to him and when they decide to engage him in on-going conversation. This status is also achieved when the child attempts to speak to adults in his everyday environments and likewise attempts to engage in or carry on conversation with them. The child's special conversational status is an invariant condition of conversational contacts between the cultures. . . .

[For instance] Adults can exercise their right *to enforce silence upon a child speaker or a group of children* . . . They often monitor . . . children's activity from a distance, and . . . are specially entitled with the *right to intervene* if deemed necessary. Such interventional behaviour does not rely on the normal politeness rules shown to other adults. The overseeing function of adults and parents allows for categorical use of asymmetrical rights of intervention. Children, conversely, must not intervene without some care to display politeness rituals as acceptable *pre-intervention behaviour* . . .

I propose the following modification in our sociological reasoning about childhood studies. Adult . . . conventions (what sociologists might also think of as theoretical suppositions) must be re-allocated from being a purely natural resource for analysis to the position of being a basic topic for the analysis itself. That is, the classical formulation of socialization theory is not the special provenance of the sociologist but originates from the latter's position as an adult in his society. In actuality lay socialization theories are an ideological basis for adult interaction with children.

M. Speier, 'The child as conversationalist: some culture contact features of conversational interactions between adults and children', in M. Hammersley and P. Woods (eds), *The Process of Schooling*, pp. 98–9.

Questions

1. What is the major criticism that Speier addresses to the 'classical formulation' of the problem of socialisation?
2. Speier gives us an interesting re-working of the 'generation gap' theories. What would sociologists study if they accepted his re-casting of the socialisation problem?

□ Class Differences in Socialisation

The next reading is from the final chapter of the third book in a series reporting the results of a large scale, longitudinal study of rearing children in a 'representative Midland city, Nottingham'. The research project which began in 1958 is relatively theoretically unsophisticated, for example in its concept of socialisation. Nevertheless it is empirically rigorous. Seven hundred mothers are taking part, so the authors statements are based on a mass of data concerning varying attitudes to, and practices of childcare, with class as a major variable. (A variable is any known characteristic which varies between the individuals in a sample.)

The particular book from which the extract is taken looks at the home environment of seven-year-olds. It recognises the *interaction* which occurs between parents and children – unlike Parsons, who tends to see socialisation as operating from the top downwards. It stresses that the control parents exercise over children must be set against the individualised care they give; but that class-related differences in parental behaviour produce class-related differences of personality and expectations in children.

Reading 4

In teaching the child the inner controls which are expected of him, parents also modify their expectations to suit the individuality of the child, and in all sorts of ways make it clear to him that the standards which prevail in the world outside can be relaxed a little to meet his private needs within the family circle. In a sense, parents strike a bargain with their children that, in return for 'socialised' behaviour outside, a sanctuary will be preserved within the home in which the child can revert to his more uncontrolled and primitive self. Thus the parents at once uphold a dual role: as advocates of society's demands, and as defenders of the child against those same demands once he is in the privacy of his family.

Numerous examples of this can be found in early upbringing, . . . In many, many families, for instance, infantile behaviour such as comfort-sucking of bottles and dummies goes on in private long after the mother has made the child understand that this indulgence is not for the public eye. Similarly, between four and seven children are allowed to 'play' with truth and falsehood in the form of fantasy within the home when it is considered both inappropriate and risky to stray from the exact truth outside the family. . . .

What all this adds up to is a concept of parents as a uniquely caring force in the child's development. Parents have an involvement with their own child which nobody else can simulate. In this lies both their strength and their vulnerability. The crucial characteristic of the parental role is its *partiality* for the individual child. This is why all the other caring agencies that we can devise can never be quite as satisfactory as the 'good-enough' parent (to use Winnicott's term). The best that community care can offer is impartiality – to be fair to every child in its care. But a developing personality needs more than that: it needs to know that to someone it matters more than other children; that someone will go to *un*reasonable lengths, not just reasonable ones, for its sake. This is the parental role which may well be of the greatest importance of all; and this is the role which society is unlikely to replace successfully, in whatever directions it may develop.

If we stopped there, this chapter could be re-titled *In Praise of Parents*, and we could end with three cheers; but, although we believe that parents are irreplaceable, we are not totally optimistic about every aspect of the parental role. It is a major part of that role to mediate and interpret cultural expectations to the child; but cultural expectations, . . . do not come in one big convenient package. They vary within the culture, so that parents in one social group are likely to pass on the attitudes of that social group, while parents in another will transmit a subcultural package that differs in various ways. An obvious example . . . is that attitudes to literacy vary so much from one social group to another that a child's progress through school is significantly predetermined before he even sets foot in the place. [Another example is the use of physical punishment.]

From TABLE 43. High . . . scorers on [a] corporal punishment index

High scorers	social class					summary	
	I&II	IIIwc	III man	IV	V	I&II, IIIwc	IIIman, IV,V
	%	%	%	%	%	% m.class	% w.class
boys	29	33	44	41	44	31	43
girls	12	20	24	21	36	16	25
both	21	27	34	31	40	24	34

The most obvious conclusion from Table 43 is that physical punishment is invoked considerably more for boys than for girls at . . . [seven years of] age. Though slightly less marked, there is also a distinct and significant tendency for physical punishment to feature more strongly as we descend the social class scale. In particular, physical methods of controlling behaviour are much more likely to be stressed among families in the unskilled manual group, and their girls enjoy a lesser degree of comparative favour than do girls in other social classes. . . .

The implications of systematic variation in the principles of child discipline held by different social groups, and in the means by which they try to enforce it, are no less important for being less obvious. Parents at the upper end of the social scale are more inclined *on principle* to use democratically based, highly verbal means of control, and this kind of discipline is likely to produce personalities who can both identify successfully with the system and use it to their own ends later on. At the bottom end of the scale, in the unskilled group, parents choose *on principle* to use a highly authoritarian, mainly non-verbal means of control, in which words are used more to threaten and bamboozle the child into obedience than to make him understand the rationale behind social behaviour: and this seems likely to result in a personality who can neither identify with nor beat the system. In short, privileged parents, by using the methods that they prefer, produce children who expect as of right to be privileged and who are very well equipped to realise those expectations; while deprived parents, *also by using the methods that they prefer*, will probably produce children who expect nothing and are not equipped to do anything about it. Thus the child born into the lowest social bracket has everything stacked against him *including his parents' principles of child upbringing*. Because we do not see how we can easily change principles which are honestly and firmly held, for this group of children we are pessimistic about the nature of the parental role.

J. and E. Newson, *Seven Years Old in the Home Environment*, pp. 403–6 and 326–8.

Questions

1. The reading refers to two ways in which classes differ in their child rearing practices. What are they? Can you suggest others?
2. Why, according to the reading, do the child rearing methods that 'privileged' parents use, lead their children to expect to grow up to be privileged themselves?

□ Intra-class Differences in Socialisation

In this rather complex reading Basil Bernstein develops Durkheim's ideas about social and cultural differences between persons living in societies characterised by mechanical or organic solidarity. He suggests there are differences between persons located *within different sections of a class* within our own industrial society and that differences between members of the 'old' and the 'new' middle class relate to differences of approach to child socialisation in these sub-classes.

The new middle class owe their class position to work involving symbolic or cultural control rather than to manufacturing industry. They are the owners of skills (acquired largely in the educational system) rather than the owners of productive property. Bernstein is interested in the ways the two factions of this powerful class have developed principles for the social control and personality development of young people in their families and in 'their' schools.

The new middle class have new types of family relationships, particularly between mothers and children. These are in tune with the proponents of the teaching style often called 'progressive' (here called 'invisible') pedagogy. This encourages a child to be flexible, 'creative', 'expressive', 'spontaneous' and to become what Bernstein calls a 'person'. The old middle class favours traditional teaching (visible pedagogy) which encourages a child to be what Durkheim described as an 'individual'.

Bernstein is also interested in the different forms of middle class cohesion – their types of solidarity. The two class fractions each hold together as communities through the use of different codes that organise their cultures. One problem for the new middle class is that their codes, which stress flexibility, etc., are at a variance with the public examination system that increasingly holds the key to the possibility of gaining entry into the middle class itself. This fraction is caught within the contradiction of favouring openness and social mobility whilst wishing to ensure the reproduction of their own class position in their own children.

Reading 5

Durkheim, it seems to me, was concerned with only *one* form of [organic] solidarity – the form which created individualism . . . His analysis is based upon the old middle class. He did not foresee, although his conceptual procedures make this possible, a form of organic solidarity [developed by the new middle class.] . . . The second form of organic solidarity celebrates the apparent release, not of the individual, but of the persons and *new* forms of social control. Thus, we can distinguish *individualized* and *personalized* forms of organic solidarity *within* the middle class, each with their own distinctive and conflicting ideologies and each with their own distinctive and conflicting forms of socialization and symbolic reality. These two forms arise out of developments of the division of labour within class societies. Durkheim's individualized organic solidarity developed out of the increasing complexity of the economic division of labour; personalized organic solidarity, it is suggested, develops out of increases in the complexity of the division of labour of cultural or symbolic control which the new middle class have appropriated. . . .

This conflict within the middle class is realized sharply in different patterns of the socialization of the young. In the new middle class, socialization . . . [involves] . . . far greater ambiguity, and drives this class to make visible the ideology of its socialization; crucial to this ideology is the concept of the *person* not of the *individual*. Whereas the concept of the *individual* leads to specific, unambiguous role identities and relatively inflexible role performances, the *concept* of the person leads to ambiguous personal identity and flexible role performances . . .

The new middle class, like the proponents of the invisible peda-gogy, are caught in a contradiction; for their theories are at variance with their objective class relationship. A deep-rooted ambivalence is the ambience of this group. On the one hand, they stand for variety against inflexibility, expression against repression, the inter-personal against the inter-positional; on the other hand, there is the grim obduracy of the division of labour and of the narrow pathways to its positions of power and prestige. Under individualized organic soli-darity, property has an essentially physical nature; however, with the development of personalized organic solidarity, although property in the physical sense remains crucial, it has been partly psychologized and appears in the form of ownership of valued skills made available in educational institutions. Thus, if the new middle class is to repeat its position in the class structure, then appropriate secondary social-ization into privileged education becomes crucial. But as the relation between education and occupation becomes more direct and closer in time, . . . the new middle class take up some ambivalent enthusiasm for the invisible pedagogy for the early socialization of the child, but settle for the *visible* pedagogy of the secondary school. . . .

The shift from individualized to personalized organic solidarity changes the structure of family relationships, and in particular the role of the woman in the socializing of the child. Historically, under individualized organic solidarity, the mother was neither important as a transmitter of physical or of symbolic property. She was almost totally abstracted from the means of reproduction of either physical or symbolic property. The control of the children was delegated to others – nanny, governess, tutor. She was essentially a domestic administrator, and it follows that she could be a model only for her daughter . . . [In the new middle class] The rôle of the mother in the rearing of her children undergoes a qualitative change. The mother is transformed into a crucial preparing agent of cultural reproduction who provides access to symbolic forms and shapes the dispositions of her children so that they are better able to exploit the possibilities of public education. We can see an integration of maternal functions, as the basis of class position becomes psychologized. *Delegated* maternal caring and preparation *becomes* maternal caring and preparation. What is of interest here is the *form* of the caring and the form of the preparation. According to the thesis, the form may be constituted by either a visible or an invisible pedagogy. The old middle class perpetuated itself through a visible pedagogy, whereas the new middle class, the bearers of the structures of personalized organic solidarity, developed invisible pedagogies.

B. Bernstein, *Class, Codes and Control*, Volume 3, pp. 124–7, 130, 131.

Questions

1. What is the difference between the relationships of 'old' and 'new' middle class mothers and their children?
2. What do you think are the major differences between progressive primary school teaching and traditional secondary school teaching and can you say why such differences are relevant to a discussion of socialisation?

☐ Working Class Girl in a Grammar School

How does it feel to *live* the disjunctures between home and school expectations mentioned by the Newsons and by Bernstein? Here Irene Payne discusses elements of her life as an adolescent from a manual worker's family in a girls' grammar school in the 1960s. She describes how she negotiated the class and sexist ideology within which she was placed.

Hers was an important contribution to one of the first collections of articles from members of a feminist study group 'concerned to share their experience as a basis for an anti-sexist critique of educational theory and practice.' The sociology of education already provided vivid accounts of the difficulties that working class *boys* had when they (more frequently) made the transition to grammar schools.

Reading 6

My family was probably what could be termed 'respectable' working class, that is, a particular segment who, for a complex of reasons, had taken on a certain set of beliefs about education. Their faith in education would not have been shared by many of the parents of my contemporaries. The material sacrifice necessary for a grammar school education would certainly not have been made by all working-class families . . . Many relations and neighbours said that education wasn't really important for girls, as they only got married and had children. My brother's success was seen as much more crucial than mine. However, my own parents, and particularly my mother, never questioned the fact that I should be educated . . . My mother certainly did not have a confident attitude towards education, but accepted the advice of some 'experts' who counselled sending me to grammar school. This passivity is, I think, a significant element in being 'respectable' working class. It goes hand in hand with a desire to conform. There was no element of understanding the educational system, let alone of actively using it, . . . I want to examine the value system of my school in relation to the value system of my working-class neighbourhood . . . to look at what I learned, both implicitly and explicitly, within this school.

The first clear set of values was characterised by the school uniform. The class roots of school uniform are fairly clear because their origins are in the public schools. Institutional colours, mottoes and crests were all part of a total image derived from the ruling class. The uniform represented a sobriety and discipline whose power extended beyond the school. I can remember that prefects had the responsibility of ensuring that girls wore their berets on the bus journeys on public transport to and from school . . . These practices were part of the process of enforcing a particular set of bourgeois values, based on ideas of respectability, smartness and appearances.

However, I think there was a further dimension to this, in terms of gender. The uniform couldn't have been better designed to disguise any hints of adolescent sexuality. I suppose the shirt and tie, the 'sensible' shoes, thick socks and navy blue knickers were part of a more 'masculinised' image. It was as though femininity had to be symbolically sacrificed to the pursuit of knowledge. Modesty was implicit as there were regulations about the length of skirts and the covering of your arms. Jewellery, make-up and nylon stockings were taboo. Ideas about dress were based on notions of 'nice' girls and 'not so nice' girls, with both class and sexual connotations. We were, after all, to be turned into middle-class young ladies.

I wore the uniform without too much suffering at school but it was the greatest source of embarrassment to me beyond the school gates. I can remember being terrified that someone from my neighbourhood might see me wearing it. I was worried that I might be regarded as a 'college pud' or a snob by my peers. If they saw anyone in school uniform they would usually jeer and hurl abuse. But it had sexual as well as class connotations. As I got older, I was particularly concerned that potential boyfriends didn't see me in this 'unfeminine' garb. The first thing I always did when I got home from school was dash to my bedroom to change out of my uniform. However, my rebellion against school uniform was never very strong as I wanted to do well at school and wearing uniform was part of the process of earning approval.

The school even had an 'official' attitude to boyfriends. I can remember the head mistress insisting that her girls didn't have time for boyfriends. This was another way of denying our sexuality. Social life was disapproved of and we were inundated with homework which made it difficult to do much else in your own time. I suppose we were being prevented from growing up so that we would conform to the demands of the school. Saturday jobs were totally disapproved of which shows the middle-class ideology of the school. I needed to work as my parents found it a struggle to keep me. These jobs also provided one of the few opportunities to participate in the adult world and gain some experience of work. Our horizons, however, were supposed to be narrowed down to working for school. All these practices were part of what it was to be a 'young lady.' . . .

Another manifestation of these implicit values was in the whole area of language. Again, there were two dimensions to this. In terms of class I had to learn to 'speak properly', that is, like middle-class people, and in terms of gender I had to learn to speak politely, that is, talking like a lady. This meant learning to speak both 'correctly' and 'nicely' and the pressure to conform can be quite inhibiting for a working-class girl . . .

I managed to conform and meet the linguistic requirements of the school, but they could only be used within the school. I had to abandon them when I left the school gates and had to change my language for home. Such 'bilingualism' is not without its disadvantages and can work to make one feel inadequate and unconfident in all language use. Mistakes at school could be an offence, but so too could mistakes at home. I was in constant terror of being exposed as a 'freak'. My way of dealing with this threat was to over-react. In my home environment I made a concerted effort to appear as 'one of the girls' and to do this I felt obliged to be louder than anyone else, to swear more, just to prove I wasn't different and hadn't been corrupted by the grammar school.

It was like leading a double life, for neither side would have recognised me in the other context. I was straddling two very different worlds and felt considerably threatened by the fact that I didn't belong to either. I had a constant sense of being different, which I interpreted as inferiority . . . My Dad was a manual worker and we were pretty poor and I didn't want my classmates to know this. Nor did I want them to know that I lived in a 'rough' area, in a house that didn't have a bathroom.

At the same time I didn't want my friends in my neighbourhood to know that I was considered clever at school . . . The problem of being seen as clever was particularly acute when it came to having boyfriends. I thought that being regarded as intelligent would make me less attractive to boys. I was always careful, therefore, to make light of my grammar school education and to refrain from mentioning how many O levels I was doing. Again there was the fear of making a mistake for, to me, it seemed that it would be a mistake to be seen as being more clever than a boy.

The pressures on me were conflicting and varied. For quite a while I tried to negotiate two worlds, but the time came when such negotiation was no longer possible. The two worlds proved to be incompatible. The two sets of values ordained different futures and the point came where I had to decide which future would be mine. Eventually the pull of the school was stronger for it held out the promise of social mobility through higher education. Once I decided to stay on at school after the statutory leaving age my fate was sealed. I could no longer pretend that school was unimportant or irrelevant. It was clear to my friends at home that I had marked myself as 'different' and from this point our paths were to diverge. They entered the world of paid work and they left me behind; I could not disguise myself as one of them any more.

Irene Payne, 'A Working-Class Girl in a Grammar School' in D. Spender and E. Sarah (eds), *Learning to Lose*, pp. 13–18.

Questions

1. Which of the contradictions between her home/neighbourhood and school life do you think Payne shared with
   (a) middle class girls and
   (b) working class boys?
2. How might middle class parents 'actively use' the educational system?

□ The Clash of Cultures

Views commonly expressed in the popular press and by diverse political commentators suggest the relationships between young black people and their parents are particularly difficult. These are presented as being friction filled because there is said to be a culture 'clash' between parents with an Asian, African or Caribbean background and children born and raised in this country, who have absorbed English values. Such parents' authority is undermined and the children run wild. But equally the view is expressed that they *should* break free. Neo-racism asserts that a continuation of 'foreign' cultures here in Britain is quite unacceptable – the best 'we' can hope for is speedy assimilation.

Errol Lawrence, in two articles in the Centre for Contemporary Cultural Studies collection *The Empire Strikes Back*, argues that sociology has played a part in this pathologising of black families by focusing on 'problems' and 'crises'. He suggests that the concepts that are commonly invoked to discuss black families emphasise generational division and underplay generational unities.

Reading 7

The family is seen to transmit traditions and generate loyalties (amongst other things), at least within the immediate family. It is the family's role in reproducing a certain sort of culture, a certain 'way of life', that makes it 'the fundamental unit of society'. Not only is the 'family' structure of the black communities seen to be different; it also, as Powell and others tell us, reproduces different cultures. Blacks are different and recognized as such not just (or even) because they have different features and/or complexions, but primarily because they have different cultures, different 'ways of life' . . . This makes it possible to argue that the cultural 'obstructions' to 'fuller participation' in society are reproduced within black families by black people themselves and that like 'original sin' these 'problems' descend from the 'immigrants' to their children, their children's children and to all who came after them . . .

It is not . . . [Afro-Caribbean or Asian] cultures in themselves that are thought to constitute the main problem for British society, but the fact that . . . they are being continued 'here in Britain'. This view turns in part on the notion that British culture is inherently superior to all others. Thus the 'meeting' of the cultures on British soil is felt to put undue 'pressure on the (black) family' and to undermine . . . [their] 'traditional ways'. The children are viewed as the agents of change in this process. They go to school with white English children, imbibe certain aspects of British culture and are said to be influenced by the greater 'freedom' of their white peers. Naturally enough, so the argument runs, they would like to enjoy such 'freedoms' as well, but this introduces tensions and stress into their home life and may even bring them into conflict with their 'traditionalist' parents. Asian parents are [for instance,] thought to face 'the gentle revolt of their children' against Asian cultural practices. Arranged marriages are presented as a specific site of conflict, particularly for Asian girls who apparently yearn to adopt the 'permissive' customs of the English. They 'want to uncover their legs and wed boys they choose, not partners arranged for them by their families'. The 'freedom' to marry the partner of your choice is of course one of those cherished British freedoms which marks out British culture as 'superior'. From this point of view, the institution of arranged marriage, in which it is assumed that the girl has no say in who she marries, is indicative of the inherent 'barbarity' of Asian cultures . . . It also assumes that white English girls have complete freedom of choice in whom they marry, conveniently glossing over possible class-based determinations and even the frequently obstructive role of the parents. Similarly, the complex negotiations involved in arranging a marriage and the differing ways different communities and parents have of going about it, remain unrecognized within the common-sense view.

Arguments about the 'problems' caused by the 'cultural preferences' of Asians and the 'negative self-image' and 'weak' family structures . . . [which are alleged to exist among] Afro-Caribbeans, form the backdrop against which discussions of Asian and Afro-Caribbean youth take place. The themes here are organized around the 'one and a half' or even 'two' generation gap which is thought to afflict the Afro-Caribbean community and the 'cultural conflict' between Asian parents and their children, who are 'caught between two cultures'. The reasons put forward for this vary from author to author, although they all boil down more or less to the view that the different experiences and backgrounds of parents and youth lead to differing responses to and expectations of life in Britain, which in turn provide the occasion for conflict between parents and their children. . . .

The ideas about 'identity crisis', 'culture conflict' and 'intergenerational conflict' which power the accounts of 'race/ethnic relations' sociologists have been constructed in large part without reference to the struggles that the parents have been involved in before and since coming to Britain. They have been characterized as the passive, acquiescent victims of racism wanting only to 'integrate'; as recalcitrant 'traditionalists', suspicious and bewildered by white society, who 'withdraw' wilfully into their own 'ethnic' or 'religious' enclaves; or as a combination of both. . . .

The idea that the struggles of black youth, against police harassment, Fascist attacks and racism in schools and at work, are 'new' phenomena is hardly borne out by the facts. Who were the objects of the police's 'nigger hunting' expeditions in the fifties and early sixties when many of today's youth weren't even a glimmer in their parents' eyes? Who fought the Fascists and Teddy Boys in Nottingham and Notting Hill in 1958? Who are the people who fought trade union racism up and down the country for the last thirty years and more? Who initiated the campaigns against ESN placements and 'sinbins'? The fact that the youths have brought new understandings and different modes of struggle to bear on their communities' struggles, does not mean that they are not still following in their parents' footsteps or that they don't stand firmly *side by side* their parents in opposition to racism.

E. Lawrence, 'In the abundance of water the fool is thirsty: sociology and black "pathology"' and, 'Just plain common sense: the "roots" of racism' in Centre for Contemporary Cultural Studies, *The Empire Strikes Back*, pp. 75–6, 83, 116, 122, 132.

Questions

1. Although non-western cultures are frequently derided for being defective in various ways (see Desmond Morris, Reading 2 in Chapter 1) this is not, in the author's view, picked out as the main 'problem' by neo-racist commentaries. What is now the main 'problem'?
2. From your knowledge of Reading 1 how do you suppose that Parsons would view the socialisation of black children into black cultures?
3. If an Afro-Caribbean girl, or an Asian boy, were writing a personal account like that of Irene Payne, what contradictions do you think that they might focus upon?

☐ Inheritance

Family heads not only control their dependents by their personal authority, but also by the control they exercise over money and property. There are legal rules governing who should get what and when, especially in cases of intestate succession (i.e. when no will has been made) and a study of these, and how they have changed over time, can tell us a lot about family relationships – even among the classes who have had little wealth to transmit.

Church and state rules actually define, in the last analysis, fundamental questions such as whether a family relationship exists and what form it should take. The 'reproduction' of the ownership and disposition of capital is secured through rules invoking patriarchal family relationships.

Reading 8

Inheritance, in the enlarged sense with which we use the term, refers to . . . familial transmission . . . throughout the life of family subordinates and at crucial moments in the life cycle – death . . ., marriage, and the age of majority . . . [It is] the process of the circulation of familial capital . . . For the purpose of analysis we divide this process of transmission . . . into two types: diachronic and synchronic. Diachronic inheritance refers to transmissions over time and down the family line at specific . . . moments in the life cycle. Synchronic inheritance refers to gifts *inter vivos* and to those familial transmissions referred to by writers such as Bourdieu (1976) as 'social reproduction' . . . The logic of these transmissions tell us about the patriarchal form of the family and about the character of intergenerational relations . . .

The dependency of minors is secured in a variety of ways – their inability to act as legal subjects, to hold capital, their exclusion from waged labour, the contemporary obligation to attend school and the process of socialisation. Their dependency however, significantly derives from the status of minors within the family, particularly with respect to divisions of family labour, the familial structuring of the waged labour market, and, especially historically, the ownership of familial property ... The rules governing the circulation of this property ... give us the template of historically approved family forms and the status of family members, even with regard to that majority of families who had no property to transmit.

[From the 13th century onwards] the dependence of minors on adults (parents and guardians) was legally given by their absolute exclusion from owning property until the age of twenty-one. Through the seventeenth and eighteenth centuries, political and juridical theorists, such as Locke and Filmer, based their arguments against extending citizen and political rights to minors on this legal exclusion from property ownership ...

Diachronic inheritance, historically, operated through a relatively fixed structure, in which the rules of transmission were more clearly laid out. These fixed powers and obligations of the patriarch, despite in practice always allowing a certain freedom of movement, have given way to a highly individualised and personal form of authority.

The consequence of the historically increasing power of familial heads to [will away family property] ... meant for the wives and children of property–owning men an increasing subjection to a patriarchal power which had decreasingly fewer obligations to provide for [those who might have expected to inherit] .... This meant increased control over the lives of wives and minors. In the case of the latter, this was particularly at the crucial moments of majority and marriage, and for both categories at the death of the patriarch. It was ... possible for him, from the early modern period, to make no provision whatsoever for his familial descendants. On the other hand, later nineteenth century developments such as the creation, *de jure*, of property-owning women, had subsequent significance for their political rights and marks a small gain for the wives of the bourgeoisie. Hence, women moved increasingly towards a contemporary notion of 'citizenship'. Minors however, remained outside the polity.

With regard to wives and children within working-class families, developments such as the nineteenth century Factory Acts and the male union demands for a 'family wage' drove women and children from crucial areas of the waged labour market. The consequence of this for wives was an *increased* dependence upon their husbands and an increasing confinement within the domestic sphere. For children of the working class a concomitant dependence was coupled to an increasing obligation to attend school. This schooling meant, by the end of the nineteenth century, increased gender differentiation, increased age grading and increased infantilisation. In short, a cultural process resulting in subjects that we today consider to be 'children'. In very broad terms, we can characterise the qualitative shift in the modalities of patriarchal control, derivable from the principles of transmission, as a move from clearly specified rules, to the personalised, 'free', regimen that we recognise today.

Recent changes, such as the introduction of various forms of taxation, justify (at least in relation to increasing numbers of the middle class) the emphasis placed by social scientists upon synchronic inheritance and the reproduction of class positions through the transmission of cultural capital. Nevertheless, . . . the distinctively *familial* quality of . . . the diachronic transmission of value (both economic and cultural) . . . remains – although this frequently goes unnoticed.

J. Fitz and J. Hood-Williams, 'The generation game: playing by the rules', in D. Robbins *et al.* (eds), *Rethinking Social Inequality*, pp. 65–7, 76, 86.

Questions

1. Give examples of the ways in which minors (those under the age of majority) are made dependent and say which of these relate specifically to the family. (You might like to refer also to the readings by Fitz, Humphries and Hartmann in Chapter 6.)
2. Explain in your own words the difference between synchronic and diachronic inheritance and explain how the balance between the significance of the two has been changing?

Essay Questions

1. Outline and evaluate the sociological insights provided by viewing childhood and youth as social constructs. (AEB 1984)
2. Does it make sociological sense to describe people as undersocialised? (London 1983)
3. How far do you share the view that society transforms 'little animals' into human beings? (Cambridge 1986)
4. What is meant by the term socialisation? Illustrate its usefulness and limitations in relation to *either* gender *or* social class. (Cambridge 1985)
5. 'The orderliness of our social world does not depend on a one-sided process whereby sets of shared expectations are imposed upon individuals by means of sanctions; it depends rather upon the interpretive competencies of both adult and child.' Examine the concept of socialisation in the light of the above statement.

6. Compare the merits of two alternative ways in which sociologists can analyse parent-child relationships.
7. Whatever the society, socialisation is always the process of learning to conform to the status quo. Discuss and illustrate using comparative material. (London 1983)
8. With reference to gender or age, assess the evidence for the statement that 'we are socialised throughout life into conforming to prescribed roles'. (London 1983)

Further Reading

Stevi Jackson, *Childhood and Sexuality*, provides both a brief, readable account of the history of childhood, and a discussion of how and why children are 'protected' from knowing about sexuality. This protection is problematic – for adults who have to tell children 'the facts of life', and for children who are exposed to danger through ignorance.

I. Pinchbeck and M. Hewitt, *Children in English Society*, Vol. 1 'From Tudor Times to the Eighteenth Century', and Vol. 2 'From the Eighteenth Century to the Children Act 1948'. A classic work, mainly focussed upon children's employment and their legal status – namely social concerns and statutory provision for the welfare of children. See also the reference to J. Fitz and J. Shaw in the Further Reading for Chapter 6.

Sarah Reedy and Martin Woodhead (eds), *Family, Work and Education*, Part One 'Childhood in the Family', and Part Two 'Learning in the Early Years'.

John and Elizabeth Newson, *Patterns of Infant Care in an Urban Community, Four Years Old in an Urban Community, Seven Years Old in the Home Environment*. The major publications from the Child Development Research Unit at the University of Nottingham. Particular children and their development can be followed through successive volumes.

Denise Riley, *War in the Nursery*. A history of psychology, including an interesting discussion of key concepts in social science thinking on child development and socialisation.

Carolyn Steedman, *The Tidy House*. Starting from the story written by three eight-year-old working class girls in one of her school classes, Steedman analyses the girls' account of the house they expect to live in, the streets around, and their views on love and motherhood. She locates these within the history of children's writing, children's relationships with adults, and theories of socialisation, education and linguistics.

John Holt, *Escape from Childhood. The needs and rights of children*. Holt believes that 'children, under the pretext of being protected, are humiliated and degraded by our society. They are not allowed to be the judges of what is best for them'. He thinks they should be given freedom of choice in education, to vote, financial independence, the right to choose their guardians, and to do what any adult may legally do.

Diana Gittins, *The Family in Question*, Chapter 5 'Why do people have children?'

5 | How was the family changed by industrial capitalism?

In this chapter we are concerned with the relationship between the family and events in the wider economy. However, when we study the history of the changing relationships between the family and the economy it is important to remember that to a considerable extent in pre-industrial England, the family *was* the economy. Modern economists, whatever general theory they hold, typically have only a passing interest in the family. Economic historians of pre-seventeenth century Europe, however, such as Theodore Shanin in his *Peasants and Peasant Society*, are students of the family itself.

Today a great a deal of the goods and services (e.g. cars, clothes, food, energy, health care, education, etc.) that we use everyday are made or provided, in places outside the family (e.g. in factories, hospitals, schools and restaurants). They are made or provided predominately by people who, each day, leave their homes and go out to work for a wage. However, in preindustrial and predominately rural societies, where the range of such goods and services was much less, they were produced largely in families. Pre–industrial families farmed small farms or large gardens, and grazed animals on common ground. They cultivated and consumed their own crops; reared, killed, prepared and ate their animals; wove and sold cloth and made it into clothes and provided much of their own health care and education – as well as selling some surplus on the market. Peasants were likely to work at these activities for members of their own or other people's families rather than for non-relative employers, and their work groups were relatively small. They were more likely to be rewarded for this work by receiving subsistence, shelter and, in the longer term, inheritance rather than by receiving wages. However this is not to say that work was not also done for wages by certain sectors of the population, or alongside cultivation for self-consumption – even in peasant societies.

The questions that interest us here concern the effects on the family of moving from one form of production (i.e. the domestic or peasant mode of production) to another (i.e. the capitalist mode of production). The key features of capitalism as an economic system are that goods and services are produced for exchange on a market in a way that produces profit for the owners of the means of production – means that may as easily be land as a factory. Production proceeds by owners, one class, entering into a relationship with workers, a second class. The former buy the labouring abilities of the latter (when they require them) from an existing market of labour, for wages. Central features of a capitalist mode of production, such as a developed market in goods and services available for cash purchase and a developed market in waged labour, were certainly well in place in England by the eighteenth century. However, it was in the late eighteenth century that further changes began which lead to England becoming an industrial country.

The readings in this chapter explore some of the further effects on the family of the industrialising of society, but it is important to note that they use the term 'industrialisation' in various ways. We understand the term industrial revolution to refer to the transformation of a society from a primarily agricultural economy to one based primarily on manufacture in workshops and factories. This occurred earlier in Britain (c.1780–1840) than in any other country. Associated with the industrial revolution were dramatic increases in the levels of production, related to the development of new technologies, and equally dramatic increases in the size of the population and its concentration into fast growing towns. All this is not, of course, the same thing as the development of capitalism which preceded industrialisation in Britain. However the agrarian revolution of the eighteenth century, in which a capitalist way of producing was established in the countryside, laid the basis for the capitalist-based industrial revolution.

A debate as to whether it was capitalistic relationships or industrialisation that promoted certain changes in family life (and a debate as to what those changes were) is conducted between our first and second readings.

In studying this chapter it is worth trying to work out in what sense the authors are using the central terms. Note also that if the terms are used in very broad and inclusive ways, this may limit the substance of any argument about their effect on the family (see our remarks in Chapter 1 about too wide definitions of 'the family'). It is trivial to think of industrialisation (or capitalisation) as just about everything that was going on in society at a particular time (which therefore effectively includes the family) and then to argue that 'it' caused change in the family. If A is not specifically and logically distinct from B, A cannot be said to cause B.

There is considerable variety in the specific answers given by sociologists and historians to the questions of how family structure and family relationships changed and what caused these changes. At first you may find these arguments confusing and annoying, particularly if you have been taught that history is the story of the 'facts' of a previous life. But history, like sociology, is a continuing debate, informed by present concerns and argued from different points of view.

The relationship between the family and industrialisation is a complex one. It varied by class, region, and by period. The broad theories that sociologists of different perspectives have so far come up with are interesting but perhaps not universally applicable. Some of the debates represented here include: whether the industrial revolution was a period of dramatic change which had profoundly disruptive effects on the working class family or whether there were in fact many continuities in family life during the period; and whether the working class family merely responded to changes in the rest of society or brought to bear considerable influence, from its own values and daily practices, upon the process of industrial production itself. Did the modern form of the family emerge because it performed a new set of functions that were required by the new industrial society, or could 'traditional' families fit equally well? Is the modern family characterised by its *structure* or by its *sentiments*? Was the powerful ideology of 'separate spheres' (i.e. the idea of a woman's place being within the home, and that home being increasingly cut off from the wider world of kin, community, and, importantly, work) integral to industrial capitalism, or did it originate autonomously? And who benefitted from the idea that adult men should be paid a wage adequate for them to support a dependent wife, children and elderly relations?

These debates spill over into our next chapter on the state because the development of the modern state and its interrelationships with the family have been formed over a long period. Interventions into the family, by the state and other agencies in the nineteenth century were often related to a concern for the welfare of children (see Fitz, Chapter 6, and Brophy and Smart, Chapter 2). Whether these interventions were entirely to the benefit of children – even those involved in child labour or child prostitution (see Gorham in Further Readings) is another question.

□ The Effects of Industrialisation and Urbanisation

Reading 1 is constructed from key arguments in the extremely successful popular sociology of *The Family and Marriage in Britain* by Ronald Fletcher. First published in 1962, this book has been reprinted frequently. In it the author argues passionately that the contemporary family is a great improvement on what has gone before. The family, far from being in decline, is a modern success story, and this is for the good. It now provides a pleasant environment for warm, stable, affective relationships independent of wider kin, community and employment.

Reading 1

The new characteristics of factory employment and urbanization, . . . although not necessarily reducing their material standards of life, were such as to compel the families of the labouring classes to live in working, housing, and sanitary conditions of the utmost squalor.

. . . in the context of these conditions, the working-class family also suffered a new disunity resulting from the fact that, now, men, women, and children had to go out of the home to undertake their separate kinds of work. To go out to work, in terms of modern standards, does not seem a sufficient factor to cause any disunity of the family, until it is remembered that in these early times men, and those women and children in employment, alike worked for very long hours – as many as sixteen hours a day, sometimes more – and with no regulated meal-times or 'break-times' as we now know them. It is difficult to see, therefore, how the 'home' could have been more than a place in which to eat and sleep. Also, because of this plentiful supply of labour, wages were low and poverty persisted. . . .

It is, of course, impossible to generalize about the standards of morality of the people doomed to live in these wretched conditions, but it is feasible to suppose that among many members of the working population they were very low. Describing some of the districts of London later in the nineteenth century, the author of *The Bitter Cry of Outcast London* wrote:

'Marriage', it has been said, 'as an institution, is not fashionable in these districts'. And this is only the bare truth. Ask if the men and women living together in these rookeries are married, and your simplicity will cause a smile. Nobody knows. Nobody cares. Nobody expects that they are. In exceptional cases only could your question be answered in the affirmative. Incest is common; and no form of vice and sensuality causes surprise or attracts attention. Those who appear to be married are often separated by a mere quarrel, and they do not hesitate to form similar companionships immediately.

Those who bemoan the immorality of the present day might ponder a little upon such an account of the past. . . .

Industrialization brought with it an increasing degree of geographical and occupational movement, and an increased degree of social mobility (i.e., movement between social classes, and changes of social status between the generations). Geographical and occupational movement was made possible by the development of mechanized modes of transport and communication during the nineteenth century . . .

[The] . . . developments in transport largely promoted the growth of suburbs, since people could now live at greater distances from their work. It seems plausible to maintain, therefore, in spite of some recent criticisms of this view, that these forces must have had the effect of loosening the ties between the individual family and its wider kinship relationships, and diminishing the degree of social life which the family shared with groups of wider kindred. The family would no longer live within a particular locality and within a stable and wide network of kinship relationships to the same extent that it did before industrialization.

It seems plausible, also, to suggest that the two great wars of the present century – involving the 'masses' of the civilian population – must have accentuated this 'geographical dispersion' and this distance between families and their earlier localities and kin-groups. Families, during both wars, were compulsorily disrupted . . .

In addition to these kinds of mobility attendant upon industrialization, however, the increase in general prosperity, especially during the past two decades, must have had its effects upon the relationships between the individual family and its wider kindred. In this sense, the individual family has become not so much 'isolated' from its wider kindred as increasingly 'independent' of them. With full employment and a greater degree of economic security, families are not so dependent upon each other for mutual aid as they once were. . . . A little more must be said about this in the face of some recent qualifications of this point. In their study of *Family and Kinship in East London*, Michael Young and Peter Willmott show that, in some areas at least, the 'extended family' is still of considerable import-ance, and that the generalization that the modern family has become 'isolated' from wider kindred is too sweeping. Their study shows that, in particular among working-class families, there is a considerable relationship of dependence and mutual aid between the wife of a family and her own mother . . . the 'extended family' was of consider-able importance to them . . . There are two things, however, that might be said about this.

The first is that, although such studies show that the extended family, in this very limited sense, is important in some areas, this evidence is not such as to warrant the assertion that the kind of generalization we have made earlier is untrue. In general, the kinds of geographical, occupational, and social mobility brought about by industrialization, transport, war, education, and so on, seem certain to have diminished the extent to which the family lives in a localized and long-abiding network of wider kinship relationships. . . .

The second point, however, is that – whatever the truth in this matter, and whatever the worth of extended kinship ties – such social distance as may exist between the family and wider relationships can hardly be said to be an outcome of family 'decline' or of 'moral decline'; neither does it necessarily entail any worsening of human relationships.

R. Fletcher, *The Family and Marriage in Britain*, pp. 110–92.

Questions

1. What aspects of the industrial revolution does Fletcher suggest had affects on family life?
2. What are the features of
   (a) an 'isolated'
   (b) an 'independent' and
   (c) an 'extended' family, as discussed by Fletcher? What factors brought about the 'independent' family?
3. What criticisms might be made of Fletcher's use of the term 'com-munity' by Howard Newby, the author of Reading 6 in Chapter 2.

☐ Family Economy and Industrialisation

This reading is in disagreement with Fletcher. Michael Anderson stresses the durable nature of family relations during industrialisa-tion, the ways in which they influenced the shape of industrialisation and the many continuities between pre- and post-industrial family relations. In his view many traditional patterns survived.

Reading 2

Far from the almost universal picture of disorganisation and disruption of family relationships perceived by many contemporaries and earlier scholars, recent work has stressed the extent to which 'traditional' attitudes influenced the strategies adopted by families whose members became involved in factory and other large-scale capitalist work organisation. The strategies adopted are also seen as primarily operating at the familial and household rather than the individual level. However, the relationship is not seen only as a one-way affair; the same research also stresses the need for employers to adopt strategies of labour recruitment which did not interfere too drastically with these same 'traditional' value systems. Seen in this light, optimal outcomes were different among sections of the proletariat from different economic and cultural backgrounds, in different industries, in different countries, and at different times; so research has increasingly begun to focus on diversity of actions and reactions rather than on any single set of effects, and to emphasise the continuities – and even in some cases the strengthening of family bonds – brought about by industrialisation and mass migration.

The continuities were many . . . Much factory industrialisation took place in small village communities, and even where towns were involved only a minority of the adult employed population was usually engaged in factory work. Factories took men and women out of the home but agricultural labourers, masons, carters and many others had traditionally worked away from home, sometimes for long periods. In many areas women had worked in the fields taking their children with them and, until it was suppressed by law, they continued to do so in many early factories. In fact, few married women worked in factories and only tiny numbers of women with small children did so, in contrast to the impression given by much misinformed contemporary as well as more recent historical comment. Instead, most remained in the vital and even expanding domestic occupations such as clothing and food production – and by doing so made significant contributions to the family economy.

Moreover, most of the urban factory labour force did not consist of young men and women of peasant stock who had come alone to live in lodgings in a large city cut off from friends and relatives, working in a huge factory as part of an atomised labour force. Instead, more often than not, migration and entry to factory employment were acts pursued within a family-oriented social context; most migration was highly focused onto particular places (and jobs within places) where the opportunities available to the migrant would match if possible the skills and earning potential of himself and his family and would be set within a context which would not conflict with values brought from the sending community.

For example, in Lancashire many urban textile factory workers seem to have had some experience in rural textile industries, while girls from peasant farming backgrounds followed traditional patterns by going mainly into domestic service . . .

Similarly, research on many areas of Europe in the nineteenth century and in North America up to the inter-war period has shown that most migration was not undertaken by atomised individuals knowing nothing about where they were going or why. Rather, migrants moved, probably a majority in family groups, along networks of relatives and friends, often at the instigation of these relatives and friends, to temporary homes provided by them and to jobs obtained with their assistance – indeed, often, under the formal or informal subcontracting systems common in industry up to the First World War, to jobs under their direct control. The timing and direction of migration would often have been decided for family reasons – young men and women sent away from home to remit their surplus earnings to support their younger siblings at home or to save for their own marriages back in the rural community . . .

Interdependence . . . sometimes [extended] to relatives outside the conjugal family, encouraging them to live near and with each other as a means of securing more congenial housing and better jobs, an insurance, however meagre, against inevitable and frequent crises such as sickness, injury, and unemployment, against which no other adequate provision existed. . . .

And taking in relatives or lodgers can be seen as another strategy, used to raise the income of certain groups at certain points in the life cycle.

The pattern, then, involved an immensely flexible response to new situations and numerous continuities for many of those involved; but it also involved subtle differences between groups and industries, only a few of which have so far been fully explored. One crucial set of differences were the employment opportunities available to married women and children and the different ways in which these groups could contribute to the family economy. . . In part these differences between groups relate to what kind of work it was seen as proper for women to do and how much the work interfered with their ability to look after small children. But it also related to what was available; for

example, textile areas, which were almost unique in early industrialisation in offering factory employment to women and children of both
sexes, seem to have had distinctive patterns of kinship behaviour
(aged parents being used to care for house and young children
while mother worked in the mill) and possibly of conjugal relationships as well . . . In all respects they differed from mining areas
where, as was increasingly the case elsewhere, there was only
domestic work for women and where there was no role for the aged:
the optimal strategy here was to have as many boys as soon as
possible so that they could contribute to family income.

M. Anderson, *Approaches to the History of the Western Family*, pp. 78–82.

Questions

1. Make a list of continuities in family experience during industrialisation
   referred to in the extract.
2. What variations between occupations and regions does Anderson
   note?

□ The 'Fit' between Industrialisation and the Conjugal Family

While Anderson stresses continuities in family relationships during
the growth of industrial capitalism in various Western countries,
W.J. Goode in his book *World Revolution and Family Patterns*
stressed that a world-wide trend towards the 'conjugal' family
system was occurring alongside moves towards industrialisation.
Our extract, covering some of Goode's central ideas, is taken from
a short textbook on *The Family* which he published a year later.

The extract suggests ways in which the conjugal family form 'fits'
an industrial system – but also ways in which it does *not* 'fit', and
the proposition that the pre-existing form of the family itself
shaped the industrialisation process. (This point is also made by
Anderson in the previous reading.) Goode is careful not to tip
over from looking at the fit between two sectors of society, into
functionalism, i.e. into suggesting one sector exists, or came into
being, to fulfill the needs of the other. Nevertheless the argument
is functional*ist* in that it conceives of systems as *having* needs.

Some contemporary social theorists, such as Anthony Giddens, doubt whether there is *any* sense in which we can talk about systems having needs.

Reading 3

Family research in the post-World War II period has documented one gross empirical regularity whose processes are not yet clearly understood – that in all parts of the world and for the first time in world history all social systems are moving fast or slowly toward some form of the conjugal family system and also toward industrialization. In agreement with the intuition of social analysts for over a century is the finding that with industrialization the traditional family systems – usually, extended or joint family systems, with or without lineages or clans – are breaking down. On the other hand, since each system begins from a somewhat different base point, the direction of change in any given family pattern may be different . . . structural characteristics of the conjugal family system [are mostly] derivable from its lesser extension of kinship relations. These traits fit rather well the demands of industrialization. Under the industrial system, the individual is supposed to be hired because of his competence, and in promotion the same standards are to be applied to all who hold the same job (i.e., the standards are achievement-based and universalistic). His relationship to the job is also functionally specific – i.e., his role obligations are confined to getting the task done. Put another way, the extended family system, with its standards of ascription, particularism, and diffuseness, is ideally not permitted to interfere with the efficient functioning of a modern enterprise.

Because of its emphasis on performance, such a system requires that a person be permitted to rise or fall, and to move about wherever the job market is best. A lesser emphasis on land ownership also increases the ease of mobility. The conjugal family system is neo-local (each couple sets up its own household), and its kinship network is not strong, thus putting fewer barriers than other family systems in the way of class or geographical mobility.

In these ways the conjugal family system 'fits' the needs of industrialism. But the relationship may also be put another way. Since increasingly an industrializing society – consider, for example, the Arab countries, or India – creates formal agencies to handle the major tasks of any kinship groupings larger than the nuclear family, such units as lineages, clans, or even large extended families also lose their functions and thereby the *allegiance* they once commanded. Thus individual families go their own way, ignoring such extended kinship ties.

More important, elders no longer control the major new economic or political opportunities, so that family authority slips from the hands of such family leaders. The young groom can obtain his bride price on his own, and need not concern himself about the good will of his elders. The couple need not obey any one outside their family unit, since only their performance on the job is relevant for their advancement. They need not even rely on family elders for job instruction, since schools, the factory, or the plantation or mine will teach them the new skills. Nor do they even need to continue working on the land, still in the possession of the elders, since the jobs and political opportunities are in the city. Thus industrialization is likely to undermine gradually the traditional systems of family control and exchange. The terms of the role–bargaining between the generations have been altered . . .

The conjugal emphasis on emotionality within the family also serves somewhat the needs of industrialism. At lower job levels, the worker experiences little intrinsic job satisfaction; at higher levels, he obtains more job satisfaction, but is also subject to rather great demands. At any level, the enterprise has no responsibility for the emotional input-output balance of the individual; this is solely the responsibility of the family, in the sense that there is nowhere else to go for it. The small family, then, deals with a problem which the industrial system cannot handle. . . .

Nevertheless, we cannot, in analyzing the interaction of the great social forces making for family change, presume some sort of natural 'harmony' between the modern complex of industrialism and the conjugal family system. Both are unplanned resultants of individual desires and initiatives. Both are systems of forces, each with its own needs, and at various points either may fail to serve the needs of the other. To place everyone in his job solely on the basis of merit, for example, would require the destruction of the family system entirely. On the other hand, without a family unit to deal with the idiosyncrasies of aged parents, the emotional needs of adults, or the insecurities of children, very likely not enough adequately functioning people would be produced to man the industrial system. . . .

This is another way of reasserting a central notion of this volume, that family and industrial factors or variables are *independent* but interacting. Neither fully determines the other, although both influence each other. Consequently, we cannot assume, in looking for patterns of family change, that industrial forces shape everything (unless we *define* them as including everything) to their measure. The very *resistance* of family systems to such pressures indicates their independence as a set of forces, even if the massive political and economic changes ultimately outweigh that resistance.

Since we have analyzed some of the ways in which family systems have altered to serve the needs of industrialization, we should also consider briefly how an industrial system fails to handle some of the problems created by this change towards a conjugal family system . . .

The neolocal, independent household and its accompanying values in favor of separate lives for each couple leave the old parents in an ambiguous position . . . Every study of their situation shows that they need help, although there is disagreement over where the help should come from. People no longer accept without question an obligation to care for the old, especially in a common household.

Similarly, the obligation to rear orphan children of relatives is not so definite as in the past. Modern society has, of course, invented various procedures for locating and evaluating both foster and step-parents for such children, as well as continuing until recently the older system of orphanages; but the action of the state does not fully substitute for the active kinship system of a primitive society.

In a parallel way, as noted earlier, the modern conjugal system does not adequately deal with the structural disruptions caused by divorce.

Modern industrialism has offered women more economic freedom, but has not relieved them of their household tasks. Labor-saving devices merely raise the standards of cleanliness and general performance, permitting more work to be turned out, but do not reduce the hours of work. The primary status of women in all societies is that of housekeeper and mother, so that in spite of higher levels of technical training, women have not developed a commensurately high level of career-mindedness over the past half-century in Western countries. Indeed, toward the higher social strata, where more women are better educated, a lower percentage of women are in the labor force, but apparently a *higher* percentage would like to be. The modern egalitarianism within the family means that the man's energies are somewhat diverted into helping at household tasks, away from his job demands. . . .

Let us now consider another relationship between family factors and social change, the possibility that the family system may have an independent, facilitating effect on the modern shift toward industrialization.

No full-scale research into this hypothesis has been carried out, but a few suggestive facts may be noted here. Negatively, of course, many observers have pointed out that extended and joint family systems prevented a free utilization of talent as well as the easy introduction of innovations against the power and traditionalism of family elders. Positively, it should be kept in mind that the family systems of the West have been different from those of other major civilizations for over a thousand years. Child or early adolescent marriage was not the ideal or the statistically usual. There was no ancestor worship, and *individuals*, not families, were responsible for crimes. There was no lineage or clan system, and the eldest male was not necessarily the leader of the family. Young couples were expected to live independently, for the most part.

Moreover, these difficulties were accentuated when the individualistic, anti-traditional ideology of ascetic Protestantism began to spread. The Puritans in the U.S., for example, defined husband and wife as loving companions rather than simply part of a family network, and their children had more freedom of marital choice than was possible in the traditional European family systems. Divorce became possible, even though disapproved. It seems likely by the time the new factory jobs opened in the late eighteenth century in England that the family system of at least part of the population was in some harmony with its new demands. Their extended kinship ties and obligations, and their links with family land, did not interfere with the new type of work obligations.

W.J. Goode, *The Family*, pp. 108–10, 114.

Questions

1. In what ways does Goode claim that the conjugal family fits the industrial system and in what ways does it not fit?
2. What distinctive features of the pre-industrial Western family facilitated the development of industrialisation?

□ The Separation of Spheres

Previous readings have pointed to the importance of women and children's employment opportunities as a factor in determining the direction of changes undertaken by the family and the industrial system. Feminist historians in particular have contributed to our understanding of changes in the family through their concern to discover women's experiences and especially through their interest in the influence of the nineteenth century idea that there should be 'separate spheres' for men and women.

In this reading Catharine Hall discusses the emergence of a new private world of home associated with women and a new public world of waged work and civic life associated with men. Her research was conducted in Birmingham and she found a clear example of this developing separation in the families of the prosperous shop keepers and manufacturers of the town. She argues that this separation was, largely, *sought* by both the men and women of the middle classes in accordance with their evangelical Christian principles and as a mark of social status. However it was, largely, *forced* upon the working class by technological change and middle class philanthropists. (For the latter, see also Chapter 6 on The Family and the State.)

Reading 4

As the businesses of provincial tradesmen expanded in the late eighteenth and early nineteenth century, so their aspirations also grew. They increasingly wanted their homes to be separated from their workplace and their wives and daughters to be dependent on them; these had become powerful symbols of belonging to the middle class. By 1851 the numbers of lock-up shops in town centres, with their proprietors living elsewhere, were on the increase. This separation between work and home had important effects on the organizations of work within the family and the marking out of male and female spheres. Men were increasingly associated with business and public activities which were physically and socially separated from the home; women with the home and with children. . . .

Men went to work every day and then came home to their families. This meant that there was a much clearer distinction between work-time and leisure-time and there was also a much clearer distinction between public and private life. As long as home and workplace were combined it must often have been difficult to categorize whether activities which went on there were 'public' or 'private' and indeed it would probably have been a pretty irrelevant question. Was feeding an apprentice, for example, who would usually have been the son of a friend and who would have generally been treated as one of the family, a business or domestic matter? The point is, of course, that they were one and the same thing, and one clear demonstration of this is that shopkeepers started to keep separate household accounts only when the separation had taken place between work and home. The physical separation of the two was the culmination of a long process during which time middle-class men's activities had become increasingly differentiated from those of middle-class women. Women's participation in family businesses had always tended to be an informal affair; the fact that married women had no property rights meant that the business was always legally owned by the husband as long as he lived. Only widows and spinsters could run their own businesses in their own names. Furthermore the training and skills had always been tied to masculinity – women were not apprenticed to drapers or to tea and coffee dealers. But the increasing complexity of the commercial world and its increasing formalization in this period meant that it was becoming more difficult for women to participate even informally. Furthermore, as new retailing skills became important, the training which encouraged these skills was not available for women. The informal 'picking up' of the business which was what women relied on was no longer necessarily enough.

But in addition to the increasing difficulty of women learning how to do business, there were the aspirations for a separate domestic sphere and the positive desire to move away from the shop if this were financially possible. . . .

Women were furthermore increasingly cut off from the variety of other *public* activities which their menfolk engaged in. 1780–1850 was the age of societies, when societies were formed in aid of every possible cause. These societies ranged from ones with a primarily political orientation to those concerned with commercial activities, self-education in its broadest sense and philanthropic works. It was exceedingly difficult for women to be involved in any of these except the philanthropic, and even there they were encouraged to participate privately and informally rather than being engaged in the public activities – the meetings and the dinners. . . .

For working-class families the separation between work and home was rooted in the changes in the organization of production. A family producing woollen cloth at home in the late eighteenth century, for example, with the wife spinning and the husband weaving, would by the mid-nineteenth century have been forced into factory production because they would not have been able to compete with the cheaper cloth produced by mechanised processes in the factory. . . .

[In the] pre-industrial economy all members of the [working class] family had worked. As long as that work had been done at home there was no question of castigating married women for being employed. It was the separation which took place between work and home, and the fact that women started going out into public places such as mills to work, so that it was no longer possible simply to combine employment with domesticity, that troubled many commentators. Furthermore the fact that women might get an independent wage in a factory was another source of worry. This financial independence gave the mill girls their notorious 'cheekiness' which was much remarked upon. It is very noticeable that there was never any public outcry about women's work as domestic servants for, despite what were in many cases appalling exploitative conditions of work, that work was private, carried out in other people's homes and thus not offending against Victorian notions of the woman as the 'angel in the house'. Similarly sweated work caused little concern until later in the nineteenth century. It was the factories and the mines, with their public presence and their mixed labour force, which forced questions about the propriety of married women's paid employment into the forefront of Victorian public life . . .

Middle-class philanthropists, who took it upon themselves to improve the manners and morals of the working classes, were amongst the first to carry bourgeois notions of the perfect family to the working class. As the Registrar General defined it in his introduction to the 1851 Census, the perfect English family in its 'essential type' was composed of, 'husband, wife, children and servants, or, less perfectly but more commonly, of husband, wife, and children'.

The less perfect family might at least aspire to a non-working wife, for the middle-class critique of working wives and the belief that their employment endangered the very structure of English society, had long been current. . . .

The 1840s saw what has been described as a 'coincidence of interests' between philanthropist, the state — representing the collective interests of capital — and the male working class who were represented by the trade union movement and Chartism — which co-operated to reduce female and child labour and to limit the length of the working day.

C. Hall, 'The butcher, the baker, the candlestick maker: the shop and the family in the Industrial Revolution', in *The Changing Experience of Women*, E. Whitelegg *et al.* (ed.), pp. 4–14.

Questions

1. What is meant by the terms 'domestic service', 'factory work', 'outwork', and 'sweated trades'?
2. What factor were influential in promoting
   (a) middle class and
   (b) working class wives' separation from the new, men's world of work?

□ The Family and Work in Pre-industrial England

In this reading Rosemary O'Day disagrees with Catharine Hall. She argues that the separation between home and waged work was well advanced among all social classes by the eighteenth century – a disagreement over timing. Secondly she argues that the increasing separation was not the result of the new organisation of production (into the factory system) but of new relations of production (into capitalistic ones) – a disagreement over causes. As we said in our introduction, capitalist relations are not the same things as industrialisation, although the character of the latter was certainly influenced by the earlier development of capitalism.

Reading 5

Rural life in the seventeenth century reveals that many types of occupation were already withdrawn from the household by this date. There was, for example, already a large rural proletariat made up of agricultural labourers who owned no land and who sold their labour for hire. The labourer might spend most of his toiling life outside an independent household – he scarcely dared dream of accumulating sufficient resources to set up a household for himself and a wife. Paupers were totally unable to contemplate a step of such magnitude – the preoccupation with survival was absolute. They lacked even a 'labour' value if they were, as most were, invalided, aged or encumbered with young children. They probably spent much of their lives tramping from town to town in search of alms. Some moved to the coalfields and to the towns to find regular work. By the nineteenth century, the workhouses were filled with men, women and children.

Some rural families, while continuing to farm small holdings, were involved in the putting-out system. In the putting-out system, a central capitalist (businessman or entrepreneur) put out (distributed) materials to the head of a household of workers to make-up into products at a piece rate in their own homes. Woollen cloth, various items of clothing, and metal wares were all produced by this method in the late seventeenth and eighteenth centuries. The equipment used to make the product was sometimes owned by the worker and sometimes leased to him by the capitalist. The worker was a dependent piece-worker. There was a separation between capital and labour.

The family of the rural landowner, the nobleman of means, presents a more complicated embroidery. In it we have the earliest form of capitalistic organization. The head of the noble household controlled the means of production (land, tools, mineral resources) and hired labour to produce or mine and to sell what was not needed for immediate consumption by family members and retainers. He and his family increasingly withdrew from the reciprocal obligations acknowledged by his forebears to tenants and serfs. Even the managerial function was fulfilled by hired personnel. It was, later, perfectly natural for the noble entrepreneur to transfer this form of organization, developed in a rural context, to a new business and commercial enterprises. What was different was that the entire family, male head included, might have appeared by the nineteenth century to be separated from work. The home was less a haven for the household head than the harbour from which he never personally set sail.

If we move away from the rural to the urban environment . . . we see that work had also been removed from its household context by the late seventeenth century in many trades and crafts. Indeed, this had happened much earlier in some areas of the economy.

In the seventeenth century, it became more difficult and costly than it had been in the medieval period (down to 1500 or even later) for men who had fulfilled their terms of apprenticeship to set up as master-craftsmen with their own home-based workshops. . . .

A class of permanent journeymen emerged – fully-skilled craftsmen who were unable to set up independently in a craft because of lack of money to buy equipment and raw materials and therefore worked for another master craftsman for a wage. More and more skilled adult males were, therefore, drawn out of their own households to work for wages in a master's workshop (of between ten and twenty workers). The wives of these journeymen could not *share* in the work of the household because it was removed out of the home. The journeyman had nothing for his wife to sell at the end of the day. He did not work in the same place. He could not use his wife's or his children's labour. Just as the factory-worker of the nineteenth century did, the journeyman went *out* to work. . . .

What, then, of the wife the journeyman left behind? Her opportunities for work inside and outside the home were reduced when she could no longer engage in her husband's trade. By this time women had been excluded from many traditional female trades, such as commercial brewing, baking and milling.

In medieval England, brewing, for instance, had been a predominantly female occupation. Ale formed part of the daily diet. Because the equipment required to make it was relatively [in]expensive, some women managed to make a business producing and selling ale to their neighbours. In the sixteenth century, however, the trade was removed from female hands. An Act of Parliament of 1574 separated brewing from the selling of ale in order to simplify the collection of a tax on the beer itself and to maintain the quality of the product. The Act forbade the ale-wives to brew the beer which they sold in their houses. Brewing was, henceforth, concentrated in a few breweries and the 'common brewers' trade' established. Production was on capitalistic lines. Brewers did not take apprentices but servants who were paid a wage. (The cost of equipment was too high for an apprentice to aspire to set up independently once the term was served.) The brewers' monopoly was reinforced by the introduction of licensing in the 1620s and 1630s. The monopoly and the capitalistic organization of the trade drove the ale-wives out of business. . . .

With their husbands working outside the home and their own trades prohibited them, there is little doubt that retailing provided most married women with their chief work outside the home in the seventeenth century. This was an occupation that demanded little training; it was an occupation with which women, in countryside and town, had long been associated. Nevertheless, by the end of the seventeenth century, entry into the retail trade was also hedged about by restrictions: there was a strict apprenticeship requirement.

. . . Many poor women and the wives of skilled but wage-earning journeymen . . . thus sought paid work outside the home . . . By no stretch of the imagination can they be regarded as working within a domestic environment in family industry before the advent of factories.

The household economy of the master also seems to have changed before the late eighteenth century . . . Certainly domestic architecture indicates that the place of work was increasingly separated from the place set aside for living [in the urban middle-class household during industrialization], which seems reasonable when one considers that the average workshop now contained ten to twenty workers. The increasing separation of production and sale due to more sophisticated markets probably also discouraged the wives of masters from participating in retail of their husband's goods. But whether these changes were sudden or associated with industrialization rather than with the effects of the *gradual* infiltration of capitalistic organization, is more difficult to settle. I believe family industry had broken down in all classes in England in the urban context long before the nineteenth-century industrialization.

R. O'Day, Women in the household, Unit 7 of Open University course U221 in E. Whitehall *et al.* (eds), *The Changing Experience of Women*, pp. 33–8.

Questions

1. (a) What strata does O'Day distinguish in England in the seventeenth century?
   (b) What were the economic situations of wives, sons, and daughters within each strata at this time?
2. What does O'Day argue are the chief effects of the development of 'capitalistic relations' on the various classes of men and women to whom she refers?
3. What role does the author say the state and the guilds played in relation to women's work and how does this view compare with that of Hall?

☐ The Separation of Home and Work?

The question of the cause of the separation between the private world of family and the public world of paid work presupposes such a separation occurred. In the next reading, Leonore Davidoff is concerned to point out that this distinction is not easy to make in practice. Although much of the literature of the nineteenth century, including the census, both assumed and at the same time encouraged a sense of this separation, in practice the lives of women did not actually divide so simply. She draws on her research on landladies and lodgers in late nineteenth and early twentieth century England to argue that many women continued to earn *within* the 'private sphere' – within their own or someone else's home. She points out that a diversity of ways of making a living can continue within a wage-labour dominated economy.

Reading 6

Historians have tended to accept the literature on the separation of spheres and the domestic ideal as a description of reality, partly because the sources for historical analysis are cast in these terms. But it is equally necessary to ask what people were actually doing, how and where they were living, and whom they were living with.

Whatever the expectations within the domestic ideal, in an increasingly urban as well as cash-dominated society, women had to find ways to earn income in lieu of or in addition to support from father, husband or other male relatives. Family ties precluded residential domestic service except for the young and single. Factory work was often problematic, both practically and morally, and in many areas simply not available. One alternative was outwork – from squalid, miserably-paid fur-pulling, matchbox making, etc., to respectable work such as tinting Christmas cards. The other major sources of income were activities like casual cleaning, child minding, washing in other people's homes, taking in washing into their own homes or providing houseroom and domestic services to lodgers and boarders. In the middle class, similar strategies included becoming companion to an older woman or resident teacher of young children. For all classes of women, these surrogate family activities could contain maternal or sexual elements, evident in roles as diverse as housekeeper or prostitute. It could be argued that these marginal activities were part of an inevitable 'transitional' stage of the economy, on the way to a more clearly demarcated and rationalised labour system. But such sweeping . . . assertions often obscure many times and places where the outcome was by no means certain. . . .

The conceptual limitations of this division between the labour market and the home are clear when trying to analyse a situation such as residential domestic service: the largest single occupation for women, numbering over 1 000 000 well into the 1930s. This activity was viewed by employers as familial (and therefore particularly suitable for young women). Servants, on the other hand, despite the fact that they were performing domestic tasks in a domestic setting, stressed that they were selling their labour as in any other occupation, and where possible they rejected the paternalistic features of the situation. This divergence should prompt us to enquire what kind of an organisation this entity called a household was, and what were its goals?

Such an approach is akin to the analysis of the form and size of the enterprise in the analysis of the Third World today. As in these countries now, in nineteenth-century England it was not at all clear whether subsidiary household tasks were for producing a profit. Nor, in fact, was it clear that members of the household regarded themselves as engaged in profit-making activities. Rather, an activity such as the housing and feeding of lodgers can be understood as a kind of subsistence employment, one of a variety of forms of labour existing side by side or even carried on by the same people: a way of life, as much as making a living.

The creators of the census in the nineteenth century were aware of the contradictions in dealing with domestic activities. Some discussion of this problem can be found in the introduction to every decennial census. In the development of the census over the century, statistical categories were successively changed in the direction of a stricter demarcation between domestic and market activities. New instructions in 1911 tried once and for all to eliminate the ambiguity with regard to the occupations of women:

> The occupations of women engaged in any business or profession including women regularly engaged in assisting relatives in trade or business must be fully stated. No entry should be made in the case of wives, daughters or other female relatives wholly engaged in domestic duties at home.

It has been stated repeatedly that the post-Second World War period has witnessed an 'explosion' in the proportion of married, particularly older, women working: from 8 per cent in 1921 to 60 per cent in 1976. But perhaps what we are seeing is a shift in the location and, to a lesser extent, the kind of work that these women are doing.

This shift may ultimately affect the women's view of themselves as it brings them into contact, even if only as 'part-timers', with large-scale private or state enterprises. However, the expectation that this move would, in some way, fundamentally change their consciousness, does not, as yet at least, seem to have materialised, despite a considerable increase in women's trade union membership. This may be partly explained by the fact that in some sense the shift may be seen as a loss of autonomy as the landlady becomes the supermarket employee. The rise of lodging and boarding did not only structure opportunities: women actively helped to shape this alternative or supplementary arena, where they could at least gain a measure of financial and social indepedence. If it is impossible ever to weigh up the gains and losses, at least this examination of the recent past should be a reminder that there is no natural or fixed separation between a private and a public sphere.

L. Davidoff, 'The separation of home and work?' in S. Burman (ed.), *Fit Work for Women*, pp. 64–7.

Questions

1. What do you understand by the phrase 'the domestic ideal'? Use evidence from Readings 4–6 to support your answer.
2. What activities does the reading refer to as examples of the difficulty of making a clear distinction between 'work' and 'home', and paid and unpaid labour.
3. What are the 'familial'/'paternalistic' features of domestic service?

☐ The Marriage of Capitalism and Patriarchy

Various authors of earlier readings in this chapter have referred to the waged employment of women and children in early nineteenth century Britain, and the varied reactions of employers, politicians and philanthropists, guilds and trade unions and working class men. By the mid-century, campaigns had been launched and legislation enacted excluding women and children from the mines, most factories, and some agricultural work, and confirming their exclusion from many trades and professions – though again, the timing and extent of change varied from region to region and by occupational sector. By the end of the century, however, the 'ideal' of wives and children being protected and economically supported by husbands and fathers was generally accepted, and practised by members of both middle and respectable working classes. How and why did this come about?

Heidi Hartmann suggests it was the results of an alliance between men as heads of families and men as capitalists each supporting their own interest in using women's labour.

Reading 7

Patriarchy as a system of relations between men and women exists in capitalism, and ... in capitalist societies a healthy and strong partnership exists between patriarchy and capital. Yet. . . the partnership. . . was not inevitable; men and capitalists often have conflicting interests, particularly over the use of women's labor power . . .

Marxists ultimately underestimated the strength of the preexisting patriarchal social forces with which fledgling capital had to contend and the need for capital to adjust to these forces. The industrial revolution . . . [drew] all people into the labor force, including women and children . . . That women and children could earn wages separately from men both undermined authority relations . . . and kept wages low for everyone . . . Working men recognized the disadvantages of female wage labor. Not only were women 'cheap competition' but working women were their very wives, who could not 'serve two masters' well. . . .

Male workers resisted the wholesale entrance of women and

children into the labor force, and sought to exclude them from union membership and the labor force as well . . .

While the problem of cheap competition could have been solved by organizing the wage earning women and youths, the problem of disrupted family life could not be. Men reserved union protection for men and argued for protective labor laws for women and children. Protective labor laws, while they may have ameliorated some of the worst abuses of female and child labor, also limited the participation of adult women in many 'male' jobs. Men sought to keep high wage jobs for themselves and to raise male wages generally. They argued for wages sufficient for their wage labor alone to support their families. This 'family wage' system gradually came to be the norm for stable working class families at the end of the nineteenth century and the beginning of the twentieth. Several observers have declared the non wage-working wife to be part of the standard of living of male workers. Instead of fighting for equal wages for men and women, male workers sought the family wage, wanting to retain their wives' services at home. In the absence of patriarchy a unified working class might have confronted capitalism, but patriarchal social relations divided the working class, allowing one part (men) to be bought off at the expense of the other (women). Both the hierarchy between men and the solidarity among them were crucial in this process of resolution. Family wages may be understood as a resolution of the conflict over women's labor power which was occurring between patriarchal and capitalist interests at that time.

Family wages for most adult men imply men's acceptance, and collusion in, lower wages for others, young people, women and socially defined inferior men as well (Irish, blacks, etc., the lowest groups in the patriarchal hierarchy who are denied many of the patriarchal benefits). Lower wages for women and children and inferior men are enforced by job segregation in the labor market, in turn maintained by unions and management as well as by auxiliary institutions like schools, training programs, and even families. Job segregation by sex, by insuring that women have the lower paid jobs, both assures women's economic dependence on men and reinforces notions of appropriate spheres for women and men. For most men, then, the development of family wages, secured the material base of male domination in two ways. First, men have the better jobs in the labor market and earn higher wages than women. The lower pay women receive in the labor market both perpetuates men's material advantage over women and encourages women to choose wifery as a career. Second, then, women do housework, childcare, and perform other services at home which benefit men directly. Women's home responsibilities in turn reinforce their inferior labor market position.

The resolution that developed in the early twentieth century can be seen to benefit capitalist interests as well as patriarchal interests. Capitalists, it is often argued, recognized that in the extreme conditions which prevailed in th early nineteenth century industrialization, working class families could not adequately reproduce themselves. They realized that housewives produced and maintained healthier workers than wage-working wives and that educated children became better workers than noneducated ones. The bargain, paying family wages to men and keeping women home, suited the capitalists at the time as well as the male workers. Although the terms of the bargain have altered over time, it is still true that the family and women's work in the family serve capital by providing a labor force and serve men as the space in which they exercise their privilege. Women, working to serve men and their families, also serve capital as consumers. The family is also the place where dominance and submission are learned, as Firestone, the Frankfurt School, and many others have explained. Obedient children become obedient workers; girls and boys each learn their proper roles.

While the family wage shows that capitalism adjusts to patriarchy, the changing status of children shows that patriarchy adjusts to capital. Children, like women, came to be excluded from wage labor. As children's ability to earn money declined, their legal relationship to their parents changed. At the beginning of the industrial era in the United States, fulfilling children's need for their fathers was thought to be crucial, even primary, to their happy development; fathers had legal priority in cases of contested custody. As children's ability to contribute to the economic well-being of the family declined, mothers came increasingly to be viewed as crucial to the happy development of their children, and gained legal priority in cases of contested custody. Here patriarchy adapted to the changing economic role of children: when children were productive, men claimed them; as children became unproductive, they were given to women. . . .

The prediction of nineteenth century Marxists that patriarchy would wither away in the face of capitalism's need to proletarianize everyone has not come true. Not only did Marxists underestimate the strength and flexibility of patriarchy, they also overestimated the strength of capital. They envisioned the new social force of capitalism, which had torn feudal relations apart, as virtually all powerful. Contemporary observers are in a better position to see the difference between the tendencies of 'pure' capitalism and those of "actual"

capitalism as it confronts historical forces in everyday practice . . .
Great flexibility has been displayed by capitalism in this process.

Heidi Hartmann, 'The unhappy marriage of Marxism and feminism: towards a
more progressive union' reprinted in L. Sargent (ed.), *Women and Revolution*,
pp. 19–24.

Questions

1. List
   (a) the benefits and
   (b) the problems (if any)
   for capital and for (privileged) working class men of maintaining
   'non-working' wives.
2. Compare and contrast Hartmann's view of the reasons for changes in
   custody of children after divorce with those of Brophy and Smart
   (Chapter 2, Reading 4).

□ The Defence of Working Class Interests

Jane Humphries disagrees with Hartmann's emphasis on the benefits to men of the family wage. She argues instead that the fight for
the family wage is a form of class resistance to capital's attempt to
exploit any and every able-bodied member of the working class,
and to pauperise the sick, old and young who could not work. A
wife at home raised the standard of living of all members of the
family, the wider kin and the local community. Working class
women/wives were happy to escape the drudgery of working class
jobs. The mutual support family members gave each other, and
the values some taught their children, increased their class consciousness.

Reading 8

The resilience of the family derives in part from workers' defence of
an institution which affects their standard of living, class cohesion
and ability to wage the class struggle. . . .

Non-labouring individuals among the working class have to be
supported. If their sustenance is not forthcoming from labour, via the
primitive communism of the family, then it must come from capital in
the form of state supplied services or individual charitable impulses.
The usual argument is that capital generally finds it cheaper, more

convenient, and less politically unsettling to maintain the historically given working-class autonomy; allowing a sufficient element of surplus in wages to sustain the non-labouring family members . . . Presumably this course is less politically disruptive because any concerted attempt by capital to take over these functions, and to reduce the non-labouring members of the working class to more direct and obvious dependence on capital, would encounter resistance. Labour's opposition would arise from the realisation (which might be imperfect) that the traditional arrangements can operate to its advantage, in terms of the determination of the standard of living and the development of class consciousness and cohesion, at least in certain periods of capitalist development. . . .

The harshness of the 1834 Poor Law was an attempt to discourage recourse to the official channels and to make the poor 'self-sufficient'. It has been suggested above that individuals can never be 'self-sufficient'. What was promoted was 'class-sufficiency' via mutually reciprocal kinship ties. In the context of primary poverty the family could not always bear the weight of these ties. As a result they were rationalised as described above, and family members were put on relief even under conditions of 'less eligibility'. But the Poor Law was a refuge of last resort, to be submitted to only in times of dire distress . . . Because of the deprivation and degradation of the workhouse, bureaucratic forms of assistance were hated and feared by the working class, whose *class* resistance was thereby enhanced . . .

A second important reason for the working-class preference for traditional family forms relates to their implications for the control of the labour supply. . . . Compare two extreme situations:

(1) There is a single wage earner who receives the historical subsistence *family* wage. The activities of the other household members remain outside the jurisdiction of the capitalist and can be directed to the production of use-values, raising the family's standard of living.

(2) All the able-bodied family members are proletarianised, including the children, and the family wage is received piecemeal.

In both cases the non-labouring family members are supported out of the family product, distribution taking place according to non-market criteria. Under the assumption that the *same* family wage is received in both situations, the standard of living of the working class must be higher in (1) and surplus value creation (per family) greater in (2). . . .

It has been argued that the male-dominated trade unions selfishly sought to impede the employment of women, with whom they felt competitive in the labour market and whom they preferred to retain as dependent domestic workers. Undoubtedly the regulation of hours and occupations caused acute misery in individual cases, when women lost jobs that were vital to their survival. More important still, the opportunistic use of sexist ideology by labour must have reinforced sexism among workers and employers and so in the long run made the attainment of economic equality more difficult.

But to condemn this strategy out of hand is to be insensitive to the material conditions of 19th-century labour. One of the few sources of working-class control over the supply of labour lay in the levers that could be brought to bear on the labour supplied by married women. This was also one of the few tactics that could be accompanied by a supportive mobilisation of bourgeois ideology . . .

The tragedy is that action could not be controlled on a class basis, but had to be regulated *systematically* on the basis of *female* labour, and theoretically of *married* female labour, so reinforcing sex-based relations of dominance and subordination.

Nevertheless, the strategy was not entirely disadvantageous to working women. To think so is again to misunderstand the material conditions of working-class experience.

. . . women workers as well as being female are also members of the working class. Class action which tries to raise the price of labour usually had beneficial effects, if not directly on women's wages, then indirectly through increased *family* wages. This exposes the fallacy in the argument that women workers might be subject to disabilities in the guise of protective legislation. Such misunderstanding results from conflating the social and customary disabilities encountered by women in the professions with the constraints placed by law on women's work in industry. The two are very different. Their confusion illustrates the inability of protagonists of such views to understand the material conditions of the working class, especially as manifested in the industrial labour process.

> The mistake that some of them [i.e. liberal women's groups making such charges] have made is in transferring their own grievances to a class whose troubles are little known and less understood . . . in supposing that while they pined to spend themselves in some intolerable toil of thought Mary Brown or Jane Smith should also pine to spend herself in fourteen hours a day washing or tailoring (Hutchins and Harrison, 1903, p. 184).

. . . All too frequently in the modern literature the family is seen as engendering false consciousness, promoting capitalist ideology, undermining class cohesion and threatening the class struggle. In short, it stands charged with being a bourgeois institution acting in collaboration with capital against the real interests of the working class. . . .

In contrast with the idea that the family socialises its members into acceptance of the dominant values stands the *possibility* that the family can, and sometimes does, promote 'deviant' ideas and behaviour. Evidence supporting this perspective is easy to find; witness . . . the first all-female offshoot of the union societies, which listed among its objectives 'to instill into the minds of our children a deep and rooted hatred of our corrupt and tyrannical rulers' (Marlow, 1971, p. 79). . . .

Similarly, family responsibilities did not always discipline working men, but sometimes promoted their radicalisation. The experience of watching the suffering and oppression of their families could instigate class action. . . .

The working-class standard of living depends not only on the level of wages, the traditional trade union concern, but also on the cost of living, which is the primary concern of the administrator of the wage – the housewife. Attacks on the working-class situation through price increases have historically produced concerted action.

E.P. Thompson states that in the early 19th century the cost of bread was the most sensitive indicator of popular discontent, and that consumer consciousness was positively related to the evolution of class consciousness (Thompson, 1963). The bread riot predates the strike as an expression of workers' community of interest, and has remained in various more modern guises an important weapon in labour's arsenal down to the present day. The prominence of working-class women in these class struggles of the marketplace derives precisely from their family roles as the executors of consumption.

J. Humphries, 'Class struggle and the persistence of the working-class family', *Cambridge Journal of Economics*, 1977, pp. 241, 248, 250–6.

Questions

1. In what ways does Humphries suggest working men's strategies were
   (a) disadvantageous and
   (b) advantageous to women?
2. Compare and contrast Humphries' arguments about working class families and resistance to class oppression, with those of Carby (Chapter 3, Reading 7) on black families and the different oppressions of black and white women.
3. Humphries refers to but does not explore, the 'non-market' criteria which govern the distribution of 'the family product' to 'non-labouring family members'. Do Oren or Delphy's observations (Chapter 3,

Readings 3 and 4) on these criteria substantially undermine Humphries' overall argument or not?

Essay Questions

1. 'The isolated nuclear family uniquely "fits" the needs of modern industrial societies.' Discuss. (AEB 1984)
2. 'The extended family was typical of pre-industrial societies and the nuclear family is typical of industrial societies.' Critically examine the evidence for and against this view. (AEB 1985)
3. 'From domination to partnership'. Discuss this view of the changes in family relationships which accompany industrialisation. (Cambridge 1984)
4. 'The modern family is uniquely well adapted to meet both the requirements of industrial society and the needs of individuals.' Discuss. (AEB 1983)
5. ' . . . there is no simple pattern of extended families in pre-industrial societies and nuclear families in industrial ones'. (Bilton *et al.*, *Introductory Sociology*.) Explain and discuss. (AEB 1987)
6. 'The nuclear family is not the result of the process of industrialisation; the prior existence of the nuclear family made industrialisation possible.' Explain and evaluate this view. (Oxford 1987.)
7. 'Wherever people work for a wage, a distinction is made between "work" and "home".' Discuss. (London 1983)

Further Reading

The literature in this field is large and expanding, so we start with two overviews with good leads into wider reading.

Diana Gittins, *The Family in Question* Chapter 1, 'How Have Families Changed?' gives a general survey, including demographic data.

Michael Anderson, *Approaches to the History of the Western Family, 1500–1914*, provides a good, short account and excellent annotated bibliography, though it is rather weak on feminist work and is therefore usefully complemented by the following three references.

Louise A. Tilly and Joan W. Scott, *Women, Work and Family*, a seminal work on nineteenth and twentieth century Britain and France, pioneering the modern concept of family economy.

Sandra Burman (ed.), *Fit Work for Women*, particularly articles by:
C. Hall, 'The Early Formation of Victorian Domestic Ideology', on the role of Evangelical Christianity, and
A. Summers, 'A Home Away From Home – Women's Philanthropic work in the nineteenth Century', on how middle class women's finding activity for themselves outside the home, resulted in the imposition of their family values on working class women.

Jane Lewis (ed.), *Labour and Love: Women's experience of home and family, 1850–1940*, is a collection of articles, with an introduction which

raises methodological issues, on relations between mothers and daughters, domestic violence, marital sexuality, contraception, and employment, in the middle and working classes, in various parts of the country.

Judy Lown, *With Free and Graceful Step? Women and Industrialisation in
Nineteenth Century England*. Based on a study of a Courtauld silk mill in
nineteenth century Essex, it looks at the way the pre-existing family
structure of the area influenced the organisation of an industrial business.
It describes the differential effects of factory life for men and women, and
suggests that women in fact *cushioned* the effects of industrialisation for
men.

Caroline Davidson, *A Woman's Work is Never Done. A history of
housework in the British Isles 1650–1950*. A very readable, fully illustrated
account of the effects of rapid industrialisation, urbanisation and technological changes on domestic tasks. It includes an account of the spread of
piped water, histories of cooking, heating, lighting, cleaning and laundry,
the importance of servants, as well as considering the time spent on
housework by, and the attitudes to it of men, women and children.

Leonore Davidoff, *The Best Circles*. A short, elegant account using
Weber's ideas on status to analyse how the new bourgeoisie in the
nineteenth century formalised Society (centred around the Court with its
season of events – e.g. Ascot, Cowes and shooting parties in Scotland –
country-house parties and afternoon calls) to enhance and secure its social
position *vis-à-vis* the aristocracy and gentry. Women in the domestic
sphere were the chief arbiters of social acceptance and rejection, and
skilful wives could gain their husbands important respectability and social
advancement.

Jeffrey Weeks, *Sex, Politics and Society. The regulation of sexuality since
1800*. Precisely because it is not specifically focused on the family, but
rather covers large areas of social concern relevant and related to the
family – e.g. illegitimacy, concerns around incest, hostility to homosexuality, demographic and eugenic concerns – this book enlarges our understanding of the changing social location of the family. It covers Victorian
society; the social concern, scientific investigation and reforming endea-
vour of the late nineteenth and early twentieth centuries; and twentieth
century consciousness and social policy.

James L. Watson (ed.), *Between Two Culture: migrants and minorities in
Britain*. After an introduction to issues around immigration, ethnicity and
class, this books includes accounts of ten different groups (Sikhs, Pakista-
nis, Monserratians, Jamaicans, West Africans, Chinese, Poles, Italians,
and Greek and Turkish Cypriots) who have migrated to Britain this
century. It gives information from anthropologists on, amongst other
things, past and present household structures and use of kin networks.

6 | What is the relationship between the family and the state?

In medieval England, the powers, rights, duties and liberties of people were tied to the feudal system of property ownership and the supreme powers of the monarchy. Complex historical processes, including peasant rebellions, struggles between monarchs and barons, and the increase in capitalistic relations referred to in Chapter 5, led to a move away from a system in which power was held and government conducted by the monarch and large landowners. But when these central powers were being reduced, concern was expressed as to what, if anything, should replace them.

An early systematic analysis of these issues by Thomas Hobbes, written in 1651, concluded that since human nature is basically selfish and individuals seek ways to maximise their own 'intense delight', they will very quickly come up against other individuals seeking *their* delight. In these circumstances, Hobbes asked, what is to prevent societies from collapsing into a 'warre of every one against every one'? His answer was that an impersonal, sovereign power with legal authority should act as the neutral, supreme authority to secure the overall good and to maintain social order. This supreme power – the state – could rule because citizens give their consent that it should do so, through a social contract.

In modern liberal democratic accounts, the way in which the consent of the people is conferred onto the state is through democratic elections, political parties and parliamentary government – although this is certainly not what Hobbes recommended. Today the state is regarded as a legal, public, power – with the legitimate right to use coercion and having supreme jurisdiction over a territory. In modern societies it often consists of a range of institutions and a large bureaucracy, including some sort of parliamentary apparatus, armed forces, police, judiciary, and also health, welfare and education services. Outside of the state stands 'civil society' – an area of social life which (according to liberal thought) is private and beyond the legitimate sphere of state intervention. Civil society includes the family, personal life and business and the economy.

What the precise relationship between the state and civil society, and in particular between the state and the family, *is*, is not, however, easy to determine in practice. There is the apparently straightforward proposition, that the state should limit itself to securing the rules that guarantee freedom of choice and individual liberties. But how should it best do this? And does it in practice do *only* this?

In opposition to liberal and liberal democratic views on the state, Marxism has more generally questioned the value of thinking of civil society, including the family, as a private sphere. This is not because Marx did not believe in the importance of individual freedom, liberty and democracy. Like Rousseau he was in favour of extreme forms of democracy. His worry was that if you dismiss business, and the economy in general (and the family) to a private sphere, then you de-politicise it. That is to say, you remove the possibility of discussing, in capitalist societies, whether a free market economy *is* the best or only way to organise production.

By the middle of the nineteenth century English men had won some political freedoms, such as the right of more of them to vote in elections. Marx saw these freedoms as by no means unimportant. However, he said that English people overestimated the extent of the freedoms they had achieved. He remarked that just as Christians believe themselves to be equal in heaven though unequal on earth, a people can believe itself to be equal in politics whilst unequal in life.

Marx argued that a free market left one group, the owners of the means of production, free to exploit the other larger group, the working class, who owned nothing but their labour. This latter group had to sell their labour in a manner that brought profit to the owners and inequality to them as the real producers of wealth. Marx, and subsequent Marxist writers, believed that the state is not the neutral referee in society, but rather that the state depends for its own existence on maintaining the present economic arrangements. It depends, for example, on revenue collected from taxes on the economy and therefore it is in its interests to maintain and support current economic arrangements. It therefore every day 'neutrally' supports one economic class against another.

Recent Marxist thinking on the state (and indeed much non-Marxist thinking) has been reinvigorated by Louis Althusser and proponents of his ideas (including Nicos Poulantzas), by Claus Offe and Jurgen Habermas, and by the non-Marxist challenge of Michel Foucault. Althusser argued that the struggle over the state and the need to possess state power was of absolutely central importance in political struggles. He extended the conventional Marxist definition of the state and argued that it was also composed of a diverse group of institutions which functioned 'ideologically' (i.e. were important in creating and maintaining ideas, rather than by using violence). So, for example, the media, the church and the schools are all included in Althusser's definition of 'ideological state apparatuses' (ISAs). The function of these institutions, and what provides the underlying unity to their diversity, is their contribution to the reproduction of the relations of production.

Althusser included the family among the ISAs – which was an innovation, since until the mid-1970s sociologists of the family seldom mentioned the state, except in relation to divorce; and sociologists concerned with theorising the state seldom mentioned the family. Subsequently both Althusser and Foucault's ideas have been taken up directly by those writing on the family; but the ideas of Habermas and Offe, though widely referred to amongst state theorists, have not.

It is perhaps strange that Althusser included the family in his definition of ISAs (it is hard to imagine for example what his remarks about gaining control of state power could refer to here). Nevertheless in the tradition of his thinking, Marxist-feminists have argued that the family does indeed help to reproduce the relations of production by providing cheap, amenable working class labourers for capitalist exploitation and because wives form a cheap and disposable 'reserve army of labour' that can be pulled into and pushed out of the labour market as economies expand or contract.

Such arguments claim that the nuclear family-household system is functional for sustaining capitalist relationships over generations. As such they are reminiscent of the arguments we met in the previous chapter on the relationship between the family and industrialisation. The way in which the family serves to reproduce capitalism has been, largely, conceived of in economic terms – providing cheap child rearing and care of the infirm, and cheap labour. However, more recently some attention has been focused more directly on the ideological significance of the family by this school of writing (see Further Readings).

Foucault argues that the idea that the state is central to power struggles is one that has outgrown its usefulness. He stresses a different conception of power: as something diffused throughout the society, which is to be seen, not so much as a capacity to be seized, as a quality lying within social relationships. Foucault has analysed the techniques of power which are not reducible to the sovereign state or to the law, but which lie within such things as the new human sciences. These are exercised not (just) by policemen with guns but by 'thought police': schoolmasters, doctors, psychiatrists, prison reformers and sexologists. Two readings in this chapter, by Christopher Lasch and Jacques Donzelot, involve this sort of approach. They challenge both Marxist and liberal/democratic conceptions of the character and role of the state.

Much work on the family and the state in the 1980s continues to explore the old but still relevant questions of the role and function of the state: what it does and what it should do. According to the basic liberal democratic view, the family is a private institution in which domestic concerns (including those of residence, sex, love and procreation) are met. This private realm should not be interfered with, except when things go wrong. The state *should* then lend a supporting hand, for example in cases of divorce or child abuse, to mediate and to protect the weak and the innocent.

The predominance of this view in society at large has led many to overlook the fact that the state supports a very particular kind of family life. It considers things to have gone wrong if citizens deviate from this. The first three readings are important early statements drawing attention to the existence of routine state intervention to control domestic life and family relations via the operations of the law, social work, the social security and tax and welfare systems. (Followers of Foucault would want to recast this as 'regulations through the family'.)

The subsequent readings present caveats or developments of this rather than fundamental disagreements, since it is now widely recognised that the state *does* intervene systematically in the 'private' world of the family. (However these interventions should not be overestimated. They are certainly slight compared to the intrusions of the Church and the local community in the sixteenth century when families appeared to have had little interior 'private' life.) The qualifications stress the variety and inconsistency of state interventions and the assumptions that families in Britain are white and composed of heterosexuals.

The final three readings widen the range of 'state' influences on the family to refer to groups which would be included in some definitions of the state but excluded in others – what has been termed 'the rise of the "therapeutic state"'. They disagree, however, as to the effects of these developments and who benefits from them.

☐ State Intervention in the Family

The work of Hilary Land in social administration marked a departure in the mid-1970s in pointing out the extent to which state agencies regulate our domestic lives and our relations with our parents, spouses, kin and children. The previous orthodoxy had been that, for example, the law intervened only when things went wrong (i.e. at divorce) or that social workers only controlled parents when children had to be taken into care. Land drew from her detailed knowledge of the complex web of social security, taxation and housing regulations and practice, to build up a picture of support for – indeed at times coercion towards – a particular, 'normal' family life.

Reading 1

The extent of state intervention in the family has . . . been obscured in order to maintain the illusion that the family is a private domain. Those pressing for new or different social policies and those managing existing services have presented these policies as defending the 'normal' or 'natural' pattern of dependencies and responsibilities already existing within the family. In addition benefits and services are provided to individuals defined to be without families, or at least 'normal' families. Thus, by narrowing the definition of 'normal' family, it has been possible to develop a wide range of services for children, and to a lesser extent for adults, without appearing to impose particular patterns of responsibilities within the family. At the same time those family obligations which are held to be important are emphasized.

Social policies are *implicit* family policies therefore because most, if not all, of them are based on certain assumptions about the pattern of 'normal' relationships between the sexes and the generations within the family. If these assumptions can be shown to be consistent between a variety of policies and also to persist over long periods of time then we need to know how and why these particular patterns are sustained and perpetuated. This means exposing the ideological dimensions of a range of social policies as they affect the family and abandoning the view that the state does not interfere in the family, which anyway is somehow separate from other major social, political and economic institutions. It also means recognizing that individual family members may have quite different and even opposing interests. Resources and responsibilities are not shared equally within the family. Just as the concept of 'the national interest' makes obscure crucial conflicts of interest within the nation, thus favouring the superordinate in society, the demand to preserve and protect 'the family' is to the advantage of its more powerful and privileged members, and some of those who voice such a demand may represent deeply conservative forces.

This paper will first examine the assumptions underlying a variety of social policies which concern the division of unpaid labour within the family whereby women care for the young, the sick and the old and, most important, for able-bodied adult men (their husbands). While acknowledging that the time and work involved are not the only dimensions of caring and that particularly in the context of a loving relationship there are other aspects which are positive and rewarding, it is important for us to recognize that, if we ascribe to women the primary responsibility for providing domestic services for other members of the family, their daily lives are structured in a way which profoundly affects their opportunities in the wider society in general and the labour market in particular. Moreover, the fact that this work is unpaid means that women do not acquire any direct financial independence by doing it. The second part of the paper therefore will indicate how the division of unpaid labour within the family is an important determinant of women's opportunities in the labour market.

[An example from the first part of the paper reads:] the social security system is based on the concept of one male breadwinner upon whom the rest of the family relies or *should* rely for financial support. The importance of the wife's financial contribution to the family is therefore ignored. Currently only £4 a week of a wife's earnings are disregarded. If she earns more than this then the extra dependency benefit is lost and in addition, for those on supplementary benefit, the benefit is reduced pound for pound. There is therefore a substantial incentive for a woman to give up paid work once her husband becomes unemployed, unless she has high enough earnings to maintain the whole family. Similarly there is evidence that the wives of men who become chronically sick are more likely to give up than to take up employment. In other words the social security system ignores the fact that most families are dependent on *two* earners (and for many working-class families this has always been so); it actively discourages role reversal and it encourages women to give priority to their responsibilities in the home. As a result the division of labour within the home remains unchanged even when the man is out of the labour market and dependent on state benefits. At the same time the experience of unemployment for the man is less intolerable than it might otherwise be.

Hilary Land, 'Who cares for the family?' *Journal of Social Policy*, 7, 3, 1978, pp. 258–9, 261–2.

Questions

1. What does Land mean by 'social policies'?
2. What do you understand by the term 'private domain'? Do you think that this term adequately describes the family? You may find it helpful to refer back to Chapter 5, Readings 4–6.

□ Repressive Benevolence

No one can enter a marriage without the direct intervention of the state. In the marriage 'contract' the state lays down a whole series of conditions that have profound consequences. For example the mere fact that only two adult, single, people of the opposite sex and sound mind may form a legal union has tremendous implications for society's views on heterosexuality, on coupledom, and on the relationships between affines and friends. All of this is so deeply embedded in our commonsense understanding of how the world works that it has not been easy to see its importance. In pointing it out, Diana Leonard argues that the state, under the guise of supporting the weaker partner, actually confirms an exploitative relationship between husbands and wives – its apparent benevolence is repressive.

Reading 2

Almost everyone in Britain gets married at least once, and the majority of the adult population at any one time are married. The state controls the entry into marriage, regulates what marriage should involve and punishes those who default. It also, increasingly, treats those men and women who go through some of the motions of being married (i.e. co-habitation, having children) 'as if' they were married. Why should this be?

The usual reasons advanced to justify legal regulation of, support for, and intervention into marriage and the family are: the protection of women and children (assuring support obligations and assigning responsibility for child care), ensuring family stability (for the psychic good of all its members, and hence the stability and well-being of the polity), and the promotion of public morality. A more important reason for regulation of marriage – indeed *the* most important reason – is that in supporting marriage the state supports a particular, exploitative relationship between men and women in which the wife provides unpaid domestic and sexual services, childbearing and rearing, and wage-earning and contribution to the household income when convenient (i.e. her labour for life – with limited rights to quit, and herself as an instrument of production) supposedly in exchange for protection, assured upkeep and some rights to children . . .

The law is presented as supporting the weaker party in the marital relationship. In the past the husband, and now whichever partner is better off (still almost invariably the man), has the officially imposed duty to support the other during and after the termination of the marriage. Women are seen as benefiting from marriage as a state-supported institution, and it is they who are more likely to feel a vested interest in the maintenance of their 'rights', i.e. in the *status quo*. Thus state support for marriage acts (as do the various elements of the welfare state, in a different context) to stabilise a potentially disruptive (class) struggle. It helps to mute or silence women's demands for equality of treatment in the labour market; to ensure that they continue to accept the assignment to them of the care of the young, the sick and the elderly, and that they are prepared to drop out of paid employment to provide such care; and to encourage them to put their energy, and occasionally even the money for their own food or clothing . . . into the maintenance of their husband (their current provider) and children.

[However] there has been almost no consideration of judicial (and very little of religious or welfare agency) regulation of marriage by sociologists. The bulk of the sociology of law relating to marriage and kinship, like most textbooks of family law . . . is concerned with divorce and legal separation, not with how the state via the legal system affects the start of or ongoing family life, and not at all with the regulation of sexual behaviour. . . .

One reason why lawyers can assert that the law does not interfere in or regulate ongoing marriage is that there is no place where one can find written down the rights and duties of husbands and wives. But this is not to say that there is not judicial consensus about the general nature of the marital relationship. Rather the lack of specification reflects the totality of the relationship – of the husband's appropriation of his wife's labour, time and body – and that it is a relationship of *personal* dependency. The couple work out together what the husband wants her to do – based on his needs and his ability to control her – within certain general parameters.

[But] . . . the nature of marriage, and what is involved in the change of status from single man and woman to husband and wife is, [only partly] . . . negotiable. One chooses to change status, and one chooses who to marry, but one does not choose what 'marriage' is to be. Having accepted 'to be married' a couple are free to work out an individual slant. . . . the husband works out an accommodation with his wife (e.g. he may or may not 'stop her' going out to work, he may require her to do housework or he many provide servants to release her for entertaining, etc.) But a couple cannot drastically modify the relationship in law – e.g. the spouses cannot contract out of their mutual duty to maintain, nor can the woman demand payment for her domestic work, nor can they be of the same sex, nor can it be a relationship between three people, etc.

While a commercial agreement between two parties does not, as such, confer rights or impose duties on any other person(s), the fact of being married affects the spouses' rights and duties with respect to other persons in many ways. For example, marriage affects (or may affect) the parties' nationality and domicile; they become 'next of kin' and acquire legal rights to participate in each other's estate on death over and against other individuals: it affects taxation, insurance and rights to certain welfare benefits: the wife customarily and the children legally take the husband's surname; and it may affect the rights and duties of third parties – e.g. neither spouse can agree to marry another while still married since the existing spouse is entitled to undivided consortium.

The support given to marriage – be it God's blessing in church, or the blessing of the Inland Revenue in the shape of the married man's tax allowance . . . or the ability to change a spouse's nationality – is not extended to any other domestic group or relationship between adults.

Diana Leonard, 'The regulation of marriage: repressive benevolence' in G. Littlejohn *et al.* (eds.), *Power and the State*, pp. 239–42.

Questions

1. What are the usual reasons given for the state's regulation of marriage?
2. Discuss the view that you can choose whether to marry and who to marry but you cannot choose what marriage is to be.

☐ The Protection
of Children

The argument that the state has intervened systematically in the family is supported by John Fitz but he has studied the effects on children and young people rather than on wives. Although it is commonly thought that the state has been right to act to protect children, Fitz suggests that this protection also involves control and has had three further consequences. It has resulted in children being made subject to the authority of the state itself, rather than exclusively to fathers or parents. It has prevented young people and children from doing waged work and therefore made them totally dependent in families. Finally the range of state institutions that specifically deal with young people, not least the school system, has created a special separate class of (strange!) people – individually 'the child' or 'the young person'.

Reading 3

There were over 100 pieces of legislation passed during Queen Victoria's reign which were concerned, in diverse ways, with the protection of children (ranging from the Factory Acts, Guardianship Acts and criminal law amendments through to the better known acts protecting children from physical abuse). Collectively this legislation successively demolished the near-absolute rights of the father, and later the absolute rights of parents, to regulate the lives of their children. Most legal commentators now agree that parents' *rights* over children have given way to *obligations* to their offspring. However, parental rights have not disappeared; rather these have been assumed by the state and can be acquired by a variety of means through the high courts and the juvenile courts. As I have argued . . . the state now stands as the 'wise and supreme parent' of *all* children. Natural parents may have their authority subverted by the state should they be deemed incapable of providing due care or control of their children.

This last point is particularly important because the focus of state intervention into the private sphere of the family is largely justified by the need to protect children. There is no doubt, however, that since 1839 the state has acquired the *legal right* to examine and regulate the internal relationships of the family . . .

. . . the combined effect of the Factory Acts and Agriculture Reform Acts was to limit the possibilities of children working in enterprises that were controlled and regulated by the Acts' legislative and administrative web. This did not prevent children from working in some areas of production, nor from working on a casual basis, for example selling goods in the street. What we do need to stress is that until 1880, and for some time afterwards in specific cases, it was possible for children to work, and their income in times of family crisis was central to the survival of their kin. Moreover, orphaned or abandoned children, especially in London, could make enough money from casual labour to survive without the support of families or charitable organizations. The formal separation of children from work in the nineteenth century . . . is in part the history of children being required to rely upon their parents, or on the state for the means of life. The gradual enforcement of the laws preventing children from working had profound effects on working-class families. . . .

Collectively, then, social policies which are concerned with the 'moral regulation of children can be seen as having two important effects. Firstly, the very existence of institutions such as juvenile courts, borstals, community homes, detention centres and so on designate children as subjects separate and different from adults, as a social category open to *specific* moral regulation through state action. Secondly, the power to bring sanctions against 'wandering', sexual precosity, economic independence, [or] participation in 'adult' practices such as drinking and gambling, constitutes a set of normative values which enhance the notions of childish innocence and dependence. Thus we have a clear indication of what social practices, experiences and ideas are to be regarded as 'adult' and from which children should be rigorously excluded.

John Fitz, 'Welfare, the family and the child', Unit 12 of Open University Course E353, *Society, Education and the State*, pp. 25, 32, 40.

Questions

1. Do you think that the state is the 'wise and supreme parent' of all children? Give reasons for your answer.
2. Make as full a list as you can of the laws that operate specifically on people under the age of majority and say at what age each law is effective.

☐ State Institutions and Women's Finances

The authors of the next reading warn against what they see as the over generalised perspective of the first three writers. They think it is better to regard the state as consisting of a variety of institutions and policies that may act in different and contradictory ways rather than uniformly. These agencies intervene into the family but they do not do so in any consistent way and the effects can be to undermine, rather than to support the traditional nuclear family. They also argue that it is wrong to think of the state as treating women as an homogenous group. For example there are big differences between the treatment of married women with children and married women without children. (The term 'aggregation', used in the reading, refers to the Inland Revenue's practice of treating the separate incomes of a husband and wife as if they were one single income belonging to the couple/husband.)

Reading 4

It is widely recognised that this country's present form of taxation has the effect of discriminating severely against women. On close examination, however, this discrimination is not quite as straightforward as is often supposed. In fact, it is possible that the history of taxation over recent years has resulted in discrimination *against* the classical nuclear family, rather than operating to reinforce it.

[Despite recent reforms] . . . the basic assumption of the aggregation of the couple's income has not been challenged. A married man will continue to be liable for declaring and paying tax on his wife's income, unless an application (involving the husband's permission) for separate assessment has been made. A wife's unearned income will continue to be treated as part of the husband's taxable income in any case. . . .

An examination of the history of aggregation reveals that it has not in fact operated to privilege the nuclear family, in which the woman is financially dependent on the man and not in paid work. On the contrary, the principle has resulted in favouring the married working couple with no children. There are two reasons behind this privilege, which clearly demonstrate the absence of a unified strategy towards women. Firstly, the history of aggregation itself concerns marriage and not the family and, secondly, there has been no coherent interaction between the policies of aggregation and the practices of child support. . . .

Far from supporting the idea of the nuclear family with dependent children, some aspects of taxation actually work against it. This anomaly has a definite history. In 1909, Lloyd George introduced a graduated rate of tax. This raised the problem that, if a man paid tax on a joint income, he would have to pay more tax than two single people living together, unless he could offset a bigger allowance against his income than the single person. It was recognised that the effect of this would have been a financial disincentive to marriage. Measures were introduced at the end of World War II to rectify this situation. The reason for its emergence as a contradiction was the result of two irreconcilable ideologies. On the one hand, there was the ideology of aggregation and, on the other hand, the woman was seen as a financial burden on the husband like other 'dependents', so that marriage was something to be afforded. It was during World War II that there was a drive to recruit married women into the labour force. As an inducement, married women were given the single person's allowance, whilst their husbands could still claim the higher married man's allowance. Married women have made up the bulk of the expansion in the employment market since the war. Nothing has been done to change the system of tax allowances as it affects married women since then. . . .

The history of the child tax allowances and family allowance and their subsequent replacement by child benefits follows a different logic. Relative to the personal tax allowances, the value of child support has declined. This has led to discrimination against the family with children. The various reforms, by which the family allowance and the child tax allowance have been replaced by tax free weekly payments for all children, have done little to alter this situation. These reforms took several years to be implemented, the government delaying on the grounds that this system would in fact mean a transfer of the husband's wage to the wife's purse. We now have a full system of child benefit, but this is undercut in several ways. The benefits for children at current levels are inadequate. They represent a horizontal redistribution from families with children to the childless. This situation is exacerbated by other factors relating to family income, so that the difference between having and not having children can be the difference between poverty and relative comfort.

F. Bennett *et al.*, 'The limits to "financial and legal independence": a socialist feminist perspective on taxation and social security' in D. Adlam *et al.*, *Politics and Power 1*, pp. 189–91.

Questions

1. According to the reading, what precise family household types are:
   (a) supported by current taxation and
   (b) not supported by it?
2. What does the reading see as two 'irreconcilable ideologies'? How have they developed historically? Can you think of any way in which they may be reconciled?

☐ The State is not our Protector

The obverse of the state's support (even if at times ambivalent support) for particular forms of domestic group and family obligation, is its action *against* other forms. For instance, the state has certainly not acted to support and sustain the family patterns of the Asian community. In so far as state practices assume common family and marriage values in Britain and ignore ethnic differences, they may reasonably be regarded as racist as well as patriarchal. Parita Trivedi points out that the state has passed restrictive, racist immigration legislation whilst simultaneously claiming to support Asian women by affirming liberal values regarding the choice of one's spouse. She regards this claim as bogus and merely one form of a general denigration of the Asian family by the media and welfare administrators.

Reading 5

The state has attempted to pose as a protective apparatus, legislating in favour of Asian women's interests. The ban on the entry of male fiancés (1979–1980), was patently an attempt to limit primary immigration: immigration of young male workers who would join the ranks of the Black working class, and increase its members. It was part of Thatcher's promise to the white electorate to curb primary immigration, which she fulfilled. The ban on male fiancés was presented as a benign act by the government – to 'protect' young Asian women from the 'horrors' of the arranged marriage system. It was however, challenged by Asian women because it was patently a racist weapon not to allow entry of potential workers into this country introduced to assuage xenophobic fears whipped up by the state. We challenged it not because we wanted to defend 'cultural practices' within our community (arranged marriage has nothing to do with 'culture' and everything to do with maintaining caste boundaries) but because we refused to abet the state in its racist ploys. We do not invoke the power of a racist state to deny people the right of entry into this country, or deny other women their choice of partner. Whether some of us decide to marry at all, let alone have an arranged marriage, is an issue we define and act upon autonomously of the state. We do not require the racist state to intervene on our behalf. To ally and collude with the racist state in a pseudo-feminist struggle would be crass and misguided. This has been one issue in which we have had to be clear about how the two areas of oppression − racial and sexual − operate. Today's arranged marriage system is qualitatively different from that of yester-year and given that the choices open to Asian women are limited, some actually do support the practice. This system of marriage has operated over a long period of time and cannot be wiped away by legislation. In fact the legislation was never intended to get rid of it. The state utilizes whichever weapons best serve its purpose. The state that attempted to 'protect' helpless Asian women, from 'barbaric' customs, is the very same state that conducted virginity tests on Asian women at Heathrow. . . .

The particular form that struggle takes, the particular circumstances in which relations are fought out, are historically specific. Nowhere is this more evident than in the discussions of the 'family' within the Asian community. There are various ways in which innumerable Asian families have been divided by the operations of immigration regulations; children have been separated from parents and elderly parents from their main supporters. Reuniting people of a particular family and attempting to overthrow the racist legislation have been important struggles for Asian women.

The particular Asian family form has been systematically under attack by the state not only through the workings of immigration rules, but also in other ideological ways, for example through the media and by welfare administrators who characterize the Asian families as being pathological (Parmar, 1982). Activists from within the Asian community (men and women) have come out strongly against this. Asian women have found themselves put in the position of resisting the state in its attempts to control and define our relations within the Asian community. The goal of the state is the control of the Asian community through repression and attack on one of its strongest institutions, the family, with its wide network of ties. Our goal is to resist racial and sexual oppression, and class exploitation. These goals are contradictory not complementary ones. The struggle against the state's intrusion into our political and personal lives has provided an arena of debate and discussion, as well as organizational impetus, in which the particular issues affecting us in their specificities have been taken up. In fact this is the most powerful argument for the setting up of autonomous Asian women's organizations.

The state cannot – and will not – legislate in our favour. This much is clear. Asian women involved in political work have been acutely aware of the co-opting role of the state, and the role of the media in sensationalizing the plight of individual Asian women in this country. Perhaps we have been too conscious of this: for it has hampered public debate and discussion on the specific oppression of Asian women from within the community. In a sense, this has been un-avoidable: one cannot escape the constraints imposed on political work when one is living in an intensely xenophobic, hostile society. However, if we are to move forward, the process of public debate has to begin: and is beginning. The fact that there are autonomous Asian women's groups with important bases in particular localities, who are engaged in struggle on several fronts – against racism, class exploitation, state repression, as well as against sexual in-equality within the community – is a sign of growing strength and confidence, which will enable us to engage in concerted action to combat the various facets of oppression and exploitation.

Parita Trivedi, 'To deny our fullness: Asian women in the making of history' *Feminist Review*, 17, Autumn 1984, pp. 46–8.

Questions

1. How, according to the reading, has the state appeared to act in the interests of Asian women and how has it actually hindered their interests?
2. What difficulties in political organising to improve the situation of Asian women does the author mention?

☐ Lesbian Mothers versus the Courts

Just as campaigning groups assert that the state opposes ethnic minority/black family patterns and cultural values, so the state also stands accused of heterosexual bias. The feminist legal group Rights of Women (ROW) has researched the experiences of 36 lesbian mothers and analysed cases of contested custody heard in court (as well as the few which get reported in law journals). The next reading describes a case heard in the Court of Appeal in 1976 and ROW's commentary on it and on other similar cases.

ROW's research is a rare example of public discussion of lesbian mothers – a fact which they argue is one factor in keeping the existence of lesbianism invisible. (All emphases are in the original.)

Reading 6

In 1976 a contested custody case was briefly reported in the Family Law Journal. A mother living with her lover in a lesbian relationship had sought custody of her five year old boy. The mother had been separated from her husband for 2 years at the time of the hearing and the child had lived with her and her lover for that time. After a hearing lasting six days the mother lost custody.

If the same criteria had been used as in heterosexual cases, no doubt the mother would have got custody. Both sides had an equally comfortable standard of living, and the child had been living with the mother for two years, so she had status quo. He was also of an age where the courts would usually consider he should be with his mother. The judge acknowledged the quality of the mother's care and concern for the child. However, lesbianism became the key issue as to why the mother should not have custody, and was the basis of the father's case. Three psychiatrists were called to testify to the effects of lesbianism on the child, two appearing for the father. The psychiatrist for the mother testified to the quality of the mother's and her partner's relationship with the child, and the trauma which would be caused by removing him from his established home, which he considered would be greater than any *damage* caused by a lesbian relationship. Also any possible teasing would be better coped with if he stayed with his mother.

It was also established by the mother's psychiatrist that the child had contact with heterosexual and male relatives with whom he could *identify*. On the father's side, however, both psychiatrists said that the child 'would have considerable difficulty growing up un-blemished by his abnormal situation'. In delivering his decision the judge preferred to accept the opinions of the two psychiatrists who said that the child would be 'blemished'. . . it was suggested by one psychiatrist that the mother's lover was immature because of her closeness to her own extended family. It was also suggested that the child's psychosexual development would be put at risk by his mother and her lover sleeping in the same bed.

The judge spoke of the gravity of damage from possible lesbian influence being '*inestimable*' and that the child might grow up to be 'ashamed and embarrassed by his mother'. He also spoke of the child learning to accept his mother, whilst not approving of her: 'It would mean the decay of society if people adopted the latter attitude. We definitely cannot have the approval. It would be detrimental, anyone might be influenced if it were approved of'. He stated that the boy should live in a house which he could describe as 'normal' to his friends and that he would be less likely to be teased if he had a normal background. Further, that if he lived with his father, no one need ever know of his mother's lesbianism. He talked of the boy needing to 'develop along *strong normal masculine lines*', and of 'difficult and uncharted waters'. He assumed that it is 'rare' for a child to grow up in a lesbian household and therefore, because of the unusualness of the case, it was necessary to rely on 'expert opinion'. The 'experts' in the case, as in later cases, did not however agree, and the judge chose the opinions that accorded most closely with his own views on the matter, rather than considering the reliability or otherwise of the evidence offered. . . .

The guiding principle in English custody disputes is the welfare of the child as the first and paramount consideration. Bearing this in mind there are a number of disturbing features which emerge from [this and other] cases . . . outlined.

Firstly, lesbianism has been focussed on as the dominating factor as to why the mother should not have custody, rather than an examination of the quality and care of the parental relationships. Further, a number of unfounded and speculative assumptions have been made about lesbianism, without these having to be proved. On occasion, the judges admit to being ill-formed, but then proceed to decide the case just the same on their own prejudices . . .

Also in a number of cases the judges make openly moral statements about their views on lesbianism, which suggest that, rather than considering the best interests of the child, they are more concerned with controlling the moral behaviour of society . . .

A further interesting but not surprising feature of these cases is that the father's behaviour and lifestyle were rarely put under the same scrutiny as the mother's. Indeed, in *E* v *E* (1980), despite the fact that the father was obviously thought to be unsuitable, it was speculated that he 'might' develop the appropriate qualities needed to bring up the child. Such positive speculation about the future behaviour of the father can only serve to emphasise how prejudiced the judiciary is in failing to give the benefit of the doubt to the lesbian mother. In nearly all cases (with the possible exception of child abuse), it is assumed it is better for the children to be with their fathers, whatever their behaviour or lifestyle. Where the father can provide a new wife or cohabitee and the *appearance* of a 'normal' or 'ordinary' family background, even if the new mother 'substitute' is a comparative stranger, this is considered even more preferable. A child may be removed from its familiar environment and close and loving relationship with its mother for this reason alone. . . .

Looking at the cases from 1976 to 1983, there has been a slight shift in attitude in some of the judgements. In the most recent judgement, for example, there is no reference to children being 'blemished' or 'scarred for life', and in *Re P* (1982) the corruption argument is dismissed as a reason, since there is no statistical evidence to support this view. Indeed, if corruption refers to sexual abuse or paedophilia, far from there being any evidence to suggest that lesbians abuse children, there is plenty of evidence to suggest that sexual abuse is carried out by heterosexual males (97%). . . .

Judges, court welfare officers, psychiatrists and social workers might do well to consider the fact that it may not be safe for children to grow up in the heterosexual family, when considering custody issues, rather than assuming that lesbians are a danger to children, and the heterosexual family must be a better alternative.

Rights of Women, *Lesbian Mothers on Trial: a report on lesbian mothers and child custody*, pp. 9–10, 14–16.

Questions

1. What instances of discrimination against lesbians does the extract highlight?
2. Compare this reading with Chapter 2, Reading 4. What are the criteria 'normally' used to determine who should have custody of children?

□ For Her Own Good

Those who write on the state in relationship to the maintenance of a particular labour process have found they need to include in their conception of 'the state' not only the police, judiciary and civil service, but also the media (see Miliband). Equally those who look at the state in relationship to the family need to extend the concept to include not only strictly state institutions and employees (such as immigration officers, judges and social workers and teachers) but also medicine and perhaps the media and advertising.

In a popular feminist history, Barbara Ehrenreich and Deidre English presented a growing group of scientists as increasingly 'helping' women to fulfil new roles in nineteenth and twentieth century European and North American society, when the significance of domestic production was greatly reduced. This 'help' was such as to confirm women as homemaking wives and, especially, mothers.

Reading 7

This book is about the scientific answer to the Woman Question, as elaborated over the last hundred years by a new class of experts – physicians, psychologists, domestic scientists, child-raising experts. These men – and, more rarely, women – presented themselves as authorities on the painful dilemma confronted by . . . so many . . .: What is woman's true nature? And what, in an industrial world which no longer honored women's traditional skills, was she to *do*? Physicians were the first of the new experts. With claims to knowledge encompassing all of human biological existence, they were the first to pass judgment on the social consequences of female anatomy and to prescribe the 'natural' life plan for women . . . [Other later] experts used their authority to define women's domestic activities down to the smallest details of housework and child raising. . . .

The relationship between women and the experts was not unlike conventional relationships between women and men. The experts wooed their female constituency, promising the 'right' and scientific way to live, and women responded – most eagerly in the upper and middle classes, more slowly among the poor – with dependency and trust. It was never an equal relationship, for the experts' authority rested on the denial or destruction of women's autonomous sources of knowledge: the old networks of skill-sharing, the accumulated lore of generations of mothers. But it was a relationship that lasted right up to our own time, when women began to discover that the experts' answer to the Woman Question was not science after all, but only the ideology of a masculinist society, dressed up as objective truth.

B. Ehrenreich and D. English, *For Her Own Good; 150 Years of the Experts' Advice to Women*, pp. 3–4.

Questions

1. Which group of scientists do the authors specify as advising women, and what did and do they advise women to do?
2. The authors clearly see these experts as prejudicial to women's interests. Can you mount an argument that they were genuinely helpful?

□ The Policing
of Families

The French sociologist Jacques Donzelot covers similar ground to Erenreich and English, though with a very different analysis and interpretation. He sees an *alliance* between the bourgeois wife of the nineteenth century, seeking to raise her status via control of the home and children, and the increasingly influential medical profession (and later 'relational technicians' using psychoanalysis). Together – they advising, she executing – they undermined paternal authority and opened the family to outside governance. For bourgeoise children they produced benevolent maternalism ('supervised freedom') and for working class children, surveillance.

Unlike Marxism (and feminism) Donzelot rejects the concept of a capitalist state and its agents seeking to secure bourgeoise class interests (or a patriarchal state seeking men's interests). He uses instead Foucault's view of the importance of the development, since the seventeenth and eighteenth centuries, of different forms of power exercised outside the state. These new techniques are diffused throughout the society, they are part of other relations rather than outside and acting upon them, and they may have no institutional basis but work instead in 'power networks' within for example sexuality, images of the body, kinship, knowledge, technology and so forth.

Donzelot argues that the changes meant that an eighteenth century family in which the head wielded power was transformed into a mid-twentieth century family which appears 'as if colonised', a relay for machinery exterior to it. We have moved from government *of* families to 'government *through* families', and from physical to psychological control. This he terms the 'tutelary complex', or in its twentieth century version, 'the psy complex'.

Reading 8

In 1876, the hygienist Fonssagrives introduced his *Dictionnaire de la santé*. . . [with the] warning:. . .

It is my ambition to make women into accomplished nurses who are understanding of all things, but who understand most of all that their role is there with the sick, and that it is as exalted as it is helpful. The role of the mother and that of the doctor are, and must remain, clearly distinct. The one prepares and facilitates the other; they are, or rather they should be, complementary to each other in the interest of the patient. The doctor prescribes the mother executes.

This organic link between doctor and family was to have profound repercussions on family life, leading to its reorganization in at least three directions: (1) the closing up of the family against the negative influences of the older educative milieu, against the methods and prejudices of domestic servants. . . (2) the making of a privileged alliance with the mother, favoring the advancement of women by virtue of this recognition of their educative usefulness; (3) the utilisation of the family by the doctor against all the old structures of education, religious discipline, and the practice of the boarding school. . .

This was an alliance profitable to both parties: with the mother's help, the doctor prevailed against the stubborn hegemony of that popular medicine of the old wives; and on the other hand, owing to the increased importance of maternal functions, he conceded a new power to the bourgeois woman in the domestic sphere. It became evident as early as the end of the eighteenth century that this alliance was capable of shaking paternal authority. In 1785, the Academy of Berlin offered the following questions for competitive discussion: (1) In a state of nature, what are the foundations and limits of paternal authority? (2) Is there a difference between the rights of the mother and those of the father? (3) To what degree can the laws extend or restrict this authority? Among the award-winning replies, that of Peuchet, the author of the *Encyclopédie méthodique*, took a position clearly in favor of a revaluation of the powers of the mother:

> If the grounds for the power that parents hold with respect to their children during their age of weakness and ignorance reside for the most part in the obligation they are under to attend to the welfare and preservation of these fragile beings, there is no question that the extent of this power grows in proportion to the duties one has to fulfill [on] their behalf. Owing to her position as mother, nurse, and protectress, the woman is prescribed duties that are unknown to men, and consequently she has a more positive right to obedience. The best reason for asserting that the mother has a more genuine right to the submission of her children is that she has greater need of it.

By augmenting the civil authority of the mother, the doctor furnished her with a social status. It was this promotion of the woman as mother, educator, and medical auxilliary that was to serve as a point of support for the main feminist currents of the nineteenth century. . . .

Of course all this applied only to families who were well-off, those who had servants, those in which the wives could devote themselves to the organization of the household, who could pay for their children's studies at the *lycée*, and those, finally, who had enough education themselves to benefit from these kinds of texts. The intervention in the affairs of working-class families went through other channels than the circulation of books and the establishment of an organic alliance between the family and medicine. In the first place, the illiteracy rate among these families was substantial up to the end of the nineteenth century; secondly, people of the lower classes could not afford a family doctor; but most important, the problems they presented were entirely unlike those discussed above. Seemingly, what was at issue was a similar concern to ensure the preservation of children, to spread the same hygienic precepts; but as regards *social economy*, the operations that were undertaken were completely different in nature from those conducted under the auspices of domestic medicine, and they produced results that were virtually opposite. The aim was no longer to free children from awkward constraints but to call a halt to the liberties that were being taken (abandonment in foundling hospitals, the disguised abandonment of putting children out to nurse), to control unauthorized associations (the growth of concubinage that accompanied urbanization in the first half of the nineteenth century), to block lines of escape (the vagabondage of individuals, of children in particular). In this case, it was no longer a question of enacting discreet protective measures but of establishing direct surveillance.

J. Donzelot, *The Policing of Families*, pp. 18, 20, 22.

Questions

1. List three adjectives or phrases in the extract to describe what was being done for bourgeois women's role as mothers.
2. How do Oren (Chapter 3, Reading 3) and Donzelot's views differ on the significance of the growth of the welfare state/the 'tutelary complex' for the lives of working class of children?
3. Compare and contrast Brophy and Smart (Chapter 2, Reading 4) and Donzelot on the growth of maternal rights and their relationship to 'the best interests of children'.

□ A Haven
in a Heartless
World

In the last hundred years, according to the American cultural critic and historian Christopher Lasch, the greatest intervention, change and undermining of traditional family values has come not only from the rise of the helping professions but also from civil society in the shape of advertising, increasing consumerism and market forces. The latter have been directed at turning women and children into self-interested consumers, making family relations combative and similar to the social relations of factory and market. Lasch feels much has been lost with the passing of the authoritarian, patriarchal family. The private world of the family has been opened out, 'experts' reign where parents used to, and women and children have been turned against the power of their husbands and fathers.

Reading 9

With the rise of the 'helping professions' in the first three decades of the twentieth century, society in the guise of a 'nurturing mother' invaded the family, the stronghold of those private rights, and took over many of its functions. The diffusion of the new ideology of social welfare had the effect of a self-fulfilling prophecy. By persuading the housewife, and finally even her husband as well, to rely on outside technology and the advice of outside experts, the apparatus of mass tuition – the successor to the church in a secularized society – undermined the family's capacity to provide for itself and thereby justified the continuing expansion of health, education, and welfare services. . . .

Like the helping professions, [the propaganda of commodities] undermined puritanical morality and patriarchal authority, subtly allying itself with women against men, children against parents. Consumerism dictated a larger role for women and a limited equality with men. Women had to become equals in the management of household expenditures. They had to become more nearly equal to men in order to enjoy sex and satisfy their husbands. From the moment it began to glimpse its 'civilizing' mission, advertising identified itself with the pseudo-emancipation of women recently epitomized in the slogan 'You've come a long way, baby.'

Similarly, advertising glorified youth. Advertising men, like psychiatrists and professional experts, claimed to understand the 'needs' of the young better than their parents did. On the one hand, advertisers insisted that the needs of the young should occupy the first place in parents' thoughts. On the other hand, they undermined parents' confidence in their ability to provide for those needs. Only modern science and technology, it appeared, could provide the growing child with the proper nutrition, the proper medical care, and the social skills he needed in order to function in the modern world. . . .

In the twenties, the first results of the combined attack on the old-style family began to come into view: the rise of the flapper, the revolt of youth, the 'revolution in manners and morals.' At the time, many observers saw in these developments the complete collapse of public order, but in retrospect it is clear that they merely facilitated the incorporation of women and youth into the market as full-fledged consumers, perpetually restless and dissatisfied. The combined influence of advertising and the 'helping professions' had liberated people from old constrictions only to expose them to more subtle forms of control. These agencies freed personal life from the repressive scrutiny of church and state only to subject it to medical and psychiatric scrutiny or the manipulation of the advertising industry. Insisting on the privacy of sex and marriage, they gave the most intimate acts unprecedented publicity. Upholding the family as the last stronghold of spontaneity, they sought to expel from marriage, love, and sex precisely the irregular, the unpredictable, the unmanageable. The 'repeal of reticence' lifted the shroud of sexual ignorance but imposed the new constraint of an allegedly scientific technique, in the light of which sexual 'performance' would be judged and usually found wanting. Lawgiver and priest retired from sexual supervision only to make way for the doctor, whose supervision was far more thorough. The older authorities had proscribed acts that threatened the stability of the community; the rest they left to discretion. Doctors, on the other hand, sought to shore up the psychic stability of the individual and therefore omitted nothing from their gaze. The disenchantment of erotic life dispelled many superstitions but reduced it to a routine. The establishment of medical and industrial jurisdiction over marriage thus defeated its own purpose, to strengthen the last bastion of privacy.

C. Lasch, *Haven in a Heartless World*, pp. 18–19.

Questions

1. From the reading make a full list of
   (a) the old forces influencing the family and
   (b) the new ones that are said to have taken over.

2. To what extent do you think that family relations have become like those of the market and factory and to what extent is this due to advertising/the propaganda of commodities?

Essay Questions

1. Despite suggestions that our society is pluralistic the state routinely acts to support very specific family relationships. Discuss.
2. What areas of agreement and disagreement exist between those who regard the state as acting in the interests of capitalism and those who regard it as acting in the interests of patriarchy?
3. Discuss any *one* major theory of the State and explain how effectively it explains the relationship between the family and the state.
4. Can we realistically talk about 'the family and the state' or must we restrict ourselves to discussions of particular state policies and practices and their relationships to particular family forms?
5. What areas of current state activity would be of interest to someone appointed as 'Minister of the Family' and how would such an appointment best respond to what you regard as pressing family problems?
6. Explain what is meant by the 'therapeutic state' and say what effects it has had on the family.
7. Some theorists define the state as including the family and some define the state as excluding the family. Making references to both views say how this difference affects their analysis of the relationships between the family and other institutions within society.

Further Reading

F. Mount, *The Subversive Family: an alternative history of love and marriage*. This jaunty, provocative account up-ends existing orthodoxy and suggests the family is the sole institution which throughout history has consistently *undermined* the 'powers that be'/the state. Mount suggests successive religious and political movements have tried to devalue the family, but have then had to settle accounts with it – on its terms. See particularly Chapter 2.

Mary McIntosh, 'The state and the oppression of women', in A. Kuhn and A.M. Wolpe (eds), *Feminism and Materialism*. This article uses Althusser's work and the idea of 'capitalist reproduction' to conceptualise the part played by the state in establishing and maintaining systems in which women are oppressed and subordinated to men. Capitalist state support for a nuclear family-based form of household and for a sex-segregated wage labour market has to be understood in terms of the state's role in the production and reproduction of the conditions for capital accumulation.

D.H.J. Morgan, *The Family, Politics and Social Theory*, Part 1. The chapters in this section of Morgan's second book show how the current public 'debate' on marriage and the family has developed: how private problems become constructed as public issues; the form of involvement of the state in marital and family affairs; politics, ideology and the family; how class and gender inequalities and conflicts get written out of the debate as the issue becomes medicalised and individualised; and what is currently constructed as 'the problem of divorce'. (See also readings and Further Reading in Chapter 2.)

Claire Ungerson (ed.), *Women and Social Policy: a reader*. This collection includes good articles on a whole variety of forms of social policy and practice related to the family: family allowances, income maintenance, the cohabitation rule, housing, schooling, health services, abortion, community care of the elderly, refuges for battered women, and social worker-client interaction.

J. Brophy and C. Smart (eds), *Women and the Law: explorations in law, family and sexuality*. This collection adds specifically legal involvements in and regulation of family life to the areas of state intervention discussed in Ungerson, above; namely, sexuality, child custody, domestic violence, conciliation, abortion, court inquiry reports.

John Fitz, 'Welfare, the family and the child' and Jenny Shaw, 'Family, state and compulsory education' in Open University, Block 5 of E353, *Society, Education and the State*, and associated readings in R. Dale *et al.* (eds), *Education and the State: politics, patriarchy and practice*. These Open University teaching texts give an excellent account of the history of state involvement in the provision of welfare for, and the associated social surveillance and control of, children. They look at laws and practices, and, most importantly, ideological constructs ('the best interests of the child', 'normal families', 'reasonable parents') relating to the family and to schooling, protective legislation, and juvenile justice. They show how state involvement may overarch and supersede the relationship between parent and child.

Michele Barrett and Mary McIntosh, *The Anti-social Family*. Chapter 3 contains a good exposition and critique of Lasch and Donzelot.

Digby Anderson and Graham Dawson (eds), *Family Portraits*. A collection arguing the need for a lobby on behalf of the 'normal family', to counter threats from 'government, feminist ideology and reproductive technology' so as to produce a 'more balanced debate and better informed family policy'.

Diana Gittins *The Family in Question*. Chapter 7 'The state: creator or destroyer of family solidarity?'

7 | Are there viable alternatives to the nuclear family?

The apparent paucity of alternative domestic forms to that of the nuclear family has often been taken to demonstrate that any alternatives are minority options. Circularities in the functionalist writings of authors like Murdock, for example, lead them to regard the widespread existence of institutions looking not unlike our marriage and family to be a testament to the impossibility of alternatives (see Chapter 1). Nevertheless, as we have seen in previous historical chapters, there *have* been alternative domestic and kinship arrangements in our own society and there continue to be alternatives in other societies. As Felicity Edholm says (Chapter 1, Reading 1), there is not one characteristic we consider 'normal' that is not considered 'abnormal' by several other societies.

When people talk of 'alternatives to the family' in Western societies they usually have in mind very different, often rather exotic, forms – such as the group marriage of the Oneida community in New York State, or the celibate Shakers (see Gordon in Further Reading). However, while we have included three Readings on communes (including two on the most famous 'experiment', the Israeli kibbutzim), we have chosen to concentrate on what we see as durable, viable alternatives which are not often recognised as such. We also explore the considerable influence of the pre-eminence of the nuclear family ideal on the (lack of) success of alternatives.

As Abrams and McCulloch point out in Reading 1, the history of communes in Europe stretches back beyond the medieval period. However the extent to which they were actually intended as alternatives to the family (prior to the 1960s) – as opposed to means to some other goal, e.g. the pursuit of godliness or political change – is debatable. If they were not intended to challenge the nuclear family or common gender roles, then clearly an assessment of them in terms of their failure to do so is misguided.

In more general terms we feel that the question of alternatives to the family becomes distorted if it is thought that the family itself is a static and fixed living arrangement. Although sociologists are right to identify the *structures* of kinship systems when studying the family, this should not be mistaken for thinking that people's *experience* of family life is static. In any kinship system 'the family process' means that the domestic arrangements of people change over time, as Robert Chester pointed out in Reading 7 of Chapter 1. (Family process refers to the way in which kinship systems are affected by the processes of birth, ageing and dying, entailing changes in the composition of domestic groups even when the basic rules of kinship are unchanged.) Over a person's life cycle the composition of the domestic group they live in will, typically, change many times. They will, if you like, find themselves living in a whole series of 'alternatives' to the nuclear family in the strict sense.

One such 'alternative' is living alone – as 9% of people do in the U.K. Of these only a small proportion are the 'never married' (5% of women and 9% of men remained unmarried at 40 years of age according to the last census). However, they comprise over three million people – but being single is rarely considered an alternative to marriage. This group is also neglected by sociologists because they create the view that being single is not an option, but rather a *phase* or *failure* – despite the fact that commonsense research, by Margaret Adams for example, shows how positively single people regard their status.

In Victorian England the numbers of single adults, especially women, was very much larger than today. Reading 5 considers this group. Especially after 1850, they developed a number of interesting strategies for living that were clearly constructed to be alternatives to marriage and the family for women who wanted to have fulfilling paid work.

Among the durable alternatives to the family, we must also certainly include the homosexual sub-culture. Both male homosexuality and lesbianism have a long history, and few societies have regarded them with as much hostility as does ours. We also consider single parenting to be a viable alternative – either when women choose to bear and raise children 'illegitimately' (how telling the term is of patriarchal values!) or when women (or men) choose to remain independent after divorce or widowhood.

Finally we have included a reading that considers the situation of 'dual career' families, since such couples are attempting to re-define the conventional sexual division of labour. Instead of a male bread-winning husband/father, the arrangement here is one in which *both* partners pursue careers. (As the name implies, such arrangements are, in our society, largely limited to the middle classes – the very idea of a 'career' is class specific.) They may also be 'alternative' in that the couple may not live together all the time if their jobs are in different towns. They may meet only at weekends or even less frequently.

□ Communes

This reading points to the long history of communal living. It suggests that the flourishing of alternatives in the late 1960s, more than 50 of which were visited by the authors, was due to the problems individuals experienced in the nuclear family itself. Philip Abrams and Andrew McCulloch interpret this as a tension between family structure and the value of 'possessive individualism'.

'Individualism' refers to one of the most influential political philosophies of the Western world. Essentially it is a conception of the individual as the possessor of his or her own self and abilities. It stresses freedom from dependence on the wills of others. It sees each person as an individual, not as part of a larger unit, be it a nation or a family. Stressing individual autonomy clearly opens up the potential for a conflict with other family values that stress individuals' obligations to the group, or to put others before self.

The authors believe many people set up or moved to communes in pursuit of freedom and self fulfilment. The failures of so many communes they see as stemming, ironically, from the fact that individual freedoms cannot be guaranteed without rules to secure them.

Reading 1

At the heart of the set of problems with which communes are involved stands the family. Philippe Aries . . . has traced the development of the conjugal nuclear family as a social institution of the western middle class constructed as part of that larger and more essentially bourgeois creation, private life. The fashioning of such a family, on the basis of an 'essential withdrawal by the household from the outside world', was also of course the fashioning of a new mode of individual property: the family becomes more definitely the possession of the head of the household. As such, the withdrawn family, as we might call it, is the enemy not only of a larger sociability but also of a larger more open and unpossessive individualism. It militates against both. So it is perhaps not surprising that as women and children come to feel that they, too, are human, and that the ethos of possessive individualism therefore gives them rights as well as men, they should feel urged to rebel against the family. And as they do, of course the family must become less and less satisfactory, more and more problematic, for men as well. Possessive individualism has to break out of the shell of the conjugal family once all the members of the family have become individuals. But how successful can such a rebellion be? . . .

Communal experiments and the critique of existing social life which they imply have been a constant and significant theme of British society for a thousand years. However many particular communes perish, communalism lasts. W.H.G. Armytage (1961) has traced the history of communal experiments from the Reformation to the middle of this century, and what is at least as striking in his account as the endless founding and collapse of particular communes is just this persistence of the communal effort. When he wrote, many communes dating from the last high tide of enthusiasm around 1930 were still in being. Immediately afterwards a new movement of interest brought a host of fresh communes to life. And although Armytage chooses to take the publication of More's *Utopia* as a convenient starting point, the continuity of communes could have been traced back through monastic orders and societies of heretics and outlaws to a very early date. Communalism, the idea of a withdrawn fellowship, is a principle of wide and diffuse appeal that can be invoked in the name of many different ends. We find it in one aspect in the group of artists and craftsmen that gathered round Bede at Jarrow, and in another in the band of scholars who made their way across England in the thirteenth century to found an alternative university at Cambridge. Any given commune may be seen as a concentrated expression of some particular values . . .

Of the communes we visited about one-quarter were gathered on the basis of common activities which required a more or less forcible insulation from society for their effective pursuit: a search for the curiously private and elusive sense of transcendent unity offered by drugs or intense mystical communion, for example. Another quarter were means to the more effective pursuit of social or political projects in the outer world. But a good half were simply this-worldly ends in themselves. . . .

[In the communes of the 1960s it] . . . *did* prove possible to create domestic settings in which familial relationships and the experience of self were significantly freed from conventional modes of possession. Provided a group had the resources to seclude itself a little from the pressure and demands of the economy around it, and provided its members were selected from a fairly narrow range of possible backgrounds and circumstances, a non-possessive familism could be achieved. Of course these conditions are already somewhat compromising; they lead communes rather quickly to exclude the damaged, the disabled and the demanding and those who are potentially so. But it is when one tries to move from such a base towards a resolution of other social problems that the real difficulties of communes appear.

To begin with, the structures (or encounters) that were developed did not ensure the greater freedom of women, although they did not prevent it, either. The refusal to let communes develop the fixity and facticity of a social institution is also a refusal to let communal living guarantee any particular social effects – even such effects as a dependable freedom . . .

. . . so long as one insists on treating freedom as though it is exclusively a question of the individual, sexless, classless, owner of a self and socially unlocated, one can only be baffled by one's failure to do better. And the members of communes are baffled by that failure just as they are perplexed by their normal inability to achieve more than a partial solution to their second fundamental problem, the problem of identity.

[The] . . . same determination to minimise structure that makes it so difficult for communes to guarantee women a more liberated experience also makes the process of communal self-seeking highly precarious, variable and indeterminate . . . one man's absence of structure is another man's social fact. Lesser planets must circle around a commune's sociometric stars to reflect the full intensity of their being. The full individuation of some members of a commune, usually the core group, tends to depend upon the, usually unacknowledged, stunting of the individuation of others.

P. Abrams and A. McCulloch, *Communes, Sociology & Society*, pp. 190–2

Questions

1. The authors claim that communes are attempts at solutions to problems caused by the family. What problems do they specify?
2. What are the main reasons the authors give to explain the breakdown of modern British communes?

☐ Women in the Kibbutz

The Israeli Kibbutzim are undoubtedly the most famous of all communal living situations. They are also the example most often named to support arguments about the inevitability and naturalness of the nuclear family and associated gender roles, and parental concern for children. The 'breakdown' of shared cooking, eating and childcare, the 'reversion' to nuclear family units, and women's withdrawal from agricultural work and public affairs into more domestic roles on kibbutzim are cited as evidence that a mere will to change is not enough. 'Nature will out.'

In the next reading, drawn from the conclusions of a book that set out to study the effects of the kibbutz on gender relations, the authors list changes in women's position in kibbutz society. They go on to argue that gender relations are best explained by the existence of an innate biological programme that will always shape the ways the sexes behave – an argument that we came across in Chapter 1.

Reading 2

1. Early in kibbutz history, more than half the women worked for a considerable time in production. Then came a long, gradual process of sexual polarization of work. Today the sexual division of labor has reached about 80 per cent of maximum.
2. Sexual division of labor is more polarized in the second and kibbutz-bred generations than it is in the first generation, and more polarized in younger kibbutzim than in older ones.
3. Despite complete formal equality in political rights, women are less active in the General Assembly than men are, as measured both by their presence in the Assembly and by the incidence of their participation. Women are somewhat overrepresented in committees dealing with social, educational, and cultural problems; they are seriously underrepresented in committees dealing with economy, work, general policy-making, and security.
4. The higher the authority of an office or committee, the lower the percentage of women in it. At the highest level of the kibbutz, women make up only 14 per cent of the personnel.
5. Women seem to have special problems sustaining all-female

work groups; they usually prefer mixed-sex groups or male leadership.

6. Men and women receive nearly the same number of years of education; in fact, women have a slight edge. Advanced schooling, however, differs in kind for each sex. Women are overrepresented in higher nonacademic education leading to such jobs as elementary-school teaching, kindergarten teaching, and medical nursing. Men are overrepresented in higher academic education leading to such jobs as agriculture, engineering, economics, and management.

7. From the ninth grade on, women consistently fall below men in scholarly achievement. This discrepancy between the sexes seems to be wider here than in comparable modern societies.

8. Although women, like men, are drafted into the army, the overwhelming majority of kibbutz girls (like other Israeli girls) do secretarial and service jobs there; few do characteristically male work or occupy command positions. The conception of the women's army as essentially a substitute unit, also providing back-up aid and encouragement for the fighting men, is completely accepted by the kibbutz girls. There has, however, been a steady expansion of the range of noncombat tasks for women.

9. Even the long, demanding Yom Kippur War did not substantially change the division of labor in the kibbutzim, even though almost half the men were called up by the army for a long period.

10. The family has risen from its initial shadowy existence to become the basic unit of kibbutz social structure. It now fulfills important functions in consumption and education, and there are demands for further expanding its function. Increased familization is indicated by high and growing rates of birth and marriage, and by a decreasing divorce rate. The status of singles, especially of women, is becoming more and more problematic, to the extent that the family, the kibbutz, and even the federations now try to help them marry.

11. The main instigators of familization are women, whose attitude toward familism is more positive than men's.

12. Attitudes toward equality have always been more egalitarian than actual behavior has. This discrepancy causes recurrent soul-searching within the kibbutzim and federations.

L. Tiger and J. Shepher, *Women in the Kibbutz*, pp. 262–3.

Questions

1. What does the term 'sexual division of labour' refer to in conclusions one and two?
2. What reasons are suggested for findings one and two in the rest of the reading?

☐ The Family in a Revolutionary Movement

Yonina Talmon argues that many generalisations about the kibbutz fail to understand Israeli history. She here explains some of the background to the kibbutz movement, arguing the need to understand this social 'experiment' in its context.

In the early 'revolutionary' period, some anti-familialism in the kibbutz was a deliberate political reaction against Jewish tradition, but much was a response to the new military and ecological situation. Demographically, only 20–30 per cent of kibbutz members were women, and there were few children. The communities relied on recruitment from outside, not internal reproduction.

Nonetheless, elements of traditional Jewish family life continued, and individual/household consumption and family centredness have been allowed to develop in today's more prosperous, routinised situation. Israel as a whole, and the state religion, is highly familistic.

Reading 3

The urge to emigrate to the new country and establish a Kibbutz was an outcome of a kind of conversion which entailed a total change of world view and way of life. This overpowering urge did not affect either whole communities or whole families. It cut through and disrupted both kinship and local ties. The pioneering ideology appealed mainly to the young and unattached, and induced them to sever their relations with parents, to discard their former attachments and disentangle themselves from their social setting altogether. The young pioneers emigrated either on their own or with a group of comrades. The disposition to establish very cohesive communities and relegate the family to a secondary position is closely related to this radical dissociation from former ties and to familial discontinuity . . .

External ties and conflicting loyalties were not allowed to interfere with internal cohesion.

The formation of families of procreation within the Kibbutz confronted the collectives with the problem of internal family attachments. New families are a source of centrifugal tendencies. Family ties are based on an exclusive and particularistic loyalty which sets the members of the family more or less apart from the rest of their comrades . . . Inasmuch as they act as buffers and protect the individual from the direct impact of public opinion, they reduce the effectiveness of informal collective control over members.

The anti-familistic tendencies inherent in the revolutionary and collectivist ideology of the Kibbutz were enhanced by the conditions in which it developed and by the nature of the functions it performed for the society as a whole. The Kibbutzim acted as an avant-garde of the emergent society. They were therefore a unique combination of agricultural settlements, training centers and military outposts. Each new community served as a spearhead of the advancement of settlement into more outlying and more arid frontier regions and had to fight its way against great odds – eroded and barren soil, severe scarcity of water, lack of adequate training and experience, very little capital resources for basic investment and the heavy burden of self-defense in a hostile environment. Settlement entailed in most cases a long preparatory period of entrenchment, land reclamation and experimentation, during which cultivation did not yield any profit. The Kibbutzim could overcome the almost insurmountable difficulties facing them only by means of channeling most of their resources of manpower and capital into production and by restricting their input into consumption and services to the bare minimum. Centralized communal organization of the non-productive branches of their economy enabled the Kibbutzim to reduce their investment in these spheres and to utilize fully the productive capacity of their members.

The tendency to attend to the needs of its members directly on the community level rather than by means of family households was strongly reinforced by the demographic characteristics of the Kibbutz and by its function as a training center for the youth movements. The presence of a considerable number of young members without families of their own in the Kibbutz and the constant turnover of temporary trainees made development of communal service institutions imperative.

Last but not least of the factors operating in the same direction was the function of the Kibbutz as a first defense line in outlying regions and around more vulnerable types of settlements. Settlement in remote frontier areas was a semi-military undertaking which required a flexible combination of activities directed towards economic development on the one hand and defense on the other. The social organization and physical layout of the Kibbutz resembled in many respects that of any army camp. Settlements composed of organizationally and ecologically independent family farms were much more difficult to tend and to defend in times of emergency. The non-familistic structure of the Kibbutz facilitated the task of merging the semi-military and economic functions . . .

It should be noted that while the Kibbutzim limited the functions of the family drastically and emphasized the predominance of the Collective, they did not abolish the family altogether. The anti-familistic policy was not based on a preconceived or fully worked out anti-familistic ideology. Most early formulations of ideological position did not propose to do away with the family completely. Justification for the restrictive norms was couched in terms of liberation of the family rather than of its negation and elimination. It should be stressed also that even during the earliest phases, when the anti-familistic bias was at its strongest, the family remained an identifiable unit. Families were regarded by their own members and by outsiders as distinct subgroups. There were socially regulated patterns of mating and children were recognized as offspring of particular parents. While premarital sexual relations were permitted, there was a clear-cut distinction between casual sexual experimentation, love affairs and the more durable and publicly sanctioned unions. By asking for a room of their own, the couple made public their wish to have permanent relations and eventually have children. Residence in a common bedroom-livingroom allocated by the Kibbutz conferred legitimacy to the couple. While children did not actually share a common domicile with their parents, they visited their parents' room and it was their home by reference. The life of the child alternated between the two ecological centers and both nursery and his parents' room were in a real sense home to him.

Y. Talmon, 'The family in a revolutionary movement: The case of the Kibbutz in Israel' in Rose Laub Coser (ed.), *The Family: its structures and functions*, pp. 552–3, 559–60.

Questions

1. What factors operated in an 'anti-familistic' fashion in the early kibbutzim?
2. Why do *you* think the kibbutzim never developed into a lasting alternative to the family?
3. What seem to you to be
   (a) the greatest benefits and

(b) the worst aspects of life in a kibbutz, when compared with living in a nuclear family?

☐ Single Women

In mid-Victorian England almost one third of women aged 20–44 remained spinsters. Such women (and other people) fought to establish an ideological climate that contained a role for single people, and for material circumstances to allow women to lead respectable lives away from their families of origin. They fought for paid careers and alternative 'homes' – schools, colleges, church communities, settlement houses and nurses' homes. Most of these were for middle class women. However, some turn-of-the-century employers also provided hostels for their working class employees – shop assistants of the John Lewis partnership, telephonists, and early typists.

Reading 4

[Single women had no obvious place in middle class homes in the second half of the nineteenth century.] A natural reaction to the isolation of so many spinsters was to form their own communities, united by their own tasks, fulfilling social needs that could not be met by married women or by men. Independent women wanted their own space, apart from the domestic world of their married sisters and from the male world in which they often moved. A community was a refuge, a foothold from which to launch into the wider world, but most of all, it was a home. . . .

One of the chief attractions of the new women's communities was their gift of privacy and time for self-development. Community life validated individuality in a culture that assumed women never needed time alone and would always be at the beck and call of others. In spite of the bourgeois family's keen sense of privacy, a woman could expect none of her own at home. Jane Austen concealed her scribbling whenever anyone came into the drawing room, lest she interfere with the sociability of her family. Florence Nightingale arose before dawn in order to have time for thorough study of government reports and statistics. . . .

But the privileges of time and space would not alone make a

community. Underpinning all women's work was a sense of religious commitment. Single women of vastly different convictions felt consecrated in their work to a sacred cause. This devotion to others' welfare was the highest expression of and validation for the idea of women's self-sacrificing nature. The stigma of paid labor for many middle-class women was thus removed. The rather negative notion of doing one's duty was changed into a positive hope for the future; work for others was part of God's plan, in which single women played a crucial role. . . .

Reformers hoped to create true communities of service out of the rather heterogeneous mixture of women drawn together by a shared workplace. They constantly spoke of the need to build esprit de corps among women, of turning the duty of work into a shared mission. At midcentury, when reformers first began talking about single women living communally, they had only two models to base their new institutions upon, religious orders and boarding schools. Both aroused deep feelings of hostility and distrust; neither promulgated independence and community. Religious orders appeared to demand the complete surrender of a woman's liberty and to cut her off entirely from her family . . . Traditional boarding schools, on the other hand, suffered from the opposite extreme. They prided themselves on being run as families, offering protection without responsibilities or liberty. . . .

Without totally discarding these two models, reformers adopted some features of both. The long-established male institutions, such as the famous Oxbridge colleges or men's clubs, were rejected. Rather, women fell back on what they knew best – the family. Their new communities were to be families, but without their complications and disadvantages. The traditional family was a model that did not excite fears or hostility, problems Florence Nightingale faced when she adapted a military model for modern nursing. At its simplest, but most enduring, the model meant mothering the needy, creating homes for the friendless and weak. . . .

A philanthropy that imitated the emotional ties and obligations of one's own home was emotionally comfortable and unthreatening. But mothering alone was not sufficient. Firm leadership, steady followers, and a new generation to train were also important ingredients in most women's communities. Women in the new institutions were pioneers who had to devise new models of behaviour, public and private. Such traditional roles as dutiful daughter, loving sister, or faithful church helper did not offer many guidelines for public leadership and professional conduct. Living in a 'family' that was not a family often exacerbated the deep conflict between the old expectations of marriage and children and the new opportunities for independence and personal fulfillment. The most common solution to the stresses and strains of living together and building a new institution was to continue the traditional emotional ties of the nuclear family while attempting cool, professional ways of behaving and working in the job and in the world outside. However, since 'family' and work were often within the walls of the same institution, many women found it difficult to draw a clear line between appropriate work behavior and personal emotions.

M. Vicinus, *Independent Women: Work and Community, 1850–1920*, pp. 31–9.

Questions

1. In what ways did conventional ideas of family life influence the new women's communities?
2. What seemed to be
   (a) the major advantages to middle class women of the communities and
   (b) the major disadvantages?
   How do you think these differed from the advantages and disadvantages of the communities mentioned for men?

☐ Homosexual Couples

Ken Plummer is one of the leading British researchers on male homosexual life styles. In this extract, written as part of a popular book on *The Couple*, he is not trying to argue that gays represent an example of a long term, alternative, living arrangement in our society – though they clearly do. Instead he is exploring the reasons why many male homosexuals should want to live in stable *couples* and why they often do not do so. The pressures of family ideology on gays is made clear.

Reading 5

In 1948 Kinsey concluded that 'long-term relationships between two males are notably few', and subsequent research has largely validated this observation. Many homosexuals (between 40 per cent and 60 per cent of most samples) do form stable relationships of over a year's duration, but very few last more than ten years and almost none celebrate a 'silver anniversary'. These findings, of course, are all subject to methodological flaws, since to obtain a random sample of homosexuals is impossible. . . .

[The] problem of forming couples has its roots for homosexuals in the wider structure of society. A great deal of childhood play is concerned with preparing children for adult roles as husband and wife, father and mother. . . .

To have a stable partner is perceived as normal and mature; not to have one as worrying and unhealthy. Such a powerful ideology provides a key motivational source for the homosexual to seek couple relationships . . .

[However, I do not wish to suggest total consensus in such matters.] Indeed, in a survey in which I took part in 1970, a quarter of some 2 000 male homosexuals interviewed were not sure they wanted homosexual love relationships lasting more than six months, and about 10 per cent said they did not want such a relationship at all. Such findings emphasize that the problem is not a universal one, and that couple formation is not universally subscribed to.

Nevertheless most homosexuals as well as heterosexuals probably do seek couple relationships. This motivation may be so strong that some homosexuals marry heterosexually; but others are committed to finding a homosexual mate. The problem of finding a mate is a central problem in the lives of many.

The homosexual motivated to find a stable relationship soon finds the world running in reverse. The heterosexual is facilitated, almost dragooned, into such a relationship, the homosexual is typically thwarted. The settings in which he has to meet other homosexuals, start relationships and maintain them are not the conventional ones.

. . . Heterosexuals find access to potential partners almost anywhere. For homosexuals the search for lovers is made difficult by the need for secrecy and anonymity created by the perception of a hostile society. If a homosexual were to make advances to any man who interested him he would have to learn to cope well with ridicule, rebuttal, rage or risk of life. Only the foolhardy, the stupid or the troublesome would take such actions . . .

For heterosexuals, most boy-girl meetings are seen as bases from which couple relationships could develop; for homosexuals most relationships are seen as transient unless there are good grounds for believing otherwise. At least two factors contribute to these transient relationships. Firstly, the way in which the gay world is structured so that people meet each other primarily as sex objects, and secondly, the norms generated in the gay world partly as a defence against threats from the 'straight' world and partly as a positive response to a new situation.

First . . .people in the gay world often have virtually nothing in common but their homosexuality and their role as sexual outcasts. Heterosexual lovers may meet in many places, places associated with many interests other than sexual ones . . .

Secondly, the existing norms of the gay world encourage transient relationships. The assumption is that a relationship embarked upon with a stranger will quickly result in sex and an anonymous departure. These norms may be explained firstly as a *defence strategy*, highlighting some of the areas most at risk for homosexuals in their relationship with the wider society.

A homosexual's masculinity is made an issue for him by society. In this culture to be sexual is valued if one is a man; to be emotional is devalued if one is a *real* man. Thus, by accentuating the sexual side of his life and divorcing it from the emotional, a homosexual can protect himself from the loss of his masculine identity and from self-conception as deviant. . . .

A homosexual also has his total identity put at risk by society. He may choose to avoid being seen by others as a homosexual and thinking of himself in this way. He may give accounts of himself which suggest that he is not really a homosexual. However, embarking on a love affair and living with another homosexual means a daily confrontation with evidence of his homosexuality. Engaging in casual relationships renders the risk to self-conception less. . . .

Even when homosexuals establish couple relationships many factors work to break them up . . .

Homosexual affairs probably dissolve speedily firstly because the relationship is given little validation or recognition by the outside (heterosexual world) . . .

Heterosexual marriage involves formal institutions, the gay couple does not. The law does not protect it, nor does the church give it its blessing 'till death do us part'. Family, community and society, if not outrightly hostile, refuse to recognise the couple as a unit.

K. Plummer, 'Men in love: observations on male homosexual couples' in M. Corbin, *The Couple*, pp. 176–87.

Questions

1. Why should Plummer say it is impossible to obtain a *random sample* of homosexuals?
2. Why, according to Plummer, do homosexuals seek stable couple relationships?

3. Give four factors, from the extract, that make it difficult for male homosexuals to form stable couples. To what extent do you suppose these apply equally to lesbians?

□ Women's Families?

This is an extract from an interview with Jean 'Binta' Breeze, a Jamaican performer who uses a combination of music, poetry and dance to present political issues in a dramatic and powerful way. She argues that the Jamaican family arrangements represent alternative possibilities both in the Caribbean and for some black women living in the UK.

Reading 6

Women in Jamaica have always been a very strong force. The mother is a powerful figure in the home. The majority of teachers are women and many public roles have always been played by women, so it has not been a situation where women are dormant. This is particularly true in my own family which is at the stage of being almost totally female . . .

Women have the usual problems in terms of unemployment, or if you are working outside the home there is the problem of dealing with a family – a situation that I face myself. There are a lot more daycare or nursery centres now than there were a few years ago and this is a definite improvement for working mothers.

But all these formalised nurseries, etc, are a very urban concept. The country way of living and providing for working mothers comes very much out of the extended family. Take myself, for example, I am here in England working, my children are home with my mother and sisters. I know that they are being well looked after and so I have the freedom of mind that is necessary for me to do my work. I also have the freedom to come over here, which I would not otherwise have had. Think of the number of West Indian women who have come to Britain in the years since we started this 'reverse colonisation'. . . They were in some cases leaving three month old babies at home with their families. How many women in urbanised western society can think of leaving three or four children and going somewhere else, not knowing when they are going to see them again? The family support in Jamaica is very strong . . . this has always been the heart of organisation amongst women. The relationship I have with my mother in Jamaica would probably be very rarely found in a society such as you have in England where there are a lot of conflicts in what women's roles are all about. Most western women find it very difficult to understand the system of living that we have back home, they don't, for instance, see the importance of the grandmothers' position in the family. During the three years in which my mother was training to be a nurse I was with my grandmother. Almost everyone in Jamaica can say that their grandmother had a very definite hand in growing them up, unlike here. The family is a source of tremendous strength for women in the West Indies and it is the women in the family who provide this strength. . . .

At the same time, you can look at it from a different angle and say that it's maybe oppressive for members of the family to have to give this support, that it is oppressive to a grandmother to have children thrown back on her after she's brought up one set. But, look at the number of old people in a community like this (England) who don't even know where their children are. The children may telephone twice a year or maybe come home for Christmas if they are particularly dutiful but look at the number of old people suffering from loneliness – there is so little family contact in many westernised societies. . . .

West Indian life is matriarchal or mother-centred and this is connected to slavery . . . During slavery the nuclear family in particular was not encouraged by plantation owners – this would have caused a solidarity which they did not want. And so family life for the slaves was continually disrupted, the men were often forcibly taken away from their families and it fell upon the women to maintain and control the family. So, if West Indian life is 'falsely' matriarchal it is slavery and tradition that has made it so. Tradition takes a long time to die, and remember that when we talk of slavery it is still only five generations ago that we were emancipated and even so slavery did not end there.

J. Breeze, 'A Family of Women' in *Trouble and Strife*, 1985, No. 7, pp. 14–16.

Questions

1. What differences between Jamaican family relationships and British nuclear family relationships are identified here?
2. What evidence is there here to support the view that the Jamaican family is not mother governed – even if it may be mother centred?

□ Dual
   Career
   Families

As part of a larger study of *Women in Top Jobs*, investigating why highly qualified women (married and single, with and without children) did or did not participate in senior roles in society, Rhona and Robert Rapoport undertook a detailed study of 16 British couples with children where both husbands and wives 'successfully combined careers and family life'. Five of the these families were described in *Dual-Career Families*.

This book was given a rather luke-warm reception when it was first published in 1971, but the title has passed into common usage, and a second edition was issued in 1976. This last extract is taken from the introduction and first chapter of this second edition.

The Rapoports (a dual career family themselves) believe that families where both spouses have demanding, personally satisfying, paid employment represent a far more fundamental and enduring challenge to conventional family relationships than do any of the heterosexual alternatives discussed so far. Quite a few of the couples they interviewed in the late 1960s had not intended to be pioneers or innovators but had become dual career families by force of circumstances; but by the late 1970s the pattern was much more acceptable, and deliberately sought.

The Rapoports have promoted this form of family in their other publications and are at pains to defend it from criticisms of elitism and of being limited in scope to a small, professional middle class base.

Reading 7

The term 'dual-career families' was coined to designate a type of family structure in which both heads of household – the husband and the wife – pursue active careers and family lives. 'Career' is sometimes used to indicate any sequence of jobs, but in its more precise meaning it designates those types of job sequences that require a high degree of commitment and that have a continuous developmental character. . . .

[As] Arlene and Jerome Skolnick said, when commenting on our initial paper,

The term 'alternative family pattern' usually brings to mind the much publicised commune, group marriage, or 'swinging' couples. Yet the variant family pattern discussed here – in which husband and wife are committed to careers – may be both more widespread in the future and more of a break with the conventional family that has prevailed until recently. As the studies of communes and swingers show, far out sexual behaviour can co-exist with traditional sex-role ideologies and a conventional division of labour [between] the sexes. The commitment of the mother-wife to a career strikes at the heart of this division of labour and is the source of many of the stresses, as well as the rewards, of this family pattern . . .

While dual-career families vary in the degree to which they have developed with a self-conscious ideology, they have in common the fact that they sustain a pattern of behaviour that brings into being a fundamental social change . . .

When we first wrote about dual-career families, we saw them as 'creative variants' pioneering a breakaway from the pattern of male-breadwinner/female-housewife stereotypes. This has by the 1970s been more normalized with increases in women's participation in the labour market reinforced by equal-opportunity legislation and more accepting public opinion . . .

The study of dual-career families, though conducted under a specific mandate to examine women in 'top jobs', was sometimes criticized as being 'middle-class biased' and 'elitist'. Several assumptions (other than a disregard for the terms of reference of the study) seem to underlie this criticism, and it is useful to consider them in relation to this re-examination.

There seems to be an *assumption that the pattern is made possible only through the use of elite resources such as 'servants'.* However, many of the individuals in the dual-career families studied came from working-class backgrounds. Their use of support resources came only *after* they were committed to the pattern; and in any case they are not specific to the dual-career pattern. In the same social setting, conventional families also use domestic service personnel. And other kinds of support people (including neighbours, kin and social service facilities) are used to support both conventional and dual-worker families – working class as well as middle class.

There is *the assumption that the use of external supports for domestic work is exploitative while the use of familial supports is non-exploitative.* This ignores the fact that in many conventional nuclear families, the wife often feels (and is) exploited in the exchange pattern that is accepted. Conversely, legitimation and the establishment of an equitable basis for the use of external supports to family life is possible. Domestic work can be a job like any other, and under appropriate conditions need not be exploitative.

There is the *assumption that domestic services are 'special' and that it is irresponsible to ask non-family members to fulfil domestic obligations*. It is considered to be elitist to import these services to the home, though similar services like hairdressing, shoe-shining, feeding and catering, bathing and medical care are acceptable if performed outside the home. Yet, as income is more equalized across the classes, such services are sought by more and more people. The professionalization of service occupations can benefit the community by creating additional occupational options. In many cases, e.g. of women desirous of working away from a not very comfortable home situation, entry into one of the personal or family service occupations may be felt to increase satisfaction as well as material rewards.

Rhona and Robert N. Rapoport, *Dual-Career Families Re-examined*, pp. 9, 12, 13, 23.

Questions

1. How do 'dual-career families' differ from 'neo-conventional families' referred to by Chester in Reading 7, Chapter 1?
2. Why might the dual-career family be regarded as more profoundly different from conventional families than are communes?
3. Give two reasons why a growth in paid domestic services could be seen as a beneficial development, and two arguments against it. (You might like to look back to the reading by Davidoff, Reading 6, Chapter 5 for historical comments on domestic *service* from the point of view of the servants.)

Essay Questions

1. To what extent do communes challenge our conventional way of viewing the family? (JMB 1979)
2. The idea that the Israeli kibbutz was a failed attempt at establishing an alternative to the Western nuclear family is misleading. Discuss.
3. Does study of contemporary households and family relationships reveal a remarkable conformity of domestic arrangements or a variety of alternatives?
4. 'The difficulties of living alone, at whatever stage of one's life, have little to do with the state of being single and much to do with major features of British social life.' Answer the following questions on this statement:
   (a) what could the author have in mind as the 'major features' of social life?

(b) what are the major differences in the 'difficulties of living alone' between young adults and old people?
(c) give evidence to support *OR* to disagree with this statement.
5. Is the 'dual-career family' a challenge and an alternative to the Western nuclear family?
6. The reason why there are so few alternatives to the Western nuclear family is because this family form best suits both the needs of industrial societies and the personal desires of men and women. Discuss.
7. What are the similarities and differences in the problems facing
(a) communes and
(b) homosexual couples as they try to establish a way of living that is alternative to the family?

Further Reading

A. Skolnick, *The Intimate Environment*, aimed at American college students gives a readable account of alternative life styles. It considers the social psychology of relationships inside the family and the impact of a changing society on those relationships.

Michael Gordon, *The Nuclear Family in Crisis: the search for an alternative*. A reader containing extracts on a whole series of projected or realised, past and present, alternative societies – Plato's Republic; the Moravians, the Oneida community, and 1960s communes and group marriages in the USA; three alternative views of the Kibbutz; and the family in Russia and China after their revolutions.

R.M. Kanter, *Commitment and Community*, also covers American utopian communities of an earlier period, but with a general analysis of communes as social enterprises.

Dolores Hayden, *The Grand Domestic Revolution: a history of feminist designs for American homes, neighbourhoods, and cities*, provides a detailed, fully illustrated account of a forgotten tradition of American feminism: pioneers who proposed, and sometimes effected, a transformation of the spatial design and material culture of American homes and neighbourhoods. They wanted, for example, to socialise housework and childcare – with kitchenless houses, day care centres and community dining clubs.

Andrew Rigby, *Alternative Realities*, and *Communes in Britain*. These books derive from research undertaken at the same time as that of Abrams and McCulloch, but the author takes a more optimistic view of the potential for communal living, and accepts more of the communards self-definitions. *Communes in Britain* describes five communes of different sorts in detail, and complements the more theoretical account in *Alternative Realities*.

Caroline New and Miriam David, *For the Children's Sake: making childcare more than women's business*. The authors argue for a radical change in the way childcare is organised. They think those doing the caring should not be dependents and second-class citizens, and that men should also be involved. Childcare should be an area of *public* concern – all the time, not as a last resort (when the state takes over from parents who have 'failed'). They discuss the politics of privatised childcare, existing provision and possible alternatives, with strategies for change provided by contributions from people who have been involved in community nurseries, co-operative crèches, and children's workshops.

Rhona Rapoport and Robert N. Rapoport (eds), *Working Couples*. This contains 12 articles by researchers who have looked at how such couples organise their lives and the problems they encounter – such topics as finding two jobs, commuting, job sharing, contracts in marriage, childcare choices.

Elaine Campbell, *The Childless Marriage: an exploratory study of couples who do not want children*, and
Stephanie Dowrick and Sibyl Grundberg (eds), *Why Children?* These provide respectively an academic study and personal accounts of why people come to not have (or have) children, and their experiences.

Kenneth Plummer (ed.), *The Making of the Modern Homosexual*, a key and sophisticated collection, but certainly male biased, so see also:

Sheila Jeffreys, *The Spinster and Her Enemies: Feminism and Sexuality 1880–1930*. This book reinterprets the 'sexual revolution' of the early twentieth century, away from the sexual puritanism of Victorian England, as in fact restricting women's independence. The virtual requirement that all women (and men) engage in (hetero)sexual activity and parenthood, established via the works of Havelock Ellis and Freud – their being threatened otherwise with becoming bitter, neurotic spinsters – resulted in their confinement to marriage and motherhood, just at the point when economic independence and a strong feminist movement offered alternative possibilities.

L. Segal (ed.), *What is to be Done About the Family*, is a collection of essays, looking at early feminist critiques of the family and the views of the 1960s, from both general and personal perspectives. Women suggest how they came to their various understandings and how their ideas and experience have now moved on – including the effects of Thatcherite policies.

Bibliography

Abrams, P. and McCulloch, A. *Communes, Sociology and Society*, Cambridge University Press, 1975.

Adams, M. *Single Blessedness*, Heinemann, 1976.

Allan, Graham. *Family Life*, Blackwell, 1985.

Anderson D. and Dawson G. (eds), *Family Portraits*, Social Affairs Unit, 1986.

Anderson, Michael. *Approaches to the History of the Western Family 1500–1914*, Macmillan, 1980.

Anderson, Michael. 'How has the family changed?', *New Society*, 27 October 1983.

Armytage, W.H.G. *Heavens Below*, Routledge & Kegan Paul, 1961.

Barrett, Michèle. *Women's Oppression Today*, Verso, 1980.

Barrett, Michèle and McIntosh, Mary. *The Anti-social Family*, Verso, 1982.

Beechey, Veronica and Donald, James (eds). *Subjectivity and Social Relations*, Open University Press, 1985.

Bell, C. *Middle Class Families*, Routledge & Kegan Paul, 1968.

Bennett, F. *et al.* 'The limits to "financial and legal independence": a socialist-feminist perspective on taxation and social security', *Politics & Power* No. 1., 1980.

Bernstein, B. *Class, Codes and Control*, Volume 3, *Towards a Theory of Educational Transmissions*, Routledge & Kegan Paul, 1976.

Blood, R.O. *Marriage*, Collier-Macmillan, 1969.

Borkowski, M., Murch, M. and Walker, V. *Marital Violence. The Community Response*, Tavistock, 1983.

Bott, E. *Family & Social Network*, Tavistock, 1971.

Breeze, J. 'A Family of Women', *Trouble & Strife*, 1985.

Brennan, Julia and Wilson, Gail (eds). *Give and Take in Families*, Hutchinson, 1987.

Brophy, J. and Smart, C. 'From disregard to disrepute: the position of women in family law', *Feminist Review*, No. 9, 1981.

Brophy, J. and Smart, C. (eds). *Women and the Law: explorations in law, family and sexuality*, Routledge & Kegan Paul, 1985.

Burgess E.W. and Locke, H.J. *The Family: from Institution to Companionship*, American Book Co., 1953.

Burman, Sandra (ed.). *Fit Work for Women*, Croom Helm, 1979.

Campbell, Elaine. *The Childless Marriage: an exploratory study of couples who do not want children*, Tavistock, 1985.

Carby, H. 'White woman listen! Black feminism and the boundaries of sisterhood', in Centre for Contemporary Cultural Studies, *The Empire Strikes Back*, Hutchinson, 1982.

Chester, R. 'The rise of the neo-conventional family', *New Society*, May, 1985.

Cohen, G. 'Women's solidarity and the preservation of privilege', in P. Caplan and J.N. Bujra, (eds). *Women United, Women Divided*, Tavistock, 1978.

Coward, R. *Female Sexual Desire*, Paladin, 1984.

Dale, R. *et al.* (eds) *Education and the State: politics, patriarchy and practice*. Falmer Press, 1981.

Davidoff, Leonore. 'The separation of home and work? Landladies and lodgers in nineteenth and twentieth century England' in S. Burman (ed.), *Fit Work for Women*, Croom Helm, 1979.

Davidoff, Leonore. *The Best Circles*, Croom Helm, 1973, paperback, Cresset Library, 1986.

Davidoff, Leonore, L'Esperance, Jean, and Newby, Howard. 'Landscape with figures: home and community in English society', in J. Mitchell and A. Oakley (eds). *The Rights and Wrongs of Women*, Penguin 1976.

Davidson, Caroline. *A Woman's Work is Never Done. A history of housework in the British Isles 1650–1950*, Chatto & Windus, 1982.

Davin, Anna. 'Imperialism and motherhood', *History Workshop*, No. 5, spring 1973.

Delphy, Christine. *Close to Home*, Hutchinson 1984.

Donzelot, J. *The Policing of Families*, Hutchinson, 1980.

Dowrick, Stephanie, and Grundberg, Sibyl (eds). *Why Children?*, The Women's Press, 1980.

Drummond, M. *How to Survive as a Second Wife*, Robson Books, 1981.

Dobash, R.E. and R. *Violence Against Wives*, Free Press/Open Books, 1980.

Edgell, Stephen. *Middle-class Couples: a study of segregation, domination and inequality in marriage*, George Allen & Unwin, 1980.

Edholm, F. 'The Unnatural Family' in E. Whitelegg *et al.* (eds). *The Changing Experience of Women*, Martin Robertson in association with Open University Press, 1982.

Ehrenreich, B. and English, D. *For Her Own Good*, Pluto, 1979.

Elliot, Faith Robertson. *The Family: Change or Continuity?*, Macmillan, 1986.

Equal Opportunities Commission. *The Experience of Caring for Elderly and Handicapped Dependants: a survey report*, HMSO, 1980.

Ferri, E. *Growing up in a One-parent Family*, National Foundation for Educational Research in England and Wales, 1979.

Finch, Janet. *Married to the Job. Wives incorporation in men's work*, George Allen & Unwin, 1983.

Finer, M. and McGregor, O.R. 'The History of the Obligation to Maintain', App. 5 to Vol. 2, DHSS, *Report of the Committee on One-Parent Families,* HMSO, Cmnd. 5629, 1978

Fitz, J. 'Welfare, the family and the child' in *Education, Welfare & the Social Order*, Unit 12 Block 5 of E353, *Society, Education and the State*, Open University Press, 1981.

Fitz, J. and Hood-Williams, J. 'The generation game: playing by the rules', in D. Robbins *et al.* (eds) *Rethinking Social Inequality*, Gower, 1982.

Flandrin, J.L. *Families in Former Times*, Cambridge University Press, 1979.

Fletcher, R. *The Family and Marriage in Britain*, Penguin, 1966, Pelican, 1967.

Foucault, M. *The Birth of the Clinic*, Tavistock, 1973.

Foucault, M. *Discipline & Punish*, Allen Lane, 1977.

Foucault, M. *The History of Sexuality*, Random House, 1978.

Foucault, M. and Gordon, C. (eds). *Power/Knowledge*, Harvester Press 1980.

Frankenberg, R. *Communities in Britain*. Penguin, 1966.

Frankenberg, R. '"In the production of the their lives, men (?) . . ." Sex and gender in British community studies', in D.L. Barker, and S. Allen, (eds). *Sexual Divisions and Society: process and change*, Tavistock, 1976.

Freud, S. *On Sexuality*, Pelican, 1977.

Gamarnikow, Eva *et al.* (eds). *The Public and the Private*, Heinemann, 1983.

Gittins, Diana. *The Family in Question: changing households and familiar ideologies*, Macmillan, 1985.

Goode, W.J. *World Revolution and Family Patterns*, Free Press N.Y., 1963.

Goode, W.J. *The Family*, Prentice Hall, 1964.

Gordon, Michael. *The Nuclear Family in Crisis: the search for an alternative*, Harper and Row, 1972.

Gorham, D. 'The "Maiden Tribute of Modern Babylon" re-examined', *Victorian Studies* vol. 21, No. 3, 1978.

Gouldner, Alvin. *The Coming Crisis of Western Sociology*, Heinemann, 1977.

Hall, C. 'The butcher, the baker, the candlestick maker: the shop and the family in the Industrial Revolution' and 'The home turned upside down? The working class family in cotton textiles 1780–1850', both in E. Whitelegg, *et al.* (eds). *The Changing Experience of Women*, Martin Robertson in Association with Open University Press, 1982.

Hart, Nicky. *When Marriage Ends. A study in status passage*, Tavistock 1976.

Hartmann, H. 'The unhappy marriage of Marxism and feminism: towards a more progressive union' in L. Sargent, (ed.). *Women & Revolution*, South End Press, 1981.

Hayden, Dolores. *The Grand Domestic Revolution: a history of feminist designs for American homes, neighbourhoods, and cities*, MIT Press, 1982.

Hobbes, T. *Leviathan*, Fontana, 1962.

Holt, John. *How Children Fail*, Pelican, 1971.

Holt, John. *Escape from Childhood. The needs and rights of children*, Penguin, 1975.

Humphries, J. 'Class struggle and the persistance of the working-class family', *Cambridge Journal of Economics*, 1977. Vol. 1, pp. 241–258.

Hutchins, B. and Harrison, A. *A History of Factory Legislation*, P.S. King, 1903.

Illsley, R. and Thompson, D. 'Women from Broken Homes', *Sociological Review*, vol. 9 no. 1, 1961.

Itzin, Catherine. *Splitting Up. Single-parent liberation*, Virago, 1980.

Jackson, Stevi. *Childhood and Sexuality*, Basil Blackwell, 1982.

Jeffreys, Sheila. *The Spinster and Her Enemies: Feminism and Sexuality 1880–1930*, Pandora, 1985.
Kanter, R.M. *Commitment and Community*, Harvard University Press, 1972.
Keesing, R. *Cultural Anthropology*, Holt Rinehart & Winston, 1981.
Land, H. 'Who cares for the family?', *The Journal of Social Policy*, vol. 7, No. 3, 1978.
Land, M. 'Family Fables', *New Socialist*, May/June 1983.
Laing, R.D. *The Divided Self*, Pelican, 1965.
Laing, R.D. *Sanity, Madness & the Family*, Pelican, 1970.
La Fontaine, Jean. 'Anthropological perspectives on the family and social change', *Quarterly Journal of Social Affairs*, vol. 1, no. 1, 1985.
Lasch, C. *Haven in a Heartless World*, Basic Books Inc., 1977.
Laslett, P. *Household and Family in Past Time*, Cambridge University Press, 1972.
Lawrence, Errol. 'Just plain common sense: the "roots" of racism', and 'In the abundance of water the fool is thirsty: sociology and black "pathology"', in Centre for Contemporary Cultural Studies, *The Empire Strikes Back: race and racism in 70s Britain*, Hutchinson, 1982.
Leach, E.R. *Rethinking Anthropology*, The Athlone Press, 1966.
Lee, David and Newby, Howard. *The Problem of Sociology*, Hutchinson, 1983.
Lees, S. *Losing Out: Sexuality and Adolescent Girls*, Hutchinson, 1986.
Leibowitz, Lila. *Females, Males, Families: a biosocial approach*, Wadsworth Publishing Co., 1978.
Leonard, Diana. 'The regulation of marriage: repressive benevolence' in G. Littlejohn, *et al.* (eds). *Power & the State*, Croom Helm, 1978.
Leonard, Diana. *Sex and Generation*, Tavistock, 1980.
Leonard, Diana. 'Women in the family' in V. Beechey, and E. Whitelegg, (eds), *Women in Britain Today*, Open University Press, 1986.
Lewis, Jane (ed.) *Labour and Love: Women's experience of home and family, 1850–1940*, Blackwell, 1986.
Lown, Judy. *With Free and Graceful Step? Women and Industrialization in Nineteenth Century England*, Polity, 1987.
Lukes, S. *Power*, Macmillan, 1974.
Marlow, J. *The Peterloo Massacre*, Panther, 1971.
Maclean, Mavis. and Eekelaar, John. *Children and Divorce: economic factors*, ESRC Centre for Socio-Legal Studies, Wolfson College, Oxford, 1983.
Marx, K. *Grundrisse*, Pelican, 1975.
McIntosh, Mary. 'The state and the oppression of women', in A. Kuhn and A.M. Wolpe (eds). *Feminism and Materialism*, Routledge & Kegan Paul, 1978.
McKee, Lorna and O'Brien, Margaret. *The Father Figure*, Tavistock, 1982.
Miliband, R. *The State in Capitalist Society*, Quartet, 1980.
Morgan, D.H.J. *Social Theory and the Family*, Routledge & Kegan Paul, 1975.
Morgan, D.H.J. *The Family, Politics and Social Theory*, Routledge & Kegan Paul, 1985.
Morgan, Elaine, *The Descent of Woman*, Morgan Stein and Day, 1972.

Morris, D. *The Naked Ape*, Corgi, 1968.

Mount, F. *The Subversive Family: an alternative history of love and marriage*, Jonathan Cape, 1982.

Murdock, G. *Social Structure*, Macmillan, 1949.

Neill, A.S. *Summerhill*, Pelican, 1985.

New, Caroline and David, Miriam. *For the Children's Sake: making childcare more than women's business*, Penguin, 1985.

Newby, H. 'Community', Study Section 20 of *Social Sciences: a Second Level Course*, Open University, 1980.

Newson, John and Elizabeth. *Patterns of Infant Care in an Urban Community*, George Allen & Unwin, 1963, Pelican, 1965.

Newson, John and Elizabeth. *Four Years Old in an Urban Community*, George Allen & Unwin, 1967, Pelican, 1970.

Newson, John and Elizabeth. *Seven Years Old in the Home Environment*, George Allen & Unwin, 1976.

Nissel, Muriel and Bonnerjea, Lucy. *Family Care of the Handicapped Elderly: who pays?* Policy Studies Institute, 1982.

Oakley, A. 'Are husbands good housewives?', *New Society*, February 1972.

Oakley, A. *Housewife*, Allen Lane, 1974.

Oakley, A. *The Sociology of Housework*, Martin Robertson, 1974.

Oren, L. 'The welfare of women in laboring families: England, 1860–1950' in M. Hartman and L.W. Banner, (eds), *Clio's Consciousness Raised: New Perspectives on the History of Women*, Harper Torchbooks, 1974.

O'Day, R. 'Women in the household: an historical analysis' Unit 7 of U221 *The Changing Experience of Women*, Open University Press, 1983.

Pahl, Ray. *Divisions of Labour*, Blackwell, 1984.

Parsons, Talcott. *The Social System*, The Free Press, 1952.

Parsons, Talcott. (ed.). *Family, Socialisation & Interaction Process*, Routledge & Kegan Paul, 1956.

Parsons, Talcott. (ed.). *Essays in Sociological Theory*, The Free Press, 1964.

Parmar, Pratibha. 'Gender, Race and Class: Asian women in resistance', in The Centre for Contemporary Cultural Studies, *The Empire Strikes Back*, Hutchinson, 1982.

Payne, I. 'A working class girl in a grammar school' in D. Spender and E. Sarah (eds). *Learning to Lose*, Womens Press, 1980.

Pinchbeck, I. and Hewitt, M. *Children in English Society*, Routledge & Kegan Paul, 1973.

Pizzey, E. *Scream Quietly or the Neighbours Will Hear You*, Penguin, 1979.

Plummer, Kenneth. 'Men in love: observations on male homosexual couples' in M. Corbin (ed.) *The Couple*, Penguin, 1976.

Plummer, Kenneth (ed.). *The Making of the Modern Homosexual*, Hutchinson, 1981.

Power Cobbe, F. 'Wife torture in England' in J.H. Murray (ed.), *Strong Minded Women*, Penguin, 1984.

Radcliffe-Brown, A.R. *Structure and Function in Primitive Society*, Cohen & West, 1952.

Rapp, Raynor. 'Family and class in contemporary America' in B. Thorne and M. Yalom (eds). *Rethinking the Family*, Longman, 1982.

Rapoport, Rhona and Robert N. *Dual-Career Families Re-examined*, Martin Robertson, 1976.

Rapoport, Rhona and Robert N. (eds). *Working Couples*, Routledge & Kegan Paul, 1978.

Rapoport, Robert N., Fogarty, M.P. and Rapoport, Rhona (eds). *Families in Britain*, Routledge & Kegan Paul, 1982.

Reedy, Sarah and Woodhead, Martin (eds). *Family, Work and Education*, Hodder and Stoughton in association with the Open University, 1980.

Reiter, Rayna R. (ed.). *Towards an Anthropology of Women*, Monthly Review Press, 1975.

Rigby, Andrew. *Alternative Realities*, Routledge & Kegan Paul, 1973.

Rigby, Andrew. *Communes in Britain*, Routledge & Kegan Paul, 1974.

Rights of Women *Lesbian Mothers on Trial: a report on lesbian mothers and child custody*, Row, 1984.

Riley, Denise. *War in the Nursery*, Virago, 1983.

Roberts, B. Finnegan, R. and Gallie, D. (eds). *New Approaches to Economic Life*, Manchester University Press, 1983.

Rosser, K.C. and Harris, C.C. *The Family and Social Change*, Routledge & Kegan Paul, 1965.

Rutter, M. and Hersov, L. (eds). *Child and Adolescent Psychiatry; Modern Approaches*, Blackwell, 1985.

Segal, L. (ed.). *What is to be Done About the Family?*, Penguin, 1983.

Shaw, Jenny. 'Family, state and compulsory education', Block 5 of E353, *Society, Educational and the State*, Open University, 1981.

Skolnick, A. *The Intimate Environment*, Little Brown, Boston, 4th Edn 1986.

Social Trends, HMSO, Office of Population and Census Surveys, annual publication.

Speier, M. 'The child as conversationalist: some culture contact features of conversational interactions between adults and children' in M. Hammersley and P. Woods (eds). *The Process of Schooling*, Routledge & Kegan Paul with the Open University Press, 1976.

Steedman, Carolyn. *The Tidy House*, Virago, 1982.

Talmon, Y. 'The family in a revolutionary movement: the case of the kibbutz in Israel' in R. Laub Coser, (ed). *The Family: its structures & functions*, St Martins Press, 1974.

Thompson, E.P. 'Happy Families', *New Society*, September 1977.

Thompson, E.P. *The Making of the English Working Class*, Vintage, 1963.

Tiger, L. and Shepher, J. *Women in the Kibbutz*, Harcourt Brace Jovanovick, 1975.

Tilly, Louise A. and Scott, Joan W. *Women, Work and Family*, Holt, Rinehart and Winston, 1973.

Trivedi, P. 'To deny our fullness: Asian women in the making of history', *Feminist Review*, No. 17, Autumn 1984.

Ungerson, Claire (ed.). *Women and Social Policy: a reader*, Macmillan, 1985.

Vicinus, M. *Independent Women: Work and Community 1850–1920*, Virago, 1985.

Watson, James L. (ed.). *Between Two Cultures: migrants and minorities in Britain*, Blackwell, 1977.

Weber, M. *Economy and Society*, Bedminster Press, 1968.

Weeks, Jeffrey. *Sex, Politics and Society. The regulation of sexuality since 1800*, Longman, 1981.

Whitehead, Ann. 'Sex Antagonism in Herefordshire', in D.L. Barker and S. Allen, (eds). *Dependence and Exploitation in Work and Marriage*, Longman, 1975.

Whitelegg, E. *et al.* (eds). *The Changing Experience of Women*, Martin Robertson in association with Open University Press, 1982.

Willis, Paul. 'Youth unemployment: thinking the unthinkable', *Youth and Policy*, vol. 2, no. 4, 1984.

Wilson, E.O. *Sociobiology: The new synthesis*, Harvard University Press, 1975.

Woods, J. 'Groping towards sexism: boys' sex talk', in A. McRobbie, and M. Nava, *Gender and Generation*, Macmillan, 1984.

Wright Mills, C. *The Sociological Imagination*, Pelican, 1980.

Young M. and Willmott, P. *The Symmetrical Family*, Routledge & Kegan Paul, 1973.

Young M. and Willmott, P. *Family and Kinship in East London*, Penguin, 1957.

Index